Y0-BCL-075

THE MULTILATERAL DEVELOPMENT BANKS

Volume 2

THE ASIAN DEVELOPMENT BANK

Also Available

Volume 1, The African Development Bank
Harris M. Mule and E. Philip English

Volume 2, The Asian Development Bank
Nihal Kappagoda

Volume 3, The Caribbean Development Bank
Chandra Hardy

Volume 4, The Inter-American Development Bank
Diana Tussie

Volume 5, Titans or Behemoths?
Roy Culpeper

THE MULTILATERAL DEVELOPMENT BANKS

VOLUME 2
THE ASIAN DEVELOPMENT BANK

NIHAL KAPPAGODA

LYNNE RIENNER PUBLISHERS

THE NORTH-SOUTH INSTITUTE
L'INSTITUT NORD-SUD

Published in the United States of America in 1995 by
Lynne Rienner Publishers, Inc.
1800 30th Street, Boulder, Colorado 80301

and in the United Kingdom by
Lynne Rienner Publishers, Inc.
3 Henrietta Street, Covent Garden, London WC2E 8LU

Paperback edition published in Canada by
The North-South Institute
55 Murray Street
Ottawa, Ontario K1N 5M3 Canada

© 1995 by Lynne Rienner Publishers, Inc. All rights reserved

Library of Congress Cataloging-in-Publication Data
Multilateral development banks.
    p. cm.
    Includes bibliographical references and index.
    Contents:—2. The Asian Development Bank / Nihal Kappagoda
    ISBN 1-55587-468-1 (alk. paper : v. 2)
    ISBN 1-55587-494-0 (pbk. : alk. paper : v. 2)
    1. Development banks. 2. Asian Development Bank.
HG1975.M848 1995
332.2—dc20   94-45003
                                                                    CIP

Canadian Cataloguing in Publication Data
Main entry under title:
Multilateral development banks
    Includes bibliographical references.
    Contents: v. 2. The Asian Development Bank / Nihal
    Kappagoda.
    ISBN 0-921942-78-8 (pbk.)
    1. Development banks. I. North-South Institute
(Ottawa, Ont.)
HG1975.M85 1995   332.1'52   C95-900188-3

British Cataloguing in Publication Data
A Cataloguing in Publication record for this book
is available from the British Library.

Printed and bound in the United States of America

⊗ The paper used in this publication meets the requirements
    of the American National Standard for Permanence of
    Paper for Printed Library Materials Z39.48-1984.

5 4 3 2 1

CONTENTS

List of Tables   vii
Foreword, *Yasutami Shimomura*   ix
Preface, *Roy Culpeper*   xi
Acknowledgments   xiii
List of Acronyms   xv

1 Introduction   1

Part 1   Historical Setting and Record of Performance

2 A Brief History of the Bank   13
   Institutional Framework, *13*
   Resources, *17*
   Bank Operations, *25*
   The Political Balance of Power, *33*
   Highlights of Past Assessments, *40*

3 Borrowing Country Experience   49
   Country Studies, *49*
   Development Impact, *64*

Part 2   Development Agenda

4 Loan Performance and Institutional Governance   89
   Loan Quality and Evaluation, *89*
   Country Strategies and Programming, *96*

5 Resource Mobilization   111
   Replenishment of the Asian Development Fund, *111*
   General Capital Increases, *113*
   Issues Affecting Resource Needs, *116*
   Changes in Financial Policies, *121*

6 Looming Development Challenges for the Bank   127
   Overview of Needs, *127*
   Role of the Bank in the Pacific DMCs, *129*
   Assistance to the Private Sector, *133*
   Protecting the Environment, *141*

Incorporating Social Dimensions in Bank Operations, *144*
Good Governance, Democratic Development,
    and Human Rights, *148*
Regional Activities, *151*

7 Achievements of the Bank   157
    Some Concluding Thoughts, *160*

Appendix: Statistical Tables of the Structure and
    Operations of the Bank and DMC Indicators   167
Bibliography   185
Index   189
About the Book and Author   199

TABLES

2.1	ADF Replenishments	20
2.2	Classification of DMCs by ADF Eligibility	23
2.3	Geographical Distribution	26
2.4	Percentage Shares of the Eight Largest Borrowers from the OCR and ADF: 1970–1992	27
2.5	Sectoral Shares	30
2.6	Shares of Lending Modalities	31
2.7	Subscribed Capital, Voting Power, and ADF	34
2.8	Distribution of Contracts Awarded by Country of Origin	35
2.9	Professional Staff: 1981–1991	37
3.1	Average Real GDP Growth by Developing Region: 1972–1991	64
3.2	Average Real GDP Growth by Subregion: 1970–1990	65
3.3	Share of Public and Private Sectors in Total Investment: 1975–1990	67
3.4	Foreign Direct Investment: 1985–1990	69
3.5	Net Resource Flows	69
3.6	Net Transfers on Loans to Asian Region	71
4.1	Ratio of Successful Projects in Asia	90
4.2	Annual Planning Cycle	98
5.1	ADF Loan Commitments: 1987–1995	112
5.2	OCR Loan Operations: 1983–1992	114
5.3	Last Year of Bank Operations in Nonborrowing Countries	121
5.4	Loan Portfolio Concentration of Selected MDBs	124
6.1	Summary of Private Sector Investment Facilities	135
6.2	Military Expenditure and Economic Development	151
A1	Bank Lending by Country and Source of Funds: 1970–1992	168
A2	Bank Lending by Sector: 1970–1992	170
A3	Bank Lending by Mode: 1970–1992	171

A4   Membership by Constituency Group and
       Date of Joining   172
A5   Subscription to Capital Stock and Voting Power:
       December 31, 1992   173
A6   Net Income of the Bank   175
A7   Net Transfers of Resources to DMCs (OCR)   175
A8   Net Transfers of Resources to DMCs (ADF)   176
A9   Loan Disbursements (OCR)   177
A10 Loan Disbursements (ADF)   178
A11 Social Indicators   179
A12 Populations of Developing Asian and Pacific Countries   180
A13 GDP Growth Rate and Per Capita GNP   181
A14 Balance of Payments on Current Account   182
A15 External Debt Outstanding   183
A16 Debt Service Ratio   184

FOREWORD

Asia and the Pacific is an extremely diverse region: It contains giants, such as China and India, as well as tiny island nations in the Pacific Ocean. At the same time, Asia and the Pacific is a dynamic region. Dynamism spread first from Japan to the newly industrializing economies (NIEs), then to the Association of South East Asian Nations (ASEAN), and to the coastal region of China through successive waves of direct investment and bilateral trade.

This rapid development has caused substantial changes in the economic structures in East Asia. In addition, the former centrally planned economies in the region are making efforts to achieve a transition to market economies. These attempts at transition have had a significant impact on the economic transformation of Asia and the Pacific.

The unique characteristics of the region make the mission of the Asian Development Bank delicate as well as important. To analyze and synthesize the work of this organization is therefore a complicated task, one that Nihal Kappagoda has (I am happy to say) accomplished successfully.

The Multilateral Development Banks: Volume 2, The Asian Development Bank deals with various aspects of the Bank in a well-balanced manner, reflecting the author's long experience in observing the Bank from both the inside and the outside. Such experience has enabled him to make full use of all the available (and in many cases, unpublished) information. For example, the section entitled "The Political Balance of Power" in Chapter 2 provides a vivid picture of the relationship between Japan, a dominant regional member of relatively low profile, and the United States, an influential nonregional member. I consider this one of the valuable contributions Mr. Kappagoda makes in this book to a broader understanding of the Bank.

Professor Yasutami Shimomura
Graduate School of Policy Science
Saitama University, Japan

PREFACE

In 1991 the North-South Institute launched its research project on the multilateral development banks ("the MDB Project"). The principal focus of the project was the group of regional development banks (comprising the African, Asian, and Inter-American Development Banks) plus the subregional Caribbean Development Bank. All these banks, created more or less in the image of the World Bank, had been around for two to three decades. Yet, in contrast to the World Bank, they had been subjected to little critical scrutiny.

The project was designed to provide a consistent framework within which each of the banks could be examined. Besides providing a brief history of the origins and evolution of its subject, each study reviews the experience of a selected group of borrowing countries, as well as the bank's performance as a lender and as a mobilizer of resources. In all of the studies, the operations and policies of the regional bank are compared with those of the World Bank; also addressed are relations between the two agencies and the division of labor between them. Finally, each study looks ahead at the challenges facing the banks in the future.

In a word, the studies seek to determine the *development effectiveness* of the regional banks by examining their impact on growth, poverty, the environment, and social indicators of development. It is hoped that the project will make an important contribution to ongoing discussions regarding the future of the multilateral system of development financing, now in its fiftieth year after the Bretton Woods Conference. In addition to this volume on the Asian Bank, the project will yield four other major publications—one each on the Inter-American, Caribbean, and African Banks, as well as a "synthesis" volume. There are also two studies on Canada's role in the MDBs, one on Sweden and the MDBs, and one on Jamaica's relations with the MDBs.

The project has been generously supported through grants from the Canadian International Development Agency, the Inter-American Development Bank, the Asian Development Bank, the African Development Bank, the Ford Foundation, the Swedish Ministry for Foreign Affairs, the Caribbean Development Bank, the Norwegian Ministry of Foreign Affairs, and the Netherlands Ministry for Development Cooperation. The views contained in this volume and in others issuing from the project, however, are those of the authors alone, and do not necessarily reflect the views of the project's sponsors, the funders of the multilateral development banks project, the North-South Institute, its supporters, or its board of directors.

Roy Culpeper
MDB Project Director
The North-South Institute

ACKNOWLEDGMENTS

This book is about an institution that I have observed since it was established in 1966. I negotiated Asian Development Bank loans with staff members on behalf of the government of Sri Lanka and later worked as a Bank staff member for eighteen months during 1981–1982 on the study of the Bank's operational priorities and plans for the 1980s. Subsequently, I worked for the Bank as a consultant. The knowledge I gained about Bank operations spans both the twenty-eight years of its existence and my working life in international development.

I wish to acknowledge the Bank's willingness to provide me access to the documents that were required for the study. The information in the text is, in most cases, current up to the time of writing, while the statistics quoted are current through 1992. The staff of the Development Policy Office and Economics and Development Resource Center, who coordinated my several visits to the Bank, deserve particular mention. Many staff members, including former colleagues, spent time discussing their experience of Bank operations. I wish to thank all of them for their time and effort.

My thanks are due to the North-South Institute for giving me the opportunity to participate in this study. I wish to thank Roy Culpeper, Clyde Sanger, Andrew Clark, and Sarah Matthews for their kind assistance, guidance, counsel, and support, and the advisory group that guided the Study of Regional Development Banks for their counsel during the conduct of the study and comments on the drafts. I am grateful to many others who took the time to read the draft and offer comments. I also wish to express my personal satisfaction at being associated once again with Professor John Lewis, whom I first met when he played a similar role as myself for the Asian Development Bank when the study of the Bank's operational priorities and plans for the 1980s was conducted. The interaction with the others in the study team helped me to improve this book.

The book is intended for those with an interest in international development and the contribution of the multilateral banks. It is hoped that it will stimulate a wide circle to engage in discussion on the relevant issues. Any errors of judgment and fact are my responsibility, although every effort has been made to eliminate the latter following the comments received on earlier drafts.

Nihal Kappagoda
Ottawa, Canada

ACRONYMS

AsDB	Asian Development Bank
ASEAN	Association of South East Asian Nations
ADF	Asian Development Fund
AFIC	Asian Finance and Investment Corporation
AIDAB	Australian International Development Assistance Bureau
DANIDA	Department of International Economic Cooperation, Danish Ministry of Foreign Affairs
DFIs	development finance institutions
DMCs	developing member countries
EBRD	European Bank for Reconstruction and Development
ECAFE	United Nations Economic Commission for Asia and the Far East
EIRR	economic internal rate of return
ESCAP	Economic and Social Commission for Asia and the Pacific
FDI	foreign direct investment
FYs	financial years
GCI	general capital increase
GDP	gross domestic product
GNP	gross national product
IBRD	International Bank for Reconstruction and Development
IFC	International Finance Corporation
IMF	International Monetary Fund
MDBs	multilateral development banks
NGOs	nongovernmental organizations
NIEs	newly industrialized countries
OCR	ordinary capital resources
ODA	official development assistance
OECD	Organization of Economic Cooperation and Development
RDB	regional development bank

REPELITA V	Fifth National Plan (Indonesia)
SDRs	special drawing rights
UNDP	United Nations Development Programme
USAID	U.S. Agency for International Development
WID	women in development

1

INTRODUCTION

The momentum of Asia's economic growth achieved over the past three decades has contradicted all predictions that were made at the beginning of the 1960s. No observer of Asian affairs would have considered this to be possible, given the history of military conflicts, insurrections, and major political problems that affected many Asian countries after the end of the Second World War. India and Pakistan, the countries of Indochina, and the two Koreas had major conflicts. Indonesia, Malaysia, Myanmar, the Philippines, and Sri Lanka faced guerrilla insurrections. China loosed murderous Red Guards on their own population, while Cambodia, under the Khmer Rouge, surpassed this record by murdering 15 to 20 percent of the country's population, particularly the more educated groups.

This bleak scene gave way to a dawning of export-led growth, mainly in the countries of East and Southeast Asia.[1] Growth in Japan began in the 1950s; its real per capita income, led by a rapid increase in manufactures, increased fourfold between 1960 and 1985. Hong Kong, the Republic of Korea, Singapore, and Taipei,China* followed with a ten-year lag leading to a doubling of real gross domestic product (GDP) every eight years during the same period. Economic growth in China, Indonesia, Malaysia, and Thailand has been comparable, although it began only in the late 1970s. Consequently, these eight economies have been among the thirteen most successful in the developing world in raising real incomes during 1965–1990. Further, these countries, with the exception of China, have combined fast growth with an improvement in income equality in some instances and with no decline in the others. In comparison, the countries in the Asian subcontinent and Myanmar, the Philippines, and Vietnam

---

*The Asian Development Bank uses the name "Taipei,China" to stand for what is commonly known as Taiwan.

have fared badly. Most of these countries have reversed the policies that stifled growth in varying degrees during the past decade and are seeking to emulate the fastest-growing economies in the next ten to fifteen years.

These developments in the continent are expected to increase Asia's share of the world's gross national product (GNP) to one-third by the turn of the century, compared to 4 percent in 1960. Half the growth in world trade during the current decade will take place in Asia. In 1992, Asian central banks controlled two-fifths of foreign exchange reserves worldwide, compared to one-sixth in 1980. In many Asian countries savings rates exceed 30 percent. In spite of these major achievements, several fault lines are emerging that signal caution and the need for attention. First, by the year 2000, the population in Asia is expected to account for 3.5 billion of the world's 6.2 billion people. Second, growth has brought about heavy concentration in cities, adding tremendous political and social pressures. In 1992, fourteen cities in Asia had populations exceeding five million: four of these were in India and three in China. This concentration has produced major infrastructure bottlenecks that now impede growth. Third, conflicts continue in the region through miscalculation or irresponsible acts by political leaders. These conflicts could easily set back the achievements in growth through the destruction of physical capital and a loss of confidence that could adversely affect the flow of foreign investment that has become a major source of resource transfers in some countries of the region. Fourth, it is not clear how these countries that achieved rapid growth, obtained access to new technology, and reached high levels of education within restrictive political systems will make the transition to participatory democracy. Finally, several issues resulting from Asia's development impinge on the agenda of the global community. Among these are the growing disparity between the region's political and economic power in the world, the potential for conflict within the global trading system that may come about with the emergence of subregional blocs, Japan's increasing economic and consequent political power, and the volatility of security in the region.

The Asian Development Bank (hereinafter referred to as the AsDB or the Bank) was established in 1966 when many countries in the region adopted policies that were intended to achieve export-oriented economic growth. In the past twenty-eight years the Bank has contributed to the development of its member countries, in some to a greater extent than in others. Its share of the net transfer of resources to the region has been small, not exceeding 5 percent, although the influence the Bank wielded has been larger than this would suggest. This book sets out a brief history of Bank operations, its contribution to growth in the region, the changes that have taken place in loan operations over the years, and its response to new priorities of donors. It goes on to suggest the role it could play in helping member countries meet the challenges of the twenty-first century. It is not a comprehensive review intended for those most familiar with its operations. Instead, its aim is to inform a more general public, those with an interest in international development, of the activities and performance of Asia's regional development bank (RDB) within the context of its historical and projected growth. Asia has a dynamism of its own that was not prompted or promoted by the AsDB. Nevertheless, the Bank contributed to this growth in various significant ways that will be described in the succeeding chapters.

The second chapter provides a brief description of the Bank and its origins, functions, and membership. The different types of resources available to the Bank fall into three categories. These are the ordinary capital resources (OCR), which are dependent on the capital subscriptions of the membership (which have increased with each of the four general capital increases [GCIs] that have taken place since the Bank was set up) and borrowings from international capital markets; the Asian Development Fund (ADF), the Bank's soft loan window set up with donor contributions in 1974 and replenished five times since then; and other special funds used mainly for technical assistance. Developing member countries (DMCs) of the Bank are divided into three categories, A, B, and C, for the allocation of resources. The classification is dependent on per capita GNP, debt repayment capacity, and special circumstances (such as those prevailing in the small island economies) of the DMCs. Among the Group A countries, the least-developed countries receive priority in the allocation of resources from the ADF.

Gross loan commitments to the end of 1992 were $42,458.1 million,[2] of which 68 percent were OCR loans and the remaining 32 percent were credits from the ADF. The pace of lending accelerated in the 1980s and the early 1990s. At the end of 1982, sixteen years after the Bank was established, gross loan commitments were $10 billion. The $20 billion level was passed in 1987, $30 billion in 1990, and $40 billion in 1992, indicating the acceleration that took place over the five years from 1987. While the increase in the level of lending was a major achievement of the Bank, concerns have been raised for many years over the excessive emphasis placed on the volume of loan commitments in Bank operations rather than on the quality of the loan portfolio. Following release of the Report of the Task Force on Improving Project Quality in February 1994, the management of the Bank has indicated that it will take action on these concerns. Nevertheless, the mobilization of resources to achieve a gross lending level of $28,894.6 million from the OCR by the end of 1992, for a paid-in capital of $2,787.0 million of the members' subscribed capital of $23,100.1 million, represents a major success of the multilateral system in the leverage it could exercise in mobilizing resources.

Southeast Asia accounted for 57.9 percent of lending from the OCR, and South Asia for 80.8 percent of lending from the ADF during 1970–1992. Among the OCR borrowers, Indonesia had the largest share, accounting for 29.3 percent, followed by India with a share of 14.8 percent during the same period. Over the five years, 1987–1992, Indonesia's share of 30.8 percent was marginally higher than the long-term average, while India's share was substantially higher at 25.5 percent reflecting the growth in the lending program since it began borrowing in 1986. Pakistan had the largest share of borrowings from the ADF at 29.1 percent, followed by Bangladesh with 28.2 percent. Bangladesh's share was lower from 1987 to 1992.

The share of agriculture and agro-industry in total lending during 1970–1992 was 26.4 percent, closely followed by energy at 24.7 percent. Transport and communications, social infrastructure, and development finance institutions (DFIs) received the next largest share of allocations. The evolution of different modalities led to a decline in direct project lending from 82.0 percent during the 1970s to 59.7 percent during the 1980s. This decline was balanced by an increase in program and sector lending, which accounted for 10.4 and 15.3 percent respectively in the latter decade.

The share of regional members in the capital of the Bank at the end of 1992 was 63.0 percent, of which DMCs accounted for 38.8 percent and Japan 16.4 percent. The United States is the major nonregional member whose shareholding translates into a voting power equivalent to that of Japan, which dominates the ADF with cumulative contributions exceeding 50 percent of the total. It is significant that the share capital held by DMCs is less than 50 percent. Donor influence on the AsDB has been on Bank policy, brought about more recently in the context of ADF replenishments and the GCI, and Bank operations in which the U.S. and Japan had the largest influence.

The third chapter describes the highlights of studies of Bank operations in Indonesia, Pakistan, and Sri Lanka that were carried out for this book. It draws attention to the Bank's support of roads, ports, and urban development projects in Indonesia, power generation and irrigation projects in Pakistan, and power development and DFI projects in Sri Lanka. Overall, the emerging picture shows that the Bank made a significant contribution to achieving self-sufficiency in food in the region through irrigation and rural development projects; to increasing hydro and thermal power generation, transmission and distribution facilities with the consequent easing of bottlenecks on industrial development and extension of consumer use of power, often in rural areas; to improved access of goods and services to markets by the construction and improvements in ports and roads; and to industrial development by financing small- and medium-scale industrialists through DFIs that could not otherwise have received direct financial assistance from the Bank.

The Bank's contribution to net resource flows to the region was on the order of 5 percent of the total during 1987–1991. Although this contribution is small in the context of foreign direct investment (FDI) and private lending exceeding 50 percent during this period, other benefits accrued through the mobilization of cofinancing resources and technical assistance for institutional building. Further, the policy improvements that were introduced through Bank technical assistance would have had a beneficial impact on the volume of private flows, the exact impact of which is difficult to estimate.

Coordination between the AsDB and the World Bank is important because both banks are major donors in most DMCs and active in the same sectors. Projections of future availability of resources in both banks point to uncertain growth rates, particularly of concessional funds. It is therefore in the interests of DMCs to avoid duplication and the consequent suboptimal use of resources. Since the World Bank chairs most consultative groups and, along with the International Monetary Fund (IMF), assists DMCs to formulate and implement macroeconomic policies, coordination is essential at the sectoral level with regard to both policies and investments financed. DMCs should take the initiative in bringing about such coordination by assigning a lead role to a single donor in sectors where many donors are active based on comparative advantage, past performance, and the capacity to undertake the required economic and sector analysis. Guidelines for the lead-role function should be drawn up and reviewed periodically to improve effectiveness.

The fourth chapter examines the lessons of postevaluation studies conducted by the Bank. These have shown a recent decline in the quality of the Bank's portfolio (as has happened in other multilateral development banks [MDBs]). Careful selection of projects and programs is crucial for the success of the AsDB's assistance to any DMC. One of the lessons drawn from these studies is the need for adequate technical assistance for project preparation. This has to be followed by detailed engineering design and increased technical assistance to the implementing agencies for project supervision and institutional building. Equally important are realistic assessments of the capacity of the implementing agency for project design. Formal midterm reviews should be performed in complex projects with allowances for changes. All these issues are critical for project preparation and implementation that will improve the quality of projects financed by the Bank. They were dealt with and the need for them agreed to by two working groups during the deliberations of the Task Force on Improving Project Quality. The adoption of these changes will have implications for the project cycle, staff, and budget, including the availability of technical assistance in support of loan operations. The steering committee for a review of the Bank's organization, appointed by the president of the Bank following the release of the report of the task force in February 1994, is examining these issues.

The Bank has recently taken important steps to improve its planning process for loan and technical assistance operations. A strategic planning unit was established in 1991 that took the lead in preparing a medium-term strategic framework for the Bank for 1992–1995. This identified five strategic development objectives for lending that are to achieve economic growth, reduce poverty, and give greater consideration to gender issues, population planning, and the protection of the environment. In a revision of the strategic framework in 1993, private sector development, public sector management, human resource development, and natural resource management were identified as thematic priorities relevant for all sectors in which the Bank had loan and technical assistance operations. As well, a second generation of country operational strategies for each DMC, which were first prepared in the 1980s, is being formulated. These will have a greater analytical content and reflect both the long-term objectives of the DMC and the Bank's strategic framework. At the next level, country operational programs are prepared annually covering a four-year time frame, including the current year. These contain a detailed lending and technical assistance program for the current year only and a review of country performance, based on an assessment made during the country programming mission. As a consequence of these changes, a new planning cycle was introduced for the Bank in 1993 leading to a somewhat larger role for the Board in the formulation of the lending and technical assistance program for each borrowing country. The DMCs, fearing donor domination of the planning process, are apprehensive about a greater role for the Board and, instead, prefer to see greater management-staff freedom in the conduct of Bank operations. Nevertheless, such a move is desirable in the interests of achieving better governance of the Bank. There could be a trade-off with a lesser involvement of the Board in the approval of loans, as in the case of technical assistance grants.

The fifth chapter deals with issues surrounding the mobilization of resources for the Bank. Negotiations for the fifth replenishment of the ADF, covering 1992–1995, ended in December 1991. This amounted to $4.2 billion, which, along with the carryover from the previous replenishment period, ensured that concessional funds of more than $6.0 billion were available for commitment during 1992–1995, to be allocated on the basis of need and past performance. For the first time, a donors' report was issued after the negotiations on the agreements reached between the donors and management on the Bank's operational agenda during the replenishment period. At the time of writing, a fourth GCI of 100 percent became effective with a paid-in capital of 2 percent. This increases the Bank's authorized capital from about $24 billion to about $48 billion. The previous capital increase of 105 percent with a paid-in capital of 5 percent had been agreed on in 1983 and proved adequate for eleven years. As in the case of the ADF replenishment, an operational agenda was agreed on for the period of the GCI, bringing the two processes into line. Bank management had resisted issuing such a document, which held up the approval of the GCI for a few months in 1994.

Two previously nonactive members, Cambodia and Vietnam, started receiving ADF loans and technical assistance in 1992 and 1993. There has been no change in the suspension of loan operations in Afghanistan and Myanmar. The new DMCs admitted to membership will have an impact on Bank resources available to the traditional borrowers. The most significant of these will be the Central Asian Republics of the former Soviet Union. As before, China and India, though eligible to receive concessional funds, can only have access to the OCR. At the other end of the scale, no definitive policy has been adopted on activities that may involve graduated DMCs. However, Korea, which ceased to borrow in 1988, has agreed with the Bank on a general framework for cofinancing projects in the Asia and Pacific region.

Recent changes have brought the financial policies in the Bank relating to arrears and sanctions in line with those of the World Bank. Specific loan-loss provisions are to be made for public sector loans when service payments have been in arrears for one year. A similar policy will apply to private sector loans after a period of arrears of six months. The Bank has as yet no guidelines on loan exposure to a single country. If a ceiling (such as 25 percent) is adopted, it will take a period of time to implement and also have an impact on the capital requirements of the Bank.

The sixth chapter looks into the future at the looming development agenda and the needs of the region in broad terms. These are being met by the Bank primarily through project lending with an appropriate mix of program and sector lending. Economic growth still claims priority, but attention is being given to crosscutting issues such as protecting the environment, incorporating the social dimensions of development, and assisting the most vulnerable groups in society. This chapter describes the processes by which environmental and social dimensions issues are dealt with in projects. The agenda also involves identifying opportunities for promoting the development of the private sector and introducing governance issues in the AsDB's lending programs. Action on governance is seen by all as a sensitive matter, to be handled with caution. Coordinated action by the family of MDBs is probably the best plan.

In carving out a future role for itself, the Bank should recognize the existence of four distinct economic groups. These are the newly industrialized economies (NIEs); the countries of Southeast Asia that are better endowed with natural resources; the low-income countries of South Asia, Indochina, China, and Mongolia; and the Pacific island countries. A different agenda could be adopted for each of these groups. The NIEs should contribute to the development of other DMCs by cofinancing projects and programs, providing technical assistance, and undertaking foreign investments in less-developed DMCs where the policy environment has improved. Bank assistance in Southeast Asian countries should be focused on physical and social infrastructure that have become bottlenecks to their future development and further improvements needed in the policy environment. Further, the Bank could serve as a catalyst in promoting foreign investment by these countries and by NIEs in the low-income DMCs. The primary financing role of the Bank should be in a range of sectors in the low-income countries. It should work with the World Bank and IMF in improving the policy environment with a view to replacing concessional assistance with foreign investment, at least in some sectors.

Many of the small island economies have no demonstrable long-term viability. Priority should be given to improving the effectiveness of funds that are being provided in substantial amounts by the donor community and the remittances received from nationals living abroad, mainly in Australia and New Zealand. While the Bank's technical assistance could effectively assist the Pacific DMCs in achieving some much-needed improvements, the donor community has difficulties in working out the best means of assisting these countries. Coordination arrangements with the activities of the World Bank (keeping in mind the wishes of the Pacific nations to deal with it directly) and those of other major donors should be under constant review and improved if opportunities arise.

The seventh and final chapter provides highlights of the Bank's achievements and ends with some personal thoughts on major issues raised in the study. These are based on the observations made in the document, and I hope that they will stimulate further discussion of the issues covered. The Bank has demonstrated a willingness to adapt its operations both to meet the development needs of its DMCs and the priorities of the donor community. It has also begun to tackle the problems affecting the quality of its loan portfolio and needs the time and opportunity to make the organizational changes that are required. Both the developing and developed members have a responsibility to assist the Bank to evolve in a manner that is best suited to meet the needs of the region in the next decade.

Notes

1. Jim Rohwer, "A Billion Consumers: A Survey of Asia," *The Economist*, October 30, 1993.
2. Dollar figures throughout the text and tables refer to current U.S. dollars.

PART 1

HISTORICAL SETTING AND
RECORD OF PERFORMANCE

2

A BRIEF HISTORY
OF THE BANK

Institutional Framework

Origins

The idea for a development bank for Asia and the Pacific was first proposed in the region in the late 1950s. The AsDB had its origins in a resolution on regional economic cooperation adopted in March 1963 by the United Nations Economic Commission for Asia and the Far East (ECAFE). It was later renamed the Economic and Social Commission for Asia and the Pacific (ESCAP). This was followed by a specific proposal for the establishment of a regional bank in July 1963 at a conference on trade promotion held by the Commission. The process[1] evolved through the deliberations of a group of experts in October 1964 and a consultative committee that met from June to December 1965. The expert group made a case for the establishment of the AsDB on three grounds. These were that the AsDB should

a) be a conduit for channelling additional external resources to the region;
b) finance projects that were not adequately funded by other donor agencies; and
c) act as a focal point for regional activities that would promote economic cooperation.

The consultative committee was of the view that the principal benefit of establishing the AsDB would be to increase the total financing available for development in the region. ECAFE had estimated in the early 1960s that the region needed $3 billion in external assistance to achieve its development goals, of which $2 billion was being provided through foreign aid and investment.[2] Another consideration was the need to develop adequate local expertise for the preparation and assessment of appropriate plans and projects for development. It was recognized that, having a regional character, the AsDB would be better suited to supporting the developmental needs of the smaller and relatively less-developed countries. They had not been served adequately by the World Bank, which was perceived as concentrating its lending mainly in India and Pakistan. The committee considered that the satisfaction of Asian aspirations, by the creation of a regional institution to promote cooperation and economic development of individual countries, was more important than its economic and financial potential. It took the view that these objectives would be met by the establishment of a bank whose management and capital had an Asian majority.

The AsDB, unlike the African Development Bank (AfDB)[3] and the Inter-American Development Bank (IDB),[4] chose partnership with the industrialized countries from the beginning, because its founding fathers recognized that these countries would be major sources of funds for Bank operations. The main incentive for the industrialized countries to participate financially in the Bank lay in the opportunities it provided to promote their development policies as well as their economic and political interests. Japan played a central role in establishing the Bank. Japan looked upon the DMCs as vital sources of raw materials and food and as markets for its expanding exports and foreign investment opportunities. The Japanese proposal to establish the AsDB dates back to 1962.[5] They adopted a low-key approach during the initial discussions on the Bank within the ECAFE. A Japanese draft, similar to the AsDB charter that was finally adopted, had been prepared in early 1963 before negotiations began within the commission. Initially, the United States was reluctant to participate in the AsDB. This hesitation was overcome due to the political need to balance the increasing U.S. involvement in Vietnam during the 1960s with higher levels of development assistance to the region. The United States chose to provide that support through the AsDB. This decision was followed shortly thereafter by Japan announcing its subscription to the Bank. These deliberations led to the establishment of the AsDB in 1966. It began operations in December of that year, with its headquarters in Manila and Mr. Takeshi Watanabe as its first president.

Purpose, Functions, and Operating Principles

The overall purpose[6] of the Bank is to foster economic growth and cooperation in the region and contribute to the collective and individual economic development of the DMCs.

Several functions and operating principles set out in the Articles of Agreement of the Bank had an important bearing on its lending operations as they evolved since 1966. The more important functions[7] of the Bank listed in the Articles were those that required it to

a) promote investment of public and private capital for development purposes in the region;
b) utilize the resources at its disposal for financing development of the DMCs in the region, giving priority to those regional, subregional, and national projects and programs that contributed most effectively to the harmonious economic growth of the region, having special regard to the needs of the smaller or less-developed member countries;
c) assist DMCs to coordinate their development policies and plans with a view to achieving better utilization of their resources, making their economies complementary, and promoting the orderly expansion of foreign trade;
d) provide technical assistance for the preparation, financing, and execution of development projects and programs, including the formulation of specific project proposals; and
e) cooperate, in the manner that it may deem appropriate, with the United Nations, its organs, and subsidiary bodies and public international and other institutions that are concerned with the investment of development funds in the region in order to interest these institutions and entities in new opportunities for investment and assistance.

The main operating principle[8] of the Bank is that it should finance specific projects, including those forming part of a national, subregional, or regional development program. The Bank also provides for loans, or guarantees of loans, made to national development banks or other suitable entities to enable them to finance smaller development projects. Another principle, which became important when operations were expanded to finance private sector projects directly, was to pay due regard to the ability of the borrower to obtain financing or facilities elsewhere on terms and conditions that the Bank considers reasonable for the recipient. These principles further state that the Bank should pay due regard to the prospects of the borrower or guarantor meeting their obligations under the contract and the desirability of avoiding a disproportionate amount of its resources being used for the benefit of a single DMC. Article 36 sets out another principle that has become relevant in the context of human rights and democratic development issues raised by donors. This is that the Bank shall not interfere in the political affairs of any member, and Bank decisions shall not be influenced by the political character of the member concerned. Only economic considerations should be relevant to Bank decisions.

Membership

The Articles opened membership of the Bank to (a) ECAFE members and associate members; and (b) other regional and nonregional developed countries that are members of the United Nations or any of its specialized agencies. The AsDB had thirty-one members[9] at its inception in 1966, nineteen of which were from the region. Since Australia, Japan, and New Zealand, among the regional members, were developed countries, the DMCs had a majority of only one at that time. The inaugural Board had ten members, three representing nonregional countries. The membership[10] now stands at fifty-five of whom thirty-nine are from the region, while the Board has expanded to twelve members of whom four represent nonregional interests. Thirty-five[11] are DMCs and are now clearly in the majority. This was brought about mainly by the accession to membership of the South Pacific DMCs. Unlike other MDBs, the AsDB permitted nonsovereign entities like Hong Kong, the Cook Islands, and several other South Pacific countries to become members before they gained independence. In such cases application for membership was presented by the member responsible for the applicant's international relations. Nonregionals are considered for membership only as "developed countries." Accordingly, Turkey was admitted to membership as a nonregional developed country in 1991.

Capital Stock

The Articles of Agreement of the AsDB stipulate that the subscribed capital stock held by regional members shall not be reduced below 60 percent. At the end of 1992, their share was 62.97 percent. Appendix Table 5 lists the voting power of members, which is related to, but not directly proportional to, their capital subscriptions. If Australia, Japan, and New Zealand, the developed regional members, vote with the nonregional members on any issue, the DMCs will be outvoted 44 to 56 percent, based on the present voting power of members. This situation can be avoided only if Australia and New Zealand together or Japan separately supports the DMCs (Australia's and New Zealand's individual voting power is inadequate to provide the necessary support). Thus, if Japan decides to override the larger Asian interests in the Bank (which is unlikely), the DMCs would have to rely on support from both Australia and New Zealand against nonregional interests. This possibility has never been a major concern, although it may surface if a contentious issue were to arise. The adoption by the Board of the report on the negotiations for the fifth replenishment of the ADF is a case in point where Australia, Japan, and New Zealand sided with the nonregional countries in pushing for its acceptance, although the report was not uniformly acceptable to the DMCs.

The original capital of the AsDB set in 1966 was $1.0 billion, of which 50 percent was paid-in and the balance was callable. Fifty percent of the paid-in portion was provided in the form of gold or convertible currencies and the remaining 50 percent in the local currency of each member. As the capital of the Bank grew over the years and the Bank matured into a strong financial institution with an excellent credit rating, the paid-in portion of the capital increases has decreased. The Articles require a review of the capital stock at intervals of no less than five years. There have been four GCIs since 1966. The first was in 1971 when the capital was increased by 150 percent, of which 20 percent was paid-in. The next increase of 135 percent was in 1976, when the paid-in portion was reduced to 10 percent. The third increase in 1983 was limited to 105 percent with the paid-in portion further reduced to 5 percent. The fourth increase of 100 percent, with a paid-in portion of 2 percent, was approved in 1994. Along with the decline in the paid-in portion of each capital increase, the proportion of convertible currencies paid-in was also reduced, although at a lower rate.[12] In addition to the GCIs, there have been capital subscriptions by new members and special increases to accommodate the needs of some members. Taking these and fluctuations in exchange rates into account, the authorized capital of the AsDB at the end of December 1992 was $23,223.7 million, of which $23,100.1 million was subscribed. The paid-in portion was only $2,787.0 million, which is 12.1 percent of the subscribed capital, reflecting the decline in the paid-in portion with each capital increase. Although the third capital increase was intended to cover the needs of the Bank for 1983–1987, it proved adequate for its lending needs to the end of 1993. The AsDB completed negotiations for the fourth GCI and obtained approval from its membership in May 1994. Projections had indicated that the Bank would exhaust its ability to make new loan commitments by mid-1994, had the capital increase not been approved.

Resources

The financial resources of the Bank consist of the OCR and special fund resources, which, in terms of the Articles, shall be "held, used, committed, invested or otherwise disposed of entirely separate from each other." The OCR consist of the subscribed capital (though the amount usable is only the paid-in portion); reserves, repayments, and income received on loans made and guarantees given; and funds raised in the capital markets by borrowings. The special fund resources consist of contributions made by member countries, repayments, and amounts set aside from the paid-in capital and allocated from the net income of the OCR.[13] The Bank is currently administering three special funds. One of these is the ADF established in 1974 for lending on concessional terms to eligible DMCs. The other two are the Technical Assistance Special Fund established in 1968 and the Japan Special Fund set up in 1988 and used mainly to finance the Bank's technical assistance and related activities.

Ordinary Capital Resources (OCR)

The Articles state that the total amount outstanding of loans, equity investments, and guarantees made by the Bank in its ordinary operations should not exceed the total amount of its unimpaired subscribed capital, reserves, and surplus included in its OCR, exclusive of the special reserve. At the end of December 1992, subscribed capital of the Bank was $23,100.1 million while reserves and unallocated net income were $4,257.0 million. Against these resources, the Bank's gross lending operations from the OCR stood at $23,688.4[14] million at the end of 1992.

The OCR are lent at rates of interest determined by the market. Until 1986, these were set on the basis of the average cost of borrowing by the Bank during the preceding twelve months plus a margin of 0.5 percent. The rates of interest were fixed for the entire life of the loan when they were negotiated. A change was made to a pool-based variable rate for loans negotiated after June 30, 1986.[15] (The World Bank changed to such a system in 1982.) The interest rates applicable are the average cost of outstanding borrowings, plus a spread. Initially, the spread was set at 0.5 percent and later reduced to 0.4 percent in 1988. They are revised at the beginning of each half year. The rate was set at 7.65 percent initially for the six months beginning July 1, 1986, and has fluctuated in the range of 6.33 to 6.61 percent during 1990–1992. At the end of 1992, 51 percent of the loan amounts outstanding and 97 percent of the undisbursed loan amounts were subject to a variable lending rate.

The loans from the OCR, which accounted for about 68 percent of AsDB lending up to the end of 1992, were denominated in U.S. dollars and disbursed and repayable in various currencies. Loans outstanding at the end of 1992 were disbursed mainly in four currencies, the yen, the Swiss franc, the U.S. dollar, and the deutsche mark, in that order, with the yen accounting for 61 percent. The borrowers bear the entire exchange risk for loans from the OCR. Since July 1992, the Bank has offered borrowers the option of U.S. dollar loans, with all transactions in U.S. dollars, or traditional multicurrency loans. The former are also subject to variable interest rates, adjusted at the beginning of each half year, based on a spread of 0.4 percent above the average cost of borrowings undertaken to fund the U.S. dollar pool.[16] There was an increase in the percentage of dollars disbursed from 10.8 percent at the end of 1991 to 12.7 percent at the end of 1992, which is attributed to the introduction of the U.S. dollar lending facility.

In addition to interest payments, a commitment charge of 0.75 percent is payable on the committed undisbursed balance of each loan. In recognition of concerns expressed by borrowers who obtained funds for infrastructure projects with long disbursement periods, the AsDB changed the commitment fee to a graduated basis[17] in 1987. The repayment periods have ranged from ten to thirty years including grace periods in the range of two to ten years. This practice of varying lending terms on the basis of project rather than country considerations is similar to that followed by the IDB but differs from the International Bank for Reconstruction and Development (IBRD) where it is dependent only on country considerations.

Asian Development Fund (ADF)

In addition to its authorized capital stock, the Articles of Agreement permitted the establishment of special funds for providing technical assistance and lending on concessional terms. This led to the creation of the Agriculture, Multi-Purpose, and Technical Assistance Special Funds in 1968. These were made up largely through contributions from bilateral sources and to a lesser extent from funds set aside from the paid-in portion of the authorized capital. They became difficult to administer when demand increased because they were dependent mostly on bilateral contributions, some of which were tied. This led to the creation of the ADF in 1974, which replaced both the Agriculture and Multi-Purpose Special Funds. The ADF has since become a mechanism for the systematic mobilization of concessional resources through contributions from donors. Its allocation to the DMCs is based on their per capita GNP, debt repayment capacity, and other specific developmental criteria such as those applicable to the island economies of the Pacific. The initial fund (ADF I) of $525 million covered the period 1974 and 1975. There have been five subsequent replenishments since, as seen in Table 2.1.

Table 2.1   ADF Replenishments

	Year Effective	Resources[a]
ADF I	1974	525
ADF II	1976	809
ADF III	1979	2,150
ADF IV	1983	3,214
ADF V	1987	3,600
ADF VI	1992	4,200

Source: AsDB Annual Report, various years.
Note: a. In millions of dollars.

ADF V initially covered 1987–1990. It was extended by one year to 1991 when additional funds became available due to changes in ADF financial policies and favorable exchange rate movements between the currency of the contributing member country and the U.S. dollar. Donors concluded negotiations for ADF VI in December 1991 and obtained commitments of $4,200 million for 1992–1995. This replenishment became effective in August 1992 when the Bank received aggregate commitments from donors beyond the minimum "trigger" figure of 50 percent of the replenishment. Along with the spillover from ADF V, the funds available during the period of ADF VI will make it possible for the Bank to make the largest commitment of soft funds in U.S. dollar terms in any replenishment period since the concessional window was set up in 1974.

The total resources of the ADF amounted to $15,263.5 million at the end of December 1992. This included bilateral contributions of $14,421.5 million[18] to successive replenishments, accumulated ADF surplus of $735.5 million, and $65.5 million set aside by the Board from the OCR in earlier years. A total of $14,062.2 million, including exchange rate adjustments of $1,060.8 million, had been committed in loans by this date. Of the resources made available in bilateral contributions, 51.5 percent was provided by Japan, 13.0 percent by the U.S., 7.0 percent by Germany, and 6.2 percent by Canada, the donors who account for 77.6 percent of the total.

Until 1988, the terms of all ADF loans carried a service charge of 1 percent and a maturity of forty years including a grace period of ten years. There was no interest or commitment fee. The principal was repaid at the rate of 1 percent per annum from the eleventh year to the twentieth year and 4.5 percent per annum thereafter. These terms were equivalent to a grant element of 77 percent. In 1988, the repayment period for countries receiving blended resources from the AsDB (in other words, both OCR and ADF) was reduced to thirty-five years leaving the grace period unchanged. Along with this, the repayments were made at the rate of 2.5 percent from the eleventh to the twentieth year and 5 percent thereafter. This reduced the grant element for these loans to 75 percent. ADF loans are disbursed and repaid in various currencies although, unlike OCR loans, they are denominated in special drawing rights (SDRs).

Other Special Funds

In accordance with the provisions in the charter, the AsDB finances technical assistance for

a) project preparation intended to assist countries in preparing projects for financing by it or other donors;
b) project implementation for assisting borrowers in implementing, operating, and managing projects financed by it;
c) advisory purposes for institutional building, plan formulation, and policy, sector, and issue-oriented studies; and
d) regional activities for any of the above purposes. To date, they have been largely for advisory purposes involving two or more countries.

Regional and advisory technical assistance is funded on a grant basis while assistance for project implementation is included in the loan for the relevant project. Project preparation technical assistance is financed on a grant basis up to $600,000. If a loan is subsequently approved, the amount in excess of $250,000 is recovered from it.

All technical assistance, with the exception of project preparation that is retroactively financed from loans and project implementation, is financed from the Technical Assistance Special Fund (TASF), the Japan Special Fund, and grants received from other bilateral and multilateral sources under cofinancing arrangements. The contributions to the TASF were initially made on a voluntary basis by both developed and developing countries. During the negotiations for ADF V, the donors decided to regularize the basis of contributions and allocated 2 percent (or $72 million) of the replenishment. A similar decision was taken during ADF VI when it was decided to allocate $140 million or 3.33 percent of the replenishment to the fund. In addition, the TASF receives allocations from the net income of the OCR, investment income, and reimbursements. Some direct contributions continue to be made. On a cumulative basis, they amounted to $85.3 million by the end of 1992, and their use was mostly untied. Technical assistance to DMCs financed from the TASF totalled $318.7 million by the end of 1992.

The Japan Special Fund is the largest single fund among the other arrangements set up for financing technical assistance on a grant basis. It was established in 1988, and the funds are untied. They are also used for financing equity investments in private sector projects although allocations to these have been small up to 1994. Contracts awarded under the Japan Special Fund for technical assistance to DMCs were $133.0 million and accounted for 22 percent of the total by the end of 1992. This compares with $160.8 million or 26 percent under several cofinancing arrangements. Regional technical assistance activities totalled $113.5 million, some of which was provided by cofinancing partners.

Access to Resources

The DMCs are classified into three groups for purposes of receiving allocations from the ADF, as listed in Table 2.2. Group A countries with full eligibility to the ADF have a low per capita GNP and low debt repayment capacity or special circumstances such as those prevailing in the small island economies. The least-developed countries among these receive priority in allocations from the ADF. Of these, Bangladesh, Cambodia, Cook Islands, Lao Peoples' Democratic Republic, Nepal, and Western Samoa received loans from the ADF in 1992. Afghanistan and Myanmar are also in this category although loan operations were suspended in both countries, the former due to donor pressure resulting from the invasion of the country by the Soviet Union in 1979 and the latter due to the suppression of democracy in 1986. Similar priority is given to Vietnam and the remaining Pacific DMCs, which are the Federated States of Micronesia, Marshall Islands, Solomon Islands, Tonga, and Vanuatu. Priority is next accorded to Mongolia, Pakistan, and Sri Lanka. Some countries in Group A will receive reasonable amounts of loans from the OCR[19] if their development needs are greater than the amount of ADF resources that can be reasonably allocated to them and if they have the capacity to service such loans. Pakistan has already received such a blend of loans from the ADF and OCR. Sri Lanka is the only other country in this group that may receive loans from the OCR during ADF VI. India and China[20] are also Group A countries and eligible to receive allocations from the ADF though none has to date. There was no agreement among donors, in particular the United States, during the ADF VI negotiations on whether to make ADF resources available to either of these, the two largest eligible low-income DMCs. In view of this lack of consensus and the needs of traditional ADF recipients and other eligible borrowers, it was concluded that resources would not be made available to these countries during the period of ADF VI. Accordingly, their borrowings from the AsDB will be entirely from the OCR.

Table 2.2   Classification of DMCs by ADF Eligibility

Group A (DMCs with full eligibility for ADF)	Afghanistan, Bangladesh, Bhutan, Cambodia, China, Cook Islands, India, Kiribati, Lao PDR, Maldive Islands, Marshall Islands, Micronesia, Mongolia, Myanmar, Nepal, Pakistan, Solomon Islands, Sri Lanka, Tonga, Turalu, Vanuatu, Vietnam, and Western Samoa
Group B (DMCs with eligibility for ADF receiving a blend of ADF/OCR)	Indonesia, Papua New Guinea, the Philippines, and Thailand
Group C (DMCs not eligible for ADF)	Fiji, Hong Kong, Korea, Malaysia, Singapore, and Taipei,China

Source: Compiled from AsDB documents.

Four countries with a higher per capita GNP and/or debt repayment capacity are in Group B. These are Indonesia, a low-income country, and Papua New Guinea, the Philippines, and Thailand, all lower-middle-income countries. Papua New Guinea is provided access to the ADF and receives a blend of the OCR and ADF. Both Indonesia and the Philippines continue to be provided limited access to the ADF on a temporary basis since the mid-1980s due to their prevailing economic situation. Thailand has not had allocations from the ADF since 1982.

Group C countries, which consist of Fiji, Hong Kong, the Republic of Korea, Malaysia, Singapore, and Taipei,China are all middle- or high-income countries and have no access to the ADF. Any borrowings by them will be from the OCR although Taipei,China (1971), Hong Kong and Singapore (1980), and Korea (1988) have stopped borrowing from the AsDB. The current ceiling for ADF eligibility is per capita GNP of $850 at 1990 prices. This is the demarcation between Groups B and C countries, though the total availability of ADF resources does not provide Group B countries with full access to them.

During the negotiations for ADF VI it was agreed that the following DMCs could receive allocations from the ADF:

a) the traditional ADF recipients, in other words Group A countries that received ADF loans during ADF V, and Papua New Guinea, which received a blend of the ADF and OCR;

b) eligible DMCs that were nonactive during ADF V, in other words Afghanistan and Myanmar (if Bank operations are resumed), Cambodia,[21] and Vietnam;

c) eligible DMCs that joined the Bank after January 1990,[22] in other words the Federated States of Micronesia, the Marshall Islands, and Mongolia; and

d) Indonesia and the Philippines, depending on the availability of funds, economic performance, and the need for external support under concessional conditions.

Access to the ADF will therefore be provided to all Group A countries except China and India and to three Group B countries, Indonesia, Papua New Guinea and the Philippines, depending on availability of funds.

It is expected that the Bank would allocate the dominant share of ADF VI to the traditional recipients as a group. Priority would next be given to Group A DMCs in which no operations were conducted during ADF V, if conditions permit them to resume loan operations, and those who joined after January 1990. Finally, limited and reduced access to the ADF could be considered for Indonesia and the Philippines for projects directed at poverty reduction, the primary social sector, and protection of the environment. Within these guidelines, the Bank will seek to regulate access based on need and development performance. If performance is judged to be weak and not as a result of external conditions, the AsDB will reduce the size of ADF operations and restrict activities to those countries that promise the most productive use of concessional funds. In such cases lending will be confined to a core program, with the focus shifting to policy dialogue, economic and sector work, and technical assistance geared to improving economic performance. This was a condition laid down by the donors in their report of the ADF VI negotiations.

Group C countries are only eligible to receive loans from the OCR with repayment periods dependent on project considerations. Only Fiji and Malaysia from among this group presently borrow from the Bank, the others having ceased to do so. Group B countries borrow largely from the OCR but, apart from Thailand, also have had limited allocations from ADF depending on availability. Group A countries, on the other hand, receive ADF resources, the only exceptions being China and India. Current policy allows these countries access to the OCR provided the need can be established and they have the capacity to service these loans. Pakistan is the only Group A country that is presently borrowing from both ADF and the OCR and thus receives a blend of resources.

Bank Operations

Volume

Gross loan commitments to the DMCs totalled $42,458.9 million for 1,103 projects by the end of 1992, nearly twenty-five years after the first loan was approved in January 1968. Some 360 of these projects were cofinanced with other donors who raised a further $13,965.5 million (of which official sources contributed 69 percent) to complement the Bank's contributions to these projects of $17,469.3 million. The OCR accounted for $28,894.6 million or 68 percent of Bank lending for 641 loans[23] and the balance of $13,564.3 million or 32 percent was for 569 loans[24] from the ADF. Thirty-one of the thirty-two DMCs have received loan commitments from the AsDB to date.[25] Important milestones were passed in reaching this level of loan commitments. Cumulative loan commitments (both OCR and ADF) reached $10 billion in 1982, $20 billion in 1987, $30 billion in 1990, and $40 billion in 1992. A similar picture is conveyed in the annual loan commitments, which reached $1.0 billion in 1978, $2.0 billion in 1984, $3.0 billion in 1988, $4.0 billion in 1991, and $5.0 billion in 1992. These aggregate figures illustrate the acceleration of the lending program in the second half of the 1980s and early 1990s, particularly in the latter period.

From 1968 to 1992, the Bank financed a total of 2,316 technical assistance projects from grant funds totalling $726.0 million[26] in thirty-one countries. Of these, 1,799 were for activities in individual DMCs, for which $612.4 million was allocated. Among these, 843 were for project preparation that led to the Bank financing 502 projects out of the total of 1,103 financed to date. The balance of 956 were for advisory and operational purposes to assist in project implementation and institutional development of the executing agencies. The other 517 technical assistance operations were for regional activities covering conferences, studies, research, and training for which $113.5 million was allocated. The scope of the Bank's technical assistance activities financed from grant funds exceeds that of the World Bank.[27]

The Bank began direct assistance to the private sector in 1983. This support encompasses direct equity financing, equity lines of credit through financial intermediaries, underwriting, loans without government guarantees, and complementary financing from non-Bank sources to help financiers benefit from the preferred creditor status of the AsDB. Over 1983–1992, there were eighty-three operations that have remained small in value. These have totalled $878.5 million in support of projects and funds in eleven countries and eight regional activities. In value terms, unguaranteed loans made up the largest component ($496.3 million), followed by equity facilities ($220.6 million). Bank funds used for private sector operations accounted for only 1.7 percent of the total. Complementary loan financing accounted for another $161.6 million.

Geographical Distribution of Lending

South Asia became a larger borrower than Southeast Asia in the 1980s. Its share of borrowings increased from 31.0 percent during 1970–1981 to 46.2 percent during 1982–1992, while that of Southeast Asia decreased from 49.2 percent to 43.2 percent. Between the two periods, the South Pacific DMCs tripled their borrowings although their share rose to only 1.9 percent, whilst that of the NIEs virtually halved and has now declined to zero due to their withdrawal from borrowings.[28] In addition to this change regarding the NIEs, the other major factor that affected the pattern was the move by India to start borrowing in January 1986 (largely responsible for the increasing share of South Asia in the 1980s) and by China in November 1987. By the end of 1992, India had become the second-largest borrower from the OCR on a cumulative basis. The lending program to China could not develop as it did in India because new lending was suspended between January 1989 and November 1990 due to the incidents that resulted in the Tiananmen Square massacre.

A somewhat different picture emerges when borrowings from the OCR and ADF are compared separately. Table 2.3 shows that the

Table 2.3   Geographical Distribution

	1970–1981 Millions of Dollars	%	1982–1992 Millions of Dollars	%	1970–1992 Millions of Dollars	%
OCR						
South Asia	559.3	8.4	6,825.3	30.7	7,384.6	25.5
Southeast Asia	4,345.7	65.0	12,328.6	55.4	16,674.3	57.6
North Asia	—	—	1,905.2	8.6	1,905.2	6.6
NIEs	1,686.9	25.2	946.1	4.2	2,633.0	9.1
South Pacific DMCs	89.9	1.3	256.2	1.2	346.1	1.2
Subtotal	6,681.8	100.0	22,261.4	100.0	28.943.2	100.0
ADF						
South Asia	2,426.3	82.6	8,516.3	80.4	10,942.5	80.9
Southeast Asia	385.4	13.1	1,668.0	15.7	2,053.4	15.2
North Asia	—	—	33.8	0.3	33.8	0.2
NIEs	—	—	—	—	—	—
South Pacific DMCs	126.1	4.3	375.1	3.5	501.2	3.7
Subtotal	2,937.8	100.0	10,593.2	100.0	13,530.9	100.0

Source: AsDB.
Note: Singapore is included in the NIEs and not in South East Asia; percentages do not total 100 percent due to rounding.

share of South Asia borrowings from the OCR increased from 8.4 percent in the 1970s to 30.7 percent in the 1980s. Southeast Asia, on the other hand, had its share decline from 65.0 to 55.4 percent. The share of the NIEs declined substantially from 25.2 to 4.2 percent as the countries withdrew from borrowing. That of the South Pacific DMCs remained small at around 1.0 percent while the share of North Asia (China and Mongolia) in the 1980s was 8.6 percent. The share of South Asia in borrowings from the ADF exceeded 80 percent during both periods. That of Southeast Asia increased marginally from 13.1 percent to 15.7 percent, mainly due to Indonesia and the Philippines being provided temporary access to the ADF due to their critical economic situation from 1987 and 1986 respectively. The NIEs received no loans from the ADF in either period while the share of the South Pacific DMCs declined marginally to 3.5 percent. North Asia received marginal amounts from the ADF, which were made available only to Mongolia.

The eight largest borrowers from the OCR and ADF accounted for over 90 percent of the loan commitments in each category during 1970–1992. It is seen from Table 2.4 that three countries, Indonesia, Pakistan, and the Philippines, are in both groups. Pakistan is one of the four largest borrowers from both sources. Over 1970–1992, Indonesia received the largest commitment of OCR at 29.3 percent of the total. India, the Philippines, and Pakistan followed, in that order, accounting for a further 38.9 percent. If only the past five years are considered, from 1988 to 1992, the shares of lending from the OCR to

Table 2.4 Percentage Shares of the Eight Largest Borrowers from the OCR and ADF: 1970–1992

Country	OCR	ADF	Total
Bangladesh	—	28.2	9.2
China	6.6	—	—
India	14.8	—	10.1
Indonesia	29.3	4.9	21.5
Korea	8.0	—	5.4
Lao PDR	—	2.5	—
Malaysia	6.9	—	4.7
Myanmar	—	3.1	—
Nepal	—	8.1	—
Pakistan	10.7	29.1	16.6
Philippines	13.4	6.5	11.2
Sri Lanka	—	10.4	—
Thailand	8.4	—	5.9
Total for eight largest borrowers	98.1	92.8	84.6

Source: AsDB.
Note: This table shows only the percentage share of the eight largest borrowers for each category. Accordingly, the symbol (—) does not indicate a zero share. See p. 26 in this book for comments on the growth of lending to India and China.

Indonesia and India were 30.8 and 25.5 percent respectively, followed by China and the Philippines with 12.5 and 10.7 percent. The Bank is unique among the RDBs in that one borrower, Indonesia, consistently received more than 30 percent of loan commitments from the OCR in most of the years since 1980. Pakistan and Bangladesh were the largest borrowers from the ADF accounting for 29.1 and 28.2 percent of loan commitments during 1970–1992. They were followed by Sri Lanka and Nepal, which together accounted for a further 18.5 percent. The past five years, 1988–1992, show a different pattern with Pakistan and Bangladesh accounting for 29.0 and 25.5 percent respectively, followed by Sri Lanka and the Philippines at 11.7 percent each. The four largest borrowers from the OCR and ADF accounted for 68.2 and 73.8 percent of each total, showing that loan concentration was higher among the borrowers from the ADF over 1970–1992. The concentration was higher during 1988–1992 when the four largest borrowers from the OCR and ADF accounted for 79.5 and 77.9 percent.

When total borrowings from both sources during 1970–1992 are analyzed, it is seen that Indonesia and Pakistan are the largest borrowers with shares of 21.5 and 16.6 percent respectively. The Philippines and India followed with shares of 11.2 and 10.1 percent. The next four were Bangladesh, Thailand, Korea, and Malaysia, in that order, with shares under 10 percent. When the more recent period of 1988–1992 is reviewed, it is seen that the shares of Bangladesh, Malaysia, and Thailand are lower by 1 to 2 percent, and Korea ceased to be a borrower. Indonesia is the largest with a share of 23 percent and India second with 17.6 percent. Pakistan's share of 15.9 percent places it third, followed by China with 8.6 percent, showing its emergence as a major borrower in recent years.

Sectoral Distribution

The dominant sector in AsDB lending during 1970–1992 has consisted of agriculture and agro-industry. Its average sectoral share in the triennial periods during 1973–1990 was in the range of 26–34 percent, with the highest share reached during 1982–1984. This supported the efforts made by many DMCs to achieve self-sufficiency in food production. The Bank adopted the policy in 1979 for increasing lending to the agriculture sector by 20 percent annually during 1979–1982, and this was realized. The Advisory Group for the Study of the Operational Priorities and Plans (OPP Study) of the AsDB for the 1980s[29] agreed with the importance accorded to the sector by the Bank in its lending program. With the emergence of poverty alleviation as a priority for AsDB lending, the Report of the Panel on the Asian Development Bank in the 1990s[30] agreed that continuing support for agriculture and rural development with poverty alleviation as the focus in project design was justified.

The start of the green revolution, which had a major impact on many Asian countries achieving food self-sufficiency, preceded the establishment of the AsDB. Credit for this should be given to the successful research on food grains that led to the development of high-yielding varieties by the International Agricultural Research Centers, set up under the umbrella of the Consultative Group for International Agricultural Research and chaired by the World Bank, and to the outreach programs these centers set up in many Asian countries. The work of the International Rice Research Institute in the Philippines, the International Crop Research Institute for the Semi-Arid Tropics in India, the Asian Vegetable Research and Development Center in Taipei,China, and more recently the International Institute for Irrigation Management in Sri Lanka deserve special mention, although the research work conducted in international centers located in other regions played a major role as well. The AsDB supported research in these centers and their outreach programs. It also assisted DMC efforts to increase food production by enabling them to use the results of this research by funding irrigation, flood control, and drainage projects. The scope of the support changed gradually to raising rural incomes and increasing employment opportunities through an integrated approach to rural development. The Bank also helped in strengthening rural institutions to enable participation of smallholder farmers and landless workers in projects it funded. These widened in scope to establish complementary facilities and services such as extension, credit, storage, and distribution.

Following the increase in oil prices in the 1970s, the AsDB gave priority to the energy sector. The thrust of the lending program was toward developing indigenous energy resources, energy conservation and improvement of system efficiency, and rural electrification. The Bank undertook a regional energy survey in 1980 to improve the effectiveness of its lending. A target of $6 billion for this sector was set for 1981–1987, but this was not realized. The OPP Study for the 1980s also agreed with the priority accorded to the sector. Lending for energy projects was on the average about one-quarter of the AsDB's portfolio during 1970–1992, although it fluctuated in the range of 17.5–33.1 percent during triennial periods. The highest shares were achieved during 1970–1972 and 1982–1984 when the sector accounted for 33.1 and 29.0 percent.

Lending to social infrastructure increased from 10–11 percent in the early 1970s to over 19 percent during 1979–1981. It declined thereafter to 14–15 percent during the 1980s, although the value of loans to this sector increased. The projects financed have focused on water supply and sanitation, education, urban development, housing, and health and population activities. Both the OPP Study for the 1980s and the expert panel for the 1990s gave priority to investments in social infrastructure. In view of the long gestation period of these investments and the fact that they were neither foreign exchange earners nor savers, the need to use resources from the ADF to finance them wherever possible was recognized. At the same time, the nature of these projects requires the financing of a higher proportion of local costs.

One should interpret with caution the changes in the sectoral shares observed in social and physical infrastructure, as shown in Table 2.5. The marginal decline in the share of social infrastructure took place in the context of an increase in loan commitments in value terms. These projects, on the average, have long gestation periods. Further, two new large borrowers from the OCR, China and India, emerged in the mid–1980s. They adopted a policy of not borrowing for social sector projects from the OCR. Instead they borrowed heavily for energy and physical infrastructure. Countries such as Indonesia, Thailand, and others in South Asia are experiencing capacity bottlenecks in physical infrastructure such as transport and communications and energy. These have become major impediments to faster growth and have led to increased borrowings for new projects.

Table 2.5   Sectoral Shares (in percentages)

	1970–1981	1982–1992	1970–1992
Agriculture and agro-industry	28.8	25.6	26.4
Energy	25.3	24.6	24.7
Industry and nonfuel minerals	3.7	4.2	4.1
Transport and communications	13.8	18.5	17.4
Social infrastructure	15.3	14.6	14.7
Development finance institutions	13.1	10.1	10.8
Multisector	0.0	2.4	1.9
Total	100.0	100.0	100.0

Source: Derived from AsDB statistics.

The allocation to industry and nonfuel minerals has ranged from 0.9 to 7.2 percent during 1970–1992, leading to a cumulative average of 4.1 percent. The transport and communications sector recorded an increase of 4.7 percent in the 1980s compared to the 1970s. Lending to DFIs[31] declined from 13.1 to 10.1 percent during the same periods, the lowest average being in 1982–1984 when it was only 7.0 percent. Multisector projects, which made up 2.4 percent of Bank lending in the 1980s, was the principal mode of lending to the South Pacific DMCs and other small countries such as the Maldives and Bhutan. They covered a number of subprojects in one or more sectors. Overall, there has been a greater demand for AsDB loans for agriculture and agro-industry and energy projects by the low-income countries and social infrastructure and industry projects by the middle-income countries.

Lending Modalities

The operating principles of the Bank state that it should finance mainly "specific projects, including those forming part of a national, sub-regional or regional development program."[32] Consequently, project lending has been the main vehicle for transferring AsDB resources to DMCs. It is seen in Appendix Table 3 that direct project lending increased in absolute terms with the growth in Bank lending in each triennial period until the mid–1980s. It declined during 1985–1987 and grew thereafter. As a share of total AsDB lending it declined gradually from 85.1 percent during 1970–1972 to 54.9 percent during 1988–1990. Its share in 1991–1992 was 56.6 percent. The change in the shares of the different lending modalities between the 1970s and the 1980s is illustrated in Table 2.6.

Table 2.6   Shares of Lending Modalities (in percentages)

	1970–1981	1982–1992	1970–1992
Project loans	82.0a	59.7	64.7
DFI and agricultural credit lines	13.9	12.6	12.6
Program loans	0.9	10.4	8.3
Sector loans	2.7	15.3	12.4
TA loans	0.5	0.2	0.3
Private sector loans	—	1.5	1.2
Multiproject loans	—	0.6	0.5
Total	100.0	100.0	100.0

Source: AsDB.

The decline in project lending has been partly compensated for by the introduction of sector lending in 1980 for financing a number of subprojects in a sector or subsector covering a specific geographical area or a time-slice of an investment program. It accounted for 14.6 and 17.6 percent during 1988–1990 and 1991–1992. This introduced greater flexibility to project lending by its ability to finance smaller projects. Sector lending was reviewed in 1985, after which its share of AsDB lending increased to its present levels. The prerequisites for such lending are the availability of a sector plan, appropriate sector policies, and institutions capable of implementing the planned investments and policy changes. It has enabled the Bank to engage DMC governments in policy dialogue on the long-term development objectives of the sector, its plans, priorities, and policies covering issues such as the investment program, incentives and disincentives, pricing, subsidies and tariffs, cost recovery, and institutional changes. Specific provisions and covenants were introduced in agreements where appropriate.

The AsDB departed from purely project lending in 1978 when it introduced program lending. These loans were intended to finance essential inputs for priority sectors or subsectors and were geared to achieve greater use of installed capacity or to enhance productivity. DMCs had to demonstrate that foreign exchange shortages were causing underutilization of capacity and that well designed plans had been formulated. If such a plan was not available, the country had to be willing to prepare one with Bank technical assistance. Although all productive sectors were eligible for this support, program loans financed mostly agricultural inputs prior to 1987. Program lending to a country was limited to 20 percent of annual lending while such lending to all DMCs was limited to 7.5 percent of total Bank lending for the year.

The policy on program lending was revised in November 1987. It is now geared to supporting medium-term adjustment programs in particular sectors and has tended to be similar to the sector adjustment programs of the World Bank. A DMC receiving support should be willing to engage in a dialogue on sectoral policies and issues relating to the efficient functioning of sectoral facilities and institutions. The understandings reached are contained in a letter of development policy sent by the DMC to the AsDB. The World Bank's sector adjustment loans often include macroeconomic issues such as budget deficit targets, trade liberalization, exchange rate policy, and so on in their policy matrices, but the policy changes embodied in AsDB program loans have focused essentially on sectoral issues even in financial and industrial sector program loans. The Bank considers the leadership in any dialogue with DMCs on macroeconomic issues to be the responsibility of the World Bank and the IMF. With the change in policy in 1987, the overall Bank ceiling for program lending was increased from 7.5 to 15 percent[33] although this was exceeded during 1988–1990. It declined to 10.3 percent in 1991–1992.

Lines of credit to DFIs enabled the AsDB to support small- and medium-sized projects (mainly in the industrial sector) that it could not otherwise have done directly. Agricultural credit lines provided similar support in the agriculture sector. The share of all lines of credit in the AsDB portfolio declined from 15 percent in the early 1970s to 12–13 percent in the late 1980s and early 1990s.

The introduction of sector and program lending, both directly and through financial intermediaries, led to a decline in the share of project lending from 99.8 percent in the early 1970s to 66.9 percent in the late 1980s.

The Political Balance of Power

Nonregional Financial Support

Nonregional countries have had a significant involvement in the formulation of lending policies and in the contributions made to the financial resources for lending and technical assistance operations since the inception of the Bank. They have also had an impact on the staffing and procurement under Bank operations. The share capital of the AsDB held by the regional members was 63.0 percent of the total at the end of 1992,[34] of which the share of DMCs was 38.8 percent and Japan 16.4 percent. The membership of a major donor—Japan— among the regional countries, which is not a superpower and whose budgetary process allows contributions to ADF replenishments and GCIs in a timely manner (unlike the United States), makes the AsDB unique in the family of RDBs. Japan's shareholding translates into a 13.5 percent share in the voting power, which is balanced by an equivalent shareholding and voting power for the United States, the largest among the nonregional member countries. The largest shareholders among the DMCs are China (6.8 percent), India (6.7 percent), Indonesia (5.7 percent), and Korea (5.3 percent).

Japan dominates the ADF with a share of 52.3 percent of the amounts committed up to the end of 1992, although these contributions do not add to its voting power in the Bank (see Table 2.7). Among the DMCs, Indonesia, Korea, Hong Kong, and Taipei,China have made contributions to the ADF, although to date these amounts have been relatively small. The United States is the largest nonregional donor to the fund with a cumulative share of 11.2 percent at the end of 1992. However, the tardy nature of its payments and the significantly larger contributions by Japan make it necessary to question whether the United States should continue to wield the influence it does on AsDB policies through voting power that is based on its historical subscription to the capital structure. There appears to be a general waning of interest in the AsDB by the United States (which has not been revived by the Clinton administration), although its influence is brought to bear on matters of foreign policy concern. Its

Table 2.7   Subscribed Capital, Voting Power, and ADF (in percentages)

| | OCR | | ADF |
| | | | Cumulative Amount |
	Subscriptions	Voting Power	Committed
Regional	62.970	64.222	57.4
DMCs	38.824	43.752	0.3
Japan	16.435	13.533	52.3
Australia and New Zealand	7.711	6.937	4.8
Nonregional	37.030	35.778	42.6
United States	15.900	13.105	11.2
Canada	5.508	4.791	6.6
Others	15.622	17.882	24.8

Source: AsDB Annual Report 1992.

ability to do so depends largely on the unwillingness of Japan and other developed member countries to oppose the United States on many issues. An example of the political influence wielded by the United States was the embargo on assistance to Vietnam, which held up the implementation of a lending program until 1993, although other members were willing to start operations at a much earlier date. Some ascribe the attitude of the United States to the shift in lending patterns by the Bank in the 1980s in favor of South Asian countries that are less market-oriented in their economic policies and outlook in comparison to the countries of Southeast and East Asia. Further, the lack of Bank representation in Washington, D.C. may be another factor. Whatever motivation lies behind this trend and the unwillingness to surrender a share of its voting power, the U.S. position makes it important for Canada, the country with the second-largest voting power (4.8 percent) among the nonregionals, to maintain its strong interest and support of the AsDB. This is necessary to maintain an independent stance and to mobilize wider donor support to promote the development efforts of the DMCs through the multilateral structure of the Bank.

Procurement

Statistics in Table 2.8 indicate that there is an increasing involvement of DMCs in contracts awarded from the OCR and ADF over 1967–1976, 1977–1986, and 1987–1992. The share of their contracts for goods, related services, and civil works from both sources of funds exceeded 50 percent during 1987–1992. Indonesia, Korea, the Philippines, India, Malaysia, and Thailand, in order of decreasing

Table 2.8 Distribution of Contracts Awarded by Country of Origin

	OCR						ADF					
	1967–1976		1977–1986		1987–1992		1967–1976		1977–1986		1987–1992	
	a	b	a	b	a	b	a	b	a	b	a	b
Regional	59.93	18.83	61.14	26.64	75.74	40.09	64.58	36.41	58.26	37.55	73.50	40.64
DMCs	10.62	5.70	18.13	9.02	55.98	26.88	18.15	6.25	21.56	14.51	56.67	24.30
Bangladesh	0.00	0.00	0.00	0.03	0.00	0.01	0.00	0.00	0.27	0.01	10.91	2.14
India	1.64	3.36	1.25	0.93	4.61	0.95	4.64	1.66	7.84	8.43	3.86	3.87
Indonesia	0.00	0.00	0.30	0.25	15.72	16.42	0.00	0.00	0.01	0.33	2.67	3.25
Korea	5.32	1.31	9.30	3.35	11.15	2.36	5.79	1.86	6.82	2.06	5.81	2.40
Malaysia	0.46	0.00	0.39	0.03	4.43	0.81	0.56	1.39	0.45	0.69	1.33	0.35
Pakistan	0.01	0.00	0.00	0.04	2.62	0.41	0.00	0.00	0.14	0.00	9.65	5.67
Philippines	0.00	0.94	1.58	0.92	5.58	3.18	0.07	1.11	0.34	2.66	3.38	4.62
Singapore	0.20	0.00	1.13	0.30	1.90	0.19	4.14	0.00	2.62	0.09	4.21	0.12
Thailand	1.32	0.00	1.09	0.04	4.38	0.13	1.75	0.00	1.53	0.02	1.41	0.04
Others	1.67	0.09	3.09	3.13	5.59	2.42	1.20	0.23	1.54	0.22	13.44	1.84
Australia and New Zealand	1.49	5.33	2.67	4.61	1.82	3.61	5.72	8.69	2.56	6.39	2.21	6.24
Japan	47.82	7.35	40.34	13.01	17.94	9.60	40.71	21.47	34.14	16.65	14.62	10.10
Nonregional	40.07	81.62	38.86	73.36	24.26	59.91	35.42	63.59	41.74	62.45	26.50	59.36
Canada	2.48	2.30	1.75	6.72	0.88	6.04	0.64	18.56	0.67	9.35	0.54	5.86
France	4.27	6.06	3.58	3.88	2.04	5.44	0.14	0.00	1.61	2.26	1.65	1.36
Germany	8.55	10.38	8.09	5.95	4.92	4.07	15.36	22.95	7.69	5.02	3.91	4.73
Italy	3.80	11.08	2.63	5.83	2.39	4.16	5.97	5.57	3.89	1.58	1.94	1.63
Netherlands	2.46	2.21	1.74	2.82	0.77	3.68	1.77	5.64	1.63	2.82	1.24	4.12
Switzerland	2.16	1.07	2.42	5.63	1.71	8.11	0.35	0.00	3.10	5.43	1.63	5.31
U.K.	4.56	3.61	4.57	10.94	2.25	8.29	7.31	2.87	8.31	18.99	3.80	21.06
U.S.	7.84	41.47	10.67	27.38	6.63	16.98	3.47	6.92	10.81	15.08	8.79	12.46
Others	3.95	3.44	3.41	4.21	2.67	3.14	0.41	1.08	4.03	1.92	3.00	2.83

Source: AsDB Annual Report 1992.
Notes: Column a: Goods, related services, and civil works (%).
Column b: Consulting services (%).
Only countries with a share in excess of 4.0 percent in categories (a) and/or (b), in at least one of the time periods, have been listed.

amounts, had shares exceeding 4 percent for contracts from the OCR, with Indonesia and Korea accounting for 15.7 and 11.2 percent. As for contracts from the ADF, Bangladesh, Pakistan, Korea and Singapore, in descending order, had shares exceeding 4 percent, with Bangladesh accounting for 10.9 and Pakistan for 9.7 percent. On the other hand, Japan's share of contracts declined from almost 48 percent from the OCR to 17.9 and from 40 percent from the ADF to 14.6 percent for the period from 1967–1976 to 1987–1992. Japan retained its leading position overall in spite of the significant decline in its share of contracts. The appreciation of the yen influenced this outcome, although Japanese firms have a competitive edge in the region in price, quality, proximity, and marketing capacity. Its share of ADF contracts, be it for 1987–1992 or on a cumulative basis for the entire period since the Bank's inception, bears no relation to the major financial contribution it makes to the ADF. It does not obtain an equivalent return in procurement.

Despite these movements in country shares, the regional share increased to 75.7 and 73.5 percent for contracts from the OCR and ADF. The share of nonregional countries declined between 1967–1976 to 1987–1992 from 40.1 to 24.3 percent and 35.4 to 26.5 percent for contracts from the OCR and ADF. The United States accounted for the largest share at 8.8 percent, followed by Germany and the United Kingdom with shares of 3.9 and 3.8 percent for ADF contracts during 1987–1992. Similarly, the United States had the largest share of OCR contracts at 6.6 percent followed by Germany at 4.9 percent during the same period.

In the case of consulting services, the DMCs have been less successful in securing contracts, although performance has improved during the three time periods to reach about one-quarter of the total from both the OCR and ADF during 1987–1992. The regional share reached about 40 percent from both sources of funds mainly due to the performance of Japanese firms, whose share, although declining (as in the case of goods, related services, and civil works), remained the highest of the regional countries. Among the nonregional countries, Canada, Germany, Italy, the United Kingdom, and the United States have been major beneficiaries of consulting contracts, having received a share exceeding 10 percent during one or more of the three time periods. During 1987–1992, the United States was the largest recipient of consultancy contracts from the OCR with a share of 17.0 percent, followed by the United Kingdom, Switzerland, and Canada with 8.3, 8.1, and 6.0 percent. In the case of ADF contracts, the United Kingdom was the largest with 21.1 percent followed by the United States, Canada, and Switzerland with 12.5, 5.9, and 5.3 percent.

These statistics on contracts awarded illustrate the changing pat-

tern between regional and nonregional countries and between countries in each grouping. It is important to take note of them because
the support given to the AsDB by nonregional and nonborrowing
members is increasingly being influenced by the contracts received
by firms in their countries for the implementation of Bank-funded
projects and technical assistance operations, although this is not the
only factor.

Influence of Major Shareholders

At the end of 1992, the Bank had 624 professional staff members representing forty-three nationalities. Many donor countries sought to
place their nationals on the staff and, in some instances, in senior
positions. The success or otherwise of these efforts can be gauged by
comparing actual staff positions with a notional entitlement based on
each country's share of the capital contribution to the Bank, though
no formal quota system exists. The interplay between this and the
merit system said to operate for appointments is unclear. A commercial advantage to some countries has been that nationals have, in
some instances, provided a window of information on projects to
firms bidding for Bank-funded contracts. Table 2.9 shows that the
number of professional staff from DMCs was less than those from
other countries during the 1980s with fewer senior positions from the

Table 2.9   Professional Staff: 1981–1991

	1981		1986		1991	
	a	b	a	b	a	b
Regional	300	42	376	51	395	57
DMCs	215	32	260	34	279	39
India	41	9	48	10	48	13
Philippines	31	2	40	3	41	3
Korea	23	4	30	5	26	2
Malaysia	20	3	24	2	24	4
Other DMCs	100	14	118	14	140	17
Australia and						
New Zealand	46	3	53	7	55	9
Japan	39	7	63	10	61	9
Nonregional	155	21	219	25	203	25
United States	48	8	64	8	68	11
Canada	29	3	38	4	34	5
Others	78	10	117	13	101	9
Total	455	63	595	76	598	82
DMCs	215	32	260	34	279	39
Others	240	31	335	42	319	43

Source: AsDB.
Notes: Column a: All professional staff.
Column b: Manager and above.

manager level and above. Professional staff from regional member countries, including those at the senior level, outnumber those from nonregional countries, and these numbers correspond broadly to their share of the capital. The staff numbers from the major shareholders, which are Japan and the United States, are below their notional entitlements, as they are for senior positions, while those of other countries such as India and the Philippines exceed theirs.

It should be recalled that the consultative committee that helped establish the AsDB in 1966 expected that the regional character of the Bank would be better suited to tackling the development problems of the Asian region than bilateral channels and the World Bank. Would the Bank be better served by increasing the number of professionals from DMCs where there are a large number of highly qualified candidates even though their numbers are already higher than the notional entitlements?

The extent of Japanese influence in the Bank and the manner in which it is exercised has been a matter of considerable speculation over the years. The Bank has had Japanese presidents since it was set up (Takeshi Watanabe, 1966–1972; Shiro Inoue, 1972–1976; Taroichi Yoshida, 1976–1981; Masao Fujioka, 1981–1989; Kimimasa Tarumizu, 1989–1993; and Mitsuo Sato, who took up duties in November 1993). This is a tradition that has been established since the inception of the Bank. The nomination is made by the government of Japan, and the concurrence of the entire membership is sought thereafter. All presidents, except for Mr. Inoue, held positions in the ministry of finance (which has responsibility for managing Japan's role in the AsDB) before their appointment to the Bank.

Early presidents of the Bank adopted a relaxed approach to exercising influence on Bank operations and deferred responsibility for loan operations to the vice president of operations. There was only one vice president (an Indian national) until the late 1970s. There were instances where, even in the early 1980s, staff meetings held to discuss loan proposals, though chaired by the president, were run and dominated by the vice president of operations. A second vice president with responsibility for finance and administration was appointed from the United States in 1978. The agreed process to choose a vice president is for the president to select a candidate from a list submitted by the U.S. Treasury. The influence of the vice president of operations waned with the appointment of a third vice president[35] in the mid–1980s (the three being responsible for operations, projects, and finance and administration), with India beginning to borrow from the Bank in 1986 and with the appointment of a more activist Japanese, Masao Fujioka, as president. His departure in 1989 led the new president, Mr. Tarumizu, to seek a more cooperative role from the board and closer coordination with all member countries. No single vice president wielded the power and influence on Bank operations that the vice president of operations did in the first fifteen years of its existence. The extent of Japanese control at the present time is illustrated by the fact that, in addition to the president, the posts of director, budget, personnel and management systems; the treasurer; the directors of the two programs departments (East and West); and the manager of the strategic planning unit are held by Japanese. These appointments are made by the president. Many perceive this as providing Japan with the ability to influence the overall direction of the Bank, the content of the programs in each country, its personnel management, borrowing, and investment policies. Whatever the motivation for this dominance, it has led to the evolution of a well-run, effective institution in comparison to the other RDBs. The process has been assisted by the Japanese ability to cope with critical staff vacancies at the senior level, sometimes as result of the environment in Manila, by seconding staff from agencies in Tokyo and by subsidizing their salaries.

While Japanese influence had a large impact on personnel policies and the running of the Bank, it also made a major contribution to the mobilization of resources, in particular to the ADF. Its contributions to the ADF have increased to more than 50 percent due to the cutbacks in commitments by the United States and other members and U.S. delays in payments. The limits set by the United States effectively reduced the size of other donor contributions and consequently the size of the ADF. This general cutback followed an historic burden-sharing arrangement among donors, which Japan and a few other donors (to their credit) ignored.

Unlike the United States, Japan has avoided raising sensitive political issues in the Bank, but conflicts have often arisen between the two countries. Both Presidents Fujioka and Tarumizu had difficult relationships with U.S. executive directors. Tarumizu experienced difficulties with the U.S. Treasury[36] in the nominations for the position of vice president of operations and in the program established for GCI IV. President Tarumizu's early retirement from the Bank, although stated as being for medical reasons, is ascribed to friction with the U.S. government.

The U.S. budgetary process, which requires that individual installments to the capital increases and ADF replenishments be subject to annual approval by Congress, has given the United States considerable leverage over the Bank with regard to its operational policies. It enabled them to bring up policy issues in connection with funding negotiations, although this is now done by the donors as a group. The U.S. influence on the Bank's lending policies has been considerable over the years. The exclusion of China and India from gaining access to the ADF; the embargo on lending to Vietnam, which was only lifted in the second half of 1993; the suspension of lending to China in 1989; and the Bank's move towards lending to the private sector and privatization are some examples of U.S. influence.

Highlights of Past Assessments

There have been five reviews of AsDB operations undertaken since the early 1980s. The first was conducted as part of an overall review of the MDBs by the U.S. Treasury in 1981.[37] The second was the Bank's *Study of Operational Priorities and Plans of the Asian Development Bank for the 1980s*, which was undertaken in 1981–1982 and published in February 1983. The third was also conducted by the Bank in 1988 and published in January 1989 as *The Asian Development Bank in the 1980s: Panel Report*. This was followed by a study by the Department of International Economic Cooperation, Danish Ministry of Foreign Affairs (DANIDA) on the *Effectiveness of Multilateral Agencies at Country Level*, conducted during 1989–1990 and published in March 1991. The assessment of the AsDB was based on Bank operations in Nepal and Thailand. The last was a *Review of the Effectiveness of Australia's Membership of the MDBs in Achieving Australia's Development Assistance Objectives*, conducted by the Australian International Development Assistance Bureau (AIDAB) and published in December 1991.[38] Three of the five reviews were conducted to serve the requirements of the concerned donors as part of a larger review of multilateral agencies. The two undertaken by the AsDB were partly donor-driven, particularly the 1988 Panel Report. The first provided an opportunity for DMC views to be sought through reviews of Bank operations conducted in five countries. Apart from these reviews, the negotiations for GCI III and IV and ADF IV, V, and VI provided the donor community with opportunities for a full discussion of Bank policies during the 1980s and early 1990s. The policy papers that were produced during the protracted negotiations for ADF VI and GCI IV reviewed most of the development issues of priority to Bank operations. This list of reviews would not be complete without mention of Dick Wilson's story of the AsDB, *A Bank for Half the World* written to commemorate the twentieth anniversary of the Bank in 1986. It is not an official publication but an accurate historical record by a writer with long experience in Asian development. It does not fall into the same category as the five reviews mentioned above.

The U.S. Treasury study was an assessment of the policies and operations of the World Bank Group, IDB, AfDB, and AsDB. It was intended to establish a policy and budgetary framework for U.S. participation in the MDBs in the 1980s in light of the Reagan administration's philosophy of efficient promotion of economic development. The analysis was based mainly on IBRD/IDA loan operations rather than on the RDBs. The report surveyed the criticisms that had been made of the MDBs, which fell into two broad groups. One dealt with fundamental issues such as the use of MDBs for channelling capital to developing countries. The second dealt with lending policies and procedures and financial and administrative policies. Some criticisms were that MDBs lent in excess of the absorptive capacities of developing countries, emphasis was on quantity rather than quality of the lending program, there were anomalies in the graduation policies of the MDBs, members lacked control over the institutions, coordination among the MDBs and bilateral aid programs was inadequate, there was insufficient attention paid to loan preparation and supervision, and evaluation systems were deficient.

The study concluded that these shortcomings, which have an impact on the institutional effectiveness of the MDBs, should be kept under continuous review. Some criticisms lacked validity, the study said, while there was inadequate information available to substantiate others, such as the lack of absorptive capacity. Two areas were identified as needing corrective policies. The first related to the overemphasis on loan quantity rather than quality, which appeared to have eroded MDB policy influence. This is an issue that is still relevant in the AsDB and was also highlighted in the Report of the Task Force on Improving Project Quality. Earlier analysis in this present study has shown that lending to DMCs increased rapidly in the 1980s and early 1990s. The second was the need for an effective maturation/graduation policy for lending that is reflective of a country's need and the availability of alternative sources of financing. The AsDB does not have a specific policy in this regard, but the arrangements in place appear to be adequate, bearing in mind that there cannot be an absolute cutoff either for maturation or graduation. It is an evolutionary process that would keep each DMC actively involved in Bank operations even after graduation.

The OPP Study conducted in 1981–1982 remains the most comprehensive review of AsDB operations. It was conducted after fifteen years of experience in loan operations and was essentially an interdepartmental study. Outside expertise was blended into the study by drawing in a highly experienced set of consultants to lead missions to review AsDB loan operations in five countries. In addition, a high-level advisory group set the agenda for the country studies, reviewed their results, and advised on the outline of the overall report written by a Bank task force. This group also made a valuable contribution at the end of the study by making an assessment of the analysis and the various recommendations in the report.

The advisory group concluded that the AsDB was a good and sound development-projects Bank. Based on this solid beginning and the need to respond to changing external circumstances, the group supported the recommendation that the Bank should become a more active and versatile development promoter. It was suggested that the Bank could play a more effective catalytic role in encouraging the additional net flow of commercial and official resources to DMCs, engage in a constructive policy dialogue on sectoral planning and policy issues, and develop a livelier partnership with DMCs. The advisory group supported the priority given by the Board and management to agriculture, energy, and social infrastructure although the actual shares realized for these sectors during the 1980s did not entirely reflect this. It also recommended the adoption of a multiyear country and sectoral programming cycle within the framework of a medium-term plan and the fulfillment of lending targets within this period. The preparation of country operational strategies to strengthen country programming was proposed. The introduction of a strategic framework for the Bank is a further stage in this evolutionary process. The advisory group also recommended that the function and character of program lending be broadened and greater flexibility be introduced in lending modalities. In making these recommendations it was conscious of the need to make a substantial increase in the level of staff capable of undertaking analytical work. Many of the recommendations of the OPP Study have been acted on by management.

Development needs and priorities changed in the 1980s, making it necessary for the AsDB to request another high-level panel of experts to advise on the operational strategy and policies for the 1990s. Unfortunately, this review was not conducted in the same depth and did not benefit from the country studies that were a part of the earlier OPP Study. However, some of the priorities identified by the panel were social infrastructure, in particular public health and education; poverty alleviation with emphasis on projects that are likely to have a direct impact on the living standards of the poor; and the integration of environmental aspects in the Bank's lending program. The report did not deal with issues relating to women in development (WID), except for making a passing reference. This issue was subsequently pursued during the ADF VI negotiations, when the management of the AsDB agreed to establish mechanisms (including a specialized unit with adequate staffing) to address WID and related matters similar to those established for dealing with other cross-cutting issues, such as the environment. In accordance with these priorities, public sector investments were to be directed to areas that would help achieve these objectives such as primary education, health clinics, urban renewal, and schemes for alleviating rural poverty. The panel recommended a more active role by the AsDB in promoting the private sector and the creation of a new institution similar to the International Finance Corporation (IFC) in the World Bank Group. The Asian Finance and Investment Corporation (AFIC) was subsequently established, though the case for its creation was not made convincingly by either the panel or management. The need to expand the scope of the policy dialogue with DMCs was highlighted in this report as in the OPP Study. The staffing implications for conducting an effective dialogue and preparing projects that reflect the new priorities were recognized by the panel.

The DANIDA study, which was conducted over a two-year period, covered eleven multilateral agencies including the World Bank, AfDB, and AsDB from among the MDBs. The agencies were studied at the country level in four countries. Kenya, Nepal, Sudan, and Thailand. The AsDB report was based on the country studies of Nepal and Thailand. It concluded that the AsDB's country programming process is open and has strong government involvement but also provided a framework for seeking project opportunities that appear necessary to meet lending levels. The availability of technical assistance funds on a grant basis (which gives it a comparative advantage over the World Bank) has led to a number of capacity-building projects aimed at identifying lending opportunities. The report identified difficulties that the AsDB had of undertaking an effective policy dialogue for nonproject lending, which the World Bank does better. Similarly, the report sees difficulties for implementing institution-building technical assistance projects necessary for developing an integrated lending strategy. This is the case particularly in the low-income countries with limited absorptive capacity, where the United Nations Development Programme (UNDP) and its specialized agencies have a comparative advantage. While financial and economic feasibility studies have been made, institutional assessments were given inadequate attention during project preparation. Technical biases in design overshadowed issues such as beneficiary participation in infrastructure development projects.

According to the report, the AsDB's strengths include its access to sizeable financial resources on both commercial and concessional terms and the increasing availability of technical assistance funds on grant terms. It had a good record in supporting capital-intensive public infrastructure projects. This focus made the transition to supporting operations and maintenance projects rather than new investments more difficult. Among the weaknesses of the AsDB, the report identified its preoccupation with expanded lending. This was difficult to maintain due to the highly competitive donor environment and to easy access by some countries to international capital markets. Further, the project focus and technical bias of professional staff made it difficult for the AsDB to be a source of, or a channel for, policy advice presently needed by many DMCs.

The purpose of the AIDAB review was to examine the contribution that the membership of the World Bank Group, AsDB, and International Fund for Agricultural Development made to achieving the objectives of Australia's development assistance program. The review covered four aspects of MDB operations, namely their objectives and strategies, development operations, organizational and funding policies, and the degree to which their activities contributed to Australian interests. The report reached positive conclusions about the MDBs and endorsed Australia's continuing support.

The report observed that, while AsDB lending in support of infrastructure was project oriented, it has moved into the area of policy reform, albeit sectorally. It highlighted the need to strengthen the Bank's commitment to pursuing policy reform in its lending and its ability to deliver. A note of caution was introduced in the report on the action taken by the AsDB in including crosscutting issues such as the environment, WID, and poverty reduction into project design and policy. It stated that there were influential elements in the AsDB to whom crosscutting issues were of lower priority than market reform or project funding. Thus, the long-term will of the institution to sustain these initiatives needed to be kept under constant review. The report also highlighted weaknesses in project design and the inability to establish an appropriate policy framework as major causes of project failure. Another problem was the overemphasis of technical and engineering aspects at the expense of institutional and social factors. Inadequate monitoring of implementation also led to delays, with adverse consequences for project benefits and the economic internal rate of return (EIRR). The report identified "volume culture" as an important reason for this. In achieving lending levels, the report stated that country strategies were interpreted loosely and inadequate time was spent on project design, leading to misleading appraisal reports and implementation delays with the lessons of earlier projects being largely ignored. Many of the criticisms the AIDAB report made applied equally to the AsDB and the World Bank.

It should be noted that the DANIDA and AIDAB reviews of the Bank were parts of larger studies that did not examine the issues in great depth. Nevertheless, they documented criticisms of Bank operations that have been voiced for a long time and need to be addressed. Some of the issues have been commented on in this study as well.

Notes

1. As described in the *Study of Operational Priorities and Plans of the AsDB for the 1980s*, AsDB, June 1983.

2. *A Generation of Growth*, AsDB, March 1992.

3. Although established in 1964, the admission of nonregional members took place only in 1982 in the AfDB.

4. Initial membership of the IDB, which was set up in 1959, was restricted to members of the Organization of American States, which permitted the United States to become a member only amongst the donor community. Amendments to the charter permitted Canada to join in 1972 and Switzerland and other nonregional members, which belonged to the International Monetary Fund, in 1976.

5. Robert Wihtol, *The Asian Development Bank and Rural Development*, St. Martin's Press, New York, 1988.

6. *The Agreement Establishing the Asian Development Bank*, AsDB, Article 1.

7. Ibid., note 6, Article 2.

8. Ibid., note 6, page 13, Article 14.

9. Membership consists of developing member countries that are from the region and developed member countries that are both regional and nonregional. The nonregional group of countries can only join as developed members.

10. See Appendix Table 4 for a full list of members grouped by constituency and the year of their joining the AsDB.

11. Including Nauru, which has not been classified as a DMC.

12. Paid-in capital in local currencies by DMCs is available for bank use subject to certain restrictions.

13. Amounts have been allocated from net income to the Technical Assistance Special Fund.

14. Loans, equity investments, and guarantees at the end of 1992 were 86.6 percent of the ceiling defined in this paragraph.

15. It also applies to most OCR operations approved between September 24, 1985, and June 30, 1986.

16. The rates applicable on U.S. dollar loans during the first and second half of 1993 were 6.63 and 6.64 percent respectively. The corresponding rates for multicurrency loans were 6.47 and 6.34 percent respectively.

17. In terms of this change, the fee is applicable on 15 percent of the committed undisbursed balance in the first year, 45 percent in the second year, 85 percent in the third year, and 100 percent in the fourth year and beyond. (The International Bank for Reconstruction and Development considered a similar modification but made no change. Instead its Board waived 0.50 percent of the commitment charge, reducing it to 0.25 percent, the net effect of which is comparable to the change made by the AsDB.)

18. This total differs from the sums of ADF I-VI in Table 2.1 due to exchange rate fluctuations and the fact that all contributions had not been made.

19. This effectively means that there are two categories in Group A. One consists of countries that receive only ADF resources and the other of countries that receives a blend of ADF and OCR, similar to those in Group B but containing a lower proportion of OCR.

20. India had voluntarily decided not to borrow from the Bank when it commenced operations. This self-denial continued until China became a member in 1986.

21. A technical assistance agreement for $2.41 million was approved in April 1992, and a rehabilitation loan of $67.7 million was signed in January 1993.

22. Countries that joined the AsDB after the adoption of the resolution on ADF VI in February 1992, Tuvalu, and the Central Asian Republics that have been admitted to membership, subject to completion of procedures, awaited the agreement of donors at the midterm review to become eligible to receive ADF resources.

23. The total number of loans exceed the total number of projects as projects financed from both sources are counted as one.

24. Ibid., note 22.

25. The Federated States of Micronesia have had no loan commitments as yet, and Nauru, which has not been classified as a DMC, is not expected to borrow.

26. In addition to grant funds, loan funds have been used to finance technical assistance activities.

27. The AsDB can only provide grant assistance for institutional development from the Institutional Development Fund set up in 1992 and project preparation from the Consultant Trust Funds made available by several bilateral sources and the Policy and Human Resources Development Fund, established in 1990 with assistance from Japan.

28. NIEs: Hong Kong, Korea, Singapore, and Taipei,China.

North Asia: China and Mongolia.

Southeast Asia: Indonesia, Lao Peoples' Democratic Republic, Malaysia, the Philippines, Thailand, and Vietnam.

South Asia: Bangladesh, Bhutan, India, Myanmar, Nepal, Pakistan, and Sri Lanka.

Pacific Islands: Fiji, Papua New Guinea, Solomon Islands, Tonga, Vanuatu, and Western Samoa.

29. This study of its operations was the first since lending began in 1968 undertaken by the Bank.

30. A second study was undertaken in the late 1980s to chart the course for the Bank in the 1990s. Details on both studies are given in Chapter 2 under the section entitled "Highlights of Past Assessments."

31. DFIs are financial intermediaries who borrow funds for on-lending to the ultimate beneficiaries. The lending agencies, such as the Bank, use DFIs to reach a wider clientele than would be possible if they attempted to lend directly.

32. From Article 14 of the Operating Principles of the Articles of Agreement establishing the Asian Development Bank, August 1966.

33. The Bank interprets these averages on a three-year basis and not annually.

34. *AsDB Annual Report*, 1992.

35. The third vice president is a European national. With the departure of the first vice president appointed from India in 1988, his replacement has been from Korea.

36. The Treasury is responsible for U.S. policy towards the AsDB and its participation in capital increases and replenishments of the ADF. U.S. and Japanese policies in the Bank have been described at length in Robert Wihtol's book. Ibid., note 6, chapter 2, page 13.

37. *U.S. Participation in the MDBs in the 1980s*, U.S. Treasury, February 1982.

38. The sixth review, which is not summarized here, is the Bank's *Report of the Task Force on Improving Project Quality,* which was released in February 1994.

3

Borrowing Country Experience

Country Studies

The methodology adopted in the study called for a review of Bank operations in three or four DMCs. These were done to gain a better understanding of how the Bank functioned, the nature of its relations with DMCs, its interface with the World Bank, and the effectiveness of its operations. The countries chosen were Indonesia, a Group B country and the largest borrower both from the OCR and in total; Pakistan, a Group A country and the largest borrower from the ADF and a blend country; and Sri Lanka, a Group A low-income country with a medium-sized economy and the third largest recipient from the ADF. The succeeding sections are based on the conclusions of these studies.

Indonesia

Indonesia is by far the Bank's largest borrower, accounting for 21.5 percent of total lending during 1970–1992. Bank lending to the country fell into four distinct phases.[1] In the first, from 1969 to 1974, it was small and mostly from the ADF. Lending from the OCR began in 1973 and grew during the next phase, which extended over a decade. It coincided with increased investments by the government when oil revenues increased. It rose further during 1983–1986 in support of government efforts to adjust to lower oil revenues. The Bank provided local currency assistance to support the government's efforts to adjust to reduced resources and lent to diversify the economy from oil and gas. The present phase, which began in 1987, has seen a further increase in lending from the OCR. Sector lending and the revision of the scope of program lending made it possible for the Bank to support government policy reforms and deregulation. These complemented the macroeconomic policy reforms financed by trade policy and private sector development loans that were provided by the World Bank. AsDB support during this period covered sector loans for power, irrigation, roads, urban development, water supply, and smallholder tree crops and program lending for development of nonoil exports and the financial and food crops sectors. Indonesia has also been provided limited access to the ADF since 1987.

Cumulative gross Bank lending (excluding loans to the private sector without government guarantee), covering 179 loans, reached $9,086.4 million at the end of 1992 of which $8,369.3 million was from the OCR and the balance of $717.1 million from the ADF, accounting for 29.0 and 5.3 percent of total Bank lending from the OCR and ADF. The sectoral breakdown reflects a pattern that differs from the Bankwide average except for agriculture and agro-industry, the leading sector with 31.4 percent of the share, which is higher than the average for the Bank. Social infrastructure is next with a share of 24.0 percent compared to the Bank average of 14.7 percent, followed by energy at 17.9 percent, transport and communications at 14.3 percent, and the financial sector at 8.1 percent.

The program in Indonesia is significant for the sharp increase in lending that took place in the 1990s. It had progressed from an annual average of $100 million in the 1970s to almost $500 million in the 1980s and over $1,000 million in the early 1990s, reaching $1,191 million and $1,211 million in 1991 and 1992. The level in 1993 was $1,293 million. The loan commitments by the Bank in 1992 were a little less than 25 percent of the total $4.948 billion received by Indonesia at the first meeting of the consultative group chaired by the World Bank.[2] The largest commitment of $1.6 billion was made by the World Bank, followed by Japan with $1.32 billion (although it would be the largest if the contribution by the EXIM Bank of Japan of $0.5 billion is included), followed by the AsDB. Other bilateral pledges were from Australia, France, Germany, the United States, and the Nordic Investment Bank.

Indonesia has been the largest recipient of technical assistance from the Bank. Of the 248 projects approved up to the end of 1992, 155 were for project preparation. These resulted in 100 loans for projects. The current strategy is to move towards advisory technical assistance for institutional building and strengthening the capacity for policy analysis.

The Bank is supporting the broad strategic objectives of the Fifth National Plan (REPELITA V) covering the period 1989/90–1993/94 that aimed to promote efficient, equitable, and environmentally sustainable growth of the country. Emphasis in the Bank's lending programs was on the promotion of nonoil exports, domestic resource mobilization, employment generation, basic needs and human resources development, and the improvement of the efficiency of existing investments with optimal resource utilization. Indonesia's economy responded positively to the program of structural adjustment during the early years of the plan period, significant improvements being observed in performance indicators. The share of nonoil exports increased from 60 to 70 percent during 1989–1992. Much of this development was concentrated in Java, the most populous island, which began to experience problems of infrastructure and other supply-side bottlenecks. Income disparities increased, although the incidence of poverty appears to have decreased. Some other islands experienced faster growth than the overall economy. This made the government focus on regional dispersion and income distribution. Donor agencies have been requested to support these efforts in their lending programs. The Bank recently undertook a study of Eastern Indonesia[3] to explore opportunities for greater involvement in that region.

The World Bank's large lending program (on the order of $1.6 billion) has concentrated on achieving stable economic growth, wide participation of the people in the development process, human resource development and poverty reduction, and sustainable development. The major emphasis of its lending program in the 1990s has been on policy formulation and the development of physical infrastructure necessary to encourage the growth of the private sector. The AsDB has made an effort to coordinate and complement its relatively smaller program with those of the World Bank and Japan, in particular in the area of assistance to smallholders for irrigation and the development of tree crops. Similar coordination has been maintained in the policy dialogue in the agriculture, energy, urban development, transport, and communications sectors.

The Bank maintains that it has assisted Indonesia in developing a policy environment that is necessary to foster a competitive and efficient economy. Policy discussions have been held regularly during the project processing stage of all loans since 1983. These efforts have intensified since 1987, when the scope of program lending was revised, and have covered both program and sector lending operations. Policy dialogue on sectoral issues figured prominently in the formulation of the program loans for nonoil exports, the financial sector, and food crops. There are two differences in the nature of the policy dialogue conducted by the AsDB and the World Bank. The AsDB dialogue has dealt exclusively with sectoral issues, even in program loans that are close to the World Bank's sector adjustment loans. For example, policy conditionalities in financial sector loans by the World Bank covered relevant macroeconomic policies such as exchange and interest rate policies, while the AsDB loans dealt with reforms of the capital markets and financial institutions covered by these loans. In addition, the World Bank assists the government in setting its macroeconomic policy agenda and formulating policies. The AsDB takes note of these policies but undertakes no active dialogue on them. Even on sectoral policies, it appears that the World Bank conducts a more active policy dialogue in comparison with the Bank in ensuring performance on conditionalities. This is true in other DMCs as well.

Fifty-four Bank projects were postevaluated[4] up to the end of 1992. Of these, thirty were judged to be generally successful. This success rate of 56 percent was less than the Bank-wide average of 60 percent for projects evaluated during the same period. Two reasons have been put forward. The first is that there was a larger percentage of agriculture-related projects, which are more difficult to implement and operate than those in other sectors because they are vulnerable to external factors beyond the control of the project authorities. Transport sector projects that were evaluated had a relatively higher success rate than those in other sectors. The second is that half the number of projects evaluated were approved during the first five years of the Bank's loan operations in Indonesia, which suggests that it may have been due to inexperience of the Bank and the agencies executing the projects. This is supported by the Bank's higher-than-average rate of generally successful projects in Indonesia for those projects approved in the first half of the 1980s. Other weaknesses identified in a review of postevaluation studies of Bank projects conducted in 1988 were: defects in project design, limitations in institutional capacity, implementation problems associated with government procedures for procurement, and delays in the acquisition of land. Project sustainability has been endangered by the inadequate allocation of funds for operations and maintenance, which indicates the need for greater attention to cost recovery in the formulation of projects.

Overall, the delays in implementing projects in all sectors have averaged 2.6 years.[5] These have been caused by major problems in some projects, mainly in the urban development and education sectors. The Bank reported that the design of recent projects has taken account of factors contributing to such delays. The implementation periods of complex projects have been adjusted accordingly. More time has been allowed for processing projects where they involve policy changes, institutional and training requirements, complex technical solutions, and local involvement. The performance of local contractors, who have won bids for a substantial amount of civil works, is also a major factor affecting project performance. There is an obvious need to upgrade the capabilities of local contractors through training. Land acquisition necessary for project implementation has caused lengthy delays due to the existence of large areas of unregistered land, which leads to lengthy investigations to establish ownership, and because of institutional weaknesses in the government agencies responsible for land transfers. While these problems require government intervention to simplify procedures, the Bank needs to take them into account when drawing up a realistic implementation schedule.

Donors have raised issues of governance at meetings of the consultative group and at the intergovernmental group for Indonesia that preceded it. Repression in East Timor, human rights violations, and the lack of progress in the development of democratic institutions[6] have led some bilateral donors, such as Canada, Sweden, and the Netherlands, to withhold commitments of assistance. While this type of action can be taken in the bilateral aid relationship with recipient countries, there has been no similar action taken vis-à-vis Indonesia either at the World Bank or AsDB.

The other major issue for the AsDB is the extent of its exposure to Indonesia, which is on the order of 30 percent of the OCR. The Bank has no policy guideline restricting loan exposure, unlike the World Bank, which places a limit of 10 percent on IBRD lending for a single country, although there have been a few instances where this ceiling has been exceeded. The World Bank has global lending responsibilities and such a guideline would not restrict its lending program as it would the AsDB. On a per capita basis, total loan commitments to Indonesia are less than those to Nepal, Pakistan, the Philippines, and Sri Lanka. Thus, any reduction of lending to Indonesia to decrease the Bank's exposure would reduce this per capita level, which is not excessive compared to some other DMCs. In addition, such a reduction can only be achieved over a period of years and would have long-term implications for the resource needs of the AsDB.

Infrastructure and urban development projects have been among the more successful interventions by the Bank in Indonesia. The Bank has financed eleven road projects from the OCR in Indonesia, including some sector and maintenance projects. These have accounted for 9.5 percent of the Bank's commitments to the end of 1992. The first four of these projects have been evaluated, and all are judged to be generally successful. They led to the construction of 630 kilometers of national roads, 330 kilometers of provincial roads, and seventy-five kilometers of district roads. The Bank has financed nine port projects, mostly from OCR resources, and accounted for a further 2.3 percent of commitments to the end of 1992. Two of the loans evaluated were intended to upgrade the cargo-handling capacity of the Port of Surabaya, both of which were judged to be generally successful. These sets of roads and ports projects succeeded in improving the infrastructure base in the country that facilitated the flow of goods and services necessary for development purposes. In addition, there were eleven urban development projects that had been approved, accounting for 7.7 percent of total lending. These included two projects each for the urban development of Bandung and Medan and two sector loans for secondary cities urban development. Among other loans have been two financial sector loans totalling $450 million, including a small contribution from the ADF, that have been used successfully to promote financial sector and capital market reform.

Pakistan

Bank lending to Pakistan from the OCR and special fund resources began in 1968 and 1972 respectively. Up to the end of 1992 it had received a blend of resources for 147 loans. On a cumulative basis, borrowing from the OCR during 1970–1992 reached $3,082.5 million, which accounted for 10.7 percent of the total, the fourth largest among the DMCs. Borrowing from the ADF during the same period was higher and reached $3,942.6 million or 29.1 percent of the total, the largest among the DMCs. The main increase in the lending program took place during 1982–1992. When loan commitments are analyzed on a triennial basis, it is seen that they increased from $501.9 million during 1979–1981 to $2,078.4 million during 1988–1990. They declined during 1991–1993 to $1,464.5 million.

The Bank's operational strategy in Pakistan[7] has been to assist the development of a self-sustained, open, export-oriented economy through fiscal, financial, and other policy reforms directed towards a dynamic private sector. Bank operations based on this strategy, which was adopted in 1989 and is to be revised shortly, were intended to promote export growth and conserve foreign exchange; improve domestic resource mobilization; increase private sector participation in the economy; enhance the efficiency of existing investments while optimizing resource utilization; and meet basic needs, alleviate poverty, and develop human resources. Due to the recent political changes in Pakistan, it is expected that the lending strategy will be reviewed in the context of the Bank's medium-term strategic framework.

Support for projects in the sectors of agriculture and agro-industry and energy during 1970–1992 exceeded the Bank-wide average by over 5 percent and accounted for 31.8 and 31.0 percent of the total respectively. The operational strategy addressed the limitations in the area of additional land that can be brought under cultivation and the scarcity of domestic financing. Accordingly, assistance to the agriculture sector has aimed at increasing crop productivity by improving water management systems and building irrigation systems and farm-to-market roads. The main objective in the energy sector has been to bridge the gap between supply and demand to reduce the constraint on economic growth, mainly in the industrial sector. Private sector participation is to be increased, though assistance will continue to be provided to the public sector. Indigenous energy sources are to be developed to reduce costly petroleum imports. Although social infrastructure projects have covered education, water supply and sewerage, health, and urban development and rehabilitation, their share in total lending during 1970–1992 was only 8 percent, which was only a little over half the Bank-wide average. More will be done in this sector in the future, although the Bank is constrained in the short term by the government's limited financial and institutional capacity. The share of lending to DFIs was larger than the Bank-wide average. Some of the latter loans were used to introduce capital market reforms. Although traditional lending to private industry was through DFIs and commercial banks, this will be modified on account of the privatization of state-owned institutions. Pakistan has received almost equal amounts of project preparation and advisory and operational technical assistance. Since the beginning of 1989, the latter has been larger in recognition of the government's weak organizational and institutional capability.

As in the case of Indonesia, the World Bank chairs the Pakistan Aid Consortium. It was set up in 1960—the second aid coordination forum—and predates the establishment of the AsDB. The major donors are the same as in the other countries for which case studies of Bank operations were done, namely the United States, the World Bank Group, the AsDB, and Japan. During the financial years (FYs) 1970–1990, they accounted for 23.9, 22.4, 18.5, and 6.1 percent of total disbursements. This pattern has changed after 1990 with the World Bank becoming the largest donor and the United States reducing its new commitments.

Pakistan's economic adjustment program, begun in the early 1980s, accelerated towards the end of the decade. It has been supported by the World Bank and the IMF in the context of the government's medium-term program set out in its Policy Framework Paper. Bank support has been provided through sector adjustment loans for the agriculture, energy, and financial sectors and IMF support from standby agreements and the structural adjustment facility. Additional financial support from the World Bank and IMF was approved in

September 1993 for an expanded program of reforms, many of which were introduced during the period of the caretaker government in 1993.

The dialogue between the Bank and the government in the negotiations of the industrial sector program loan in 1988 focused on policies designed to deregulate the policy environment to achieve rapid, industry-led, export-oriented, economic growth. The third and fourth development financing loans approved in 1987 and 1989 were used to assist the government to rationalize the working of DFIs and promote a secondary market for fixed-income securities. The policy dialogue pursued through an agriculture program loan in 1990 covered the removal of the exemption from payment of wealth tax on agricultural land if the assessee's income is only from agriculture, the elimination of fertilizer subsidies, and improved recovery of operations and maintenance costs of irrigation systems. The release of the second tranche on this loan was delayed due to government noncompliance with covenants relating to these policy changes, although they were subsequently implemented during 1993.

The Bank's postevaluation of completed projects shows that 67 percent were rated to be generally successful. This is higher than the Bank-wide average. Many of the projects evaluated were implemented in the 1970s in the aftermath of the loss of East Pakistan in 1971. They were affected adversely by the general conditions prevailing in the country at the time. This created difficulties for project implementation given the need for institutional building, technology assimilation, building up of staff and management capabilities, and government policy formulation. In spite of these early difficulties, the government achieved institutional and technical maturity and a capability in counterpart agencies. The relatively high success rate of projects evaluated indicates a commitment by both the government and the Bank to overcome difficulties in implementation. It also suggests that lessons were learned from previous projects.

A Review of Post-Evaluation Findings in Pakistan prepared in October 1991 found that, of the factors within the joint control of the Bank and the government, deficiencies in project design ranked first among the causes of delay in implementation. These were due to inadequate time and resources devoted to project preparation. Lack of incentives and attention led to an exceptionally high turnover among qualified technical staff, particularly in projects involving new technology. A conclusion of the review was that a regulated economy with subsidies and price distortions made it difficult for individual projects to function within a reliable framework of prices in order for performance to be measured. There had been a tendency to respond to problems with further state intervention, which often compounded them. These problems have receded with the deregulation of the economy introduced in the late 1980s with support and assistance from the donor community. The more favorable policy environment should improve the implementation of projects in the country, though some transitional difficulties may be experienced.

Several issues need to be considered in determining the Bank's future intervention in Pakistan. One of them is that it is a moderately indebted country with a stock of debt in excess of 50 percent of GDP. However, the ratios of debt service and interest to exports are not above critical levels. This would indicate that future AsDB lending should, as far as possible, be from the ADF, although the need for a larger volume of resource transfers than available from the ADF can be easily established. Other issues are the excessive level of military expenditure, which is in excess of 30 percent of government expenditure, and the lack of stability in democratic institutions.[8] These may cause the same concerns to bilateral donors as they do in other parts of Asia and elsewhere. The Bank's position on them has yet to be determined.

Electric power generation and irrigation have been reported to be the most effective sectors of Bank intervention in Pakistan. A little under one-fifth of Bank lending, involving some 25 loans, has been for electric power development, which made a significant impact on the development of the sector. The Bank's program emphasized the expansion of generation capacity of both hydropower and thermal capacities. It also supported system planning, institutional building, and sector strategy formulation through its technical assistance program. Support for hydropower generation has primarily been for the expansion of the facilities at Tarbela and for thermal generation at the Pipri project. Seven electric power projects (involving ten loans including supplements) have been evaluated, all of which have been judged to be generally successful. Only three projects in the agriculture and agro-industry sector have been evaluated, of which two were irrigation projects. All were judged to be generally successful. There were two on-farm water management projects designed to reconstruct canals and tap additional groundwater resources. The other irrigation project was the Chasma Right Bank project. It has been extended to three stages, although only the first was evaluated. Situated in the Indus basin, this project was made possible by the construction of several major dams in northern Pakistan.

Sri Lanka

Foreign assistance to Sri Lanka is provided mainly through the aid group, which meets annually under the chair of the World Bank to consider the country's balance-of-payments needs. The group presently consists of fourteen Western bilateral donors (an increase from the original seven), the AsDB, the European Union, the UNDP, and the World Bank. On a gross disbursement basis, Sri Lanka received, on the average, about $544 million from all bilateral and multilateral sources annually during 1985–1990. The annual average for sources other than the aid group during this period was only $20 million, which means that the aid group remains the umbrella under which most of the assistance is provided to the country.

Loan and grant commitments to Sri Lanka averaged around $700 million annually during 1980–1991. Japan was the largest donor during this period, accounting for 23.2 percent of the total. It exceeded commitments by the World Bank, the second-largest donor accounting for 20.9 percent of the total, each year since 1986. The AsDB, United States, and Germany were next with 14.4, 10.3, and 5.0 percent of the total. These five donors contributed a little under three-fourths of the total. Canada and several European donors (Finland, France, the Netherlands, Sweden, and the United Kingdom) together committed 17.6 percent while the UNDP and European Union accounted for a further 4.2 percent. A feature of the assistance provided to Sri Lanka during this period was that it was either in the form of grants or concessional loans. Another aspect was the increasing influence in the aid group of Japan, the World Bank, the AsDB, and the United States. They accounted for 84 percent of total pledges at the 1993 meeting of the group compared to the average of a little over two-thirds of commitments during 1980–1991.

Bank lending operations to Sri Lanka began in 1968 with a loan for tea factory development. Up to the end of December 1992, sixty-eight loans totalling $1,423.32 million had been approved. Four were policy-based program loans, five were sector loans, and the balance of fifty-nine were for fifty-eight projects. Only six of the loans were from the OCR and accounted for $14.14 million or 1 percent of the funds committed to Sri Lanka. The last OCR loan, which was a supplement to a loan approved in 1971, was approved in 1974. The balance of sixty-two loans were from the Bank's special fund resources, which accounted for 99 percent of the loan commitments to date.

Sri Lanka was the third-largest recipient from the ADF up to the end of 1992, accounting for 10.4 percent of total commitments, compared to 28.2 and 29.1 percent for Bangladesh and Pakistan. Commitments from the ADF exceeded 11.0 percent after 1984 and reached 14.7 percent in 1991. They declined to 10.4 and 6.5 percent in 1992 and 1993. The country also benefited from the Bank's facilities for the private sector, namely equity lines and investments and unguaranteed loans. These were small operations and accounted for only $6.40 million to the end of December 1992. Sri Lanka received $29.606 million of technical assistance during 1970–1992. These funds were used for financing fifty-three project preparation and sixty-one advisory and operational technical assistance activities. The former led to the approval of thirty-six Bank loans by the end of 1992 while the latter were geared primarily to assisting in the implementation of AsDB projects by strengthening the institutional capacity of executing agencies.

The pattern of Bank lending to Sri Lanka diverged considerably from the average for the region. The agriculture and agro-industry sector received the largest share (46.7 percent) of funds committed during 1970–1992, which was much higher than the Bank-wide average of 26.4 percent for the same period. The spread of projects financed has been considerable. It includes tea (Sri Lanka's principal export until 1985, and now the second largest); coconut development and the plantation sector as a whole; fisheries and aquaculture; irrigation and settlement development; forestry; livestock; and sugar. Lending to DFIs and financial sector development accounted for 18.3 percent of Bank loans, the second-largest share, compared to 10.8 percent Bank-wide. These funds have been used for lending to small- and medium-scale industry through the Development Finance Credit Corporation and the National Development Bank of Sri Lanka, the provision of rural credit, and, more recently, low-income housing. A large financial sector program loan aimed at achieving reforms of the major financial institutions in the country was provided in 1990. Energy, social infrastructure, and transport and communications, in descending order, received considerably lower shares in Sri Lanka in comparison to total Bank lending. In the energy sector, assistance was provided for one thermal generation and two major hydropower projects, rural electrification, urban power distribution, and a sector loan. Most of the assistance classified under transport and communications was allocated for road improvement. Projects supported in the social infrastructure category were for technical education, health, and population. A sector loan was provided for water supply.

Growth of nonproject lending to Sri Lanka took place after 1984, although the major shift was in the late 1980s and early 1990s. A sector loan of $45 million was made to the plantations in 1984 to arrest the long-term deterioration of the tree crops when it was recognized that the piecemeal approach adopted had not been successful in achieving adequate rehabilitation. A loan of $30 million to the water supply sector was made in 1986 to address sectorwide issues relating to maintenance, cost recovery, and managerial reorganization. Similarly, a loan of $74.3 million was made to the power subsector in 1990 to expand the power system to rural areas. A special assistance loan of $14.3 million was made in 1983 to alleviate local currency constraints in ongoing Bank-financed projects. The AsDB's first policy-based loan was made in 1989 when $80 million was approved for an agriculture program.[9] The second program loan of $80 million, approved in 1989, was for the financial sector. A third of $60 million for a second agriculture program was approved in 1991.[10]

The basic objectives of the Bank's operational strategy adopted in 1993 is to assist the government to tackle the overriding development problems of chronic unemployment and the high incidence of poverty, particularly in rural areas. It proposes to do this by supporting projects that will accelerate economic growth, improve the access of the poor and underprivileged to productive assets such as farming equipment and transportation facilities, and protect the environment. Faster growth will raise income levels and generate opportunities for productive employment. Such improvements can be maintained in the long term only if they are achieved with gains in economic efficiency and sustainable financial and environmental regimes. The Bank will simultaneously address the distortions that limit the access of the poor to opportunities that produce income and employment. Policy-based assistance and dialogue will be an integral component of the Bank's strategy. The thrust of this strategy will be a two-part approach to Sri Lanka's problems.

> First, it involves the promotion of appropriate macroeconomic and sectoral policies to generate a faster rate of efficient and sustainable growth; and through the reforms in policies, investment programs and institutions thereby, to boost the effective demand for labour. Second, it involves the expanded provision of economic infrastructure and inputs to the disadvantaged so as to enable them to share the income-earning opportunities from accelerated growth.[11]

This will result in focusing the Bank's advisory and investment resources on the underprivileged, in particular the rural poor.

In the past, the AsDB's policy dialogue with the government with relation to loan operations has covered the agriculture, energy, financial, and industrial sectors. Under the new strategy, the focus of attention in the agriculture sector will be to reverse the declining trend in the production of traditional tree crops and to restore the viability of large state-owned plantations. Their financial losses and the consequent decline of Sri Lanka's share in the world tea market have created problems for both the internal and external balance of the economy. Further, improving the management of irrigation systems, fostering efficient import substitution through crop diversification, and the provision of enhanced producer incentives to achieving export-oriented production are added policy objectives.

In the energy sector, attention will be paid to supporting low-cost development programs in the power subsector, energy conservation, and pricing policies. Major issues are the financial viability of the main power utility (Ceylon Electricity Board), which should be strengthened, and the financial position of the power distribution company (Lanka Electric Company Ltd.) and the roles of these two institutions; and the timing and participation of the private sector in the next coal-fired power generating plant.

The main policy issues in the industrial sector are the provision of incentives, long-term credit, and reform of tariffs to enhance private sector participation, especially in the production of nontraditional exports. The AsDB will support the efforts of the World Bank to reduce the large deficits of public sector enterprises, with consequent benefits to the government budget, and to privatize programs, including the possibility of making direct investments in the privatized companies.

In the financial sector, the AsDB will continue to address issues relating to liberalizing interest rates and improving the organization and management of financial institutions. Rationalizing the operation of capital markets, including the promotion of a secondary market for government securities, and enhancing the possibility of equity financing will be added objectives. These sectoral policies will be pursued through AsDB loan and technical assistance operations.

An assessment of implementation experience of the AsDB would not be complete without a comparison with that of the World Bank in Sri Lanka. Thirty-two AsDB loans were completed during the twenty-year period of 1970–1990. Of these, thirteen had cancellations of undisbursed balances of 10 percent or more of the original loan amount, three of which were in excess of 50 percent. On the average, cancellations were 15.0 percent of the original loan amounts. In comparison to this, the World Bank had 37 projects that closed during the same twenty-year period. Of these, nineteen had cancellations of 10 percent or more, while five were in excess of 50 percent. Total cancellations on these projects averaged 26.8 percent of the original loan amounts. Although the number of projects completed by the AsDB and the World Bank during this period were comparable (though the volume of the latter was larger), cancellations appear to have affected more World Bank projects and to a larger degree, perhaps indicating a greater degree of faulty project design, cost estimates, and assessments of implementation capacity of recipient institutions. It is also possible that the World Bank demanded a higher standard of conditionality and performance that led to cancellations.

Nineteen of the projects completed by the AsDB underwent Project Performance Audit Reports that were circulated to the board up to the end of 1992. Nine of them were in the agriculture sector, four in the power sector, three in DFIs, two in industry, and one in telecommunications. Ten of these were judged to be generally successful[12] in achieving the intended objectives. This was a lower percentage than the long-term average for the Bank, although more in line with recent experience. Seven were classified as partially successful and two as unsuccessful. In analyzing the results of the audit reports, it should be remembered that most of the projects evaluated were formulated in the pre–1977 period when the government was committed to a program of greater economic regulation. It would be interesting to see whether projects that were formulated and implemented under the more liberal economic policy regime in the post–1977 period performed better. Only three of the nineteen loans evaluated have been in this period, a power project and two DFI credits, all of which were classified as generally successful. Further, some projects would have been affected by the ethnic strife in the country after 1983.

A recurring theme in the audit reports has been the weakness of the implementing agencies. Since institutional development is a major objective of the AsDB, its operations in Sri Lanka should emphasize advisory and operational technical assistance for institutional development associated with loans or as stand-alone technical assistance for this purpose. Another recurring theme has been the need to assess the requirements and perceptions of beneficiaries (such as farmers and fishermen) of the goods and services provided under Bank projects. Future project design should cope with this issue through field-level surveys of prospective beneficiaries. Project experience has indicated that, if more review missions were undertaken during implementation with a mandate to recommend changes in project scope, it would improve output. Improvements could also be made in the Bank's record in enforcing loan conditionalities.

There are considerable risks associated with the implementation of the strategy adopted by the AsDB and the World Bank in Sri Lanka. The civil conflict in the north and east continues unabated without evidence of a solution, and an escalation would lead to higher budgetary expenditures by the military. With the government already under pressure to reduce the budget deficit as a means of easing inflationary pressures, it would have difficulty in balancing these conflicting demands. It has reduced the budget deficit in recent years by cutting capital expenditure, which has halved as a ratio of GDP over 1988–1992. Further, the government will face elections towards the end of 1994, which could lead to a weakening of the political resolve to follow through on sensitive reforms. It is also possible that vested interests could succeed in weakening the reform program, particularly on the restructuring of public enterprises, including their privatization, and further economic deregulation. The government's track record on policy reform has been good in the recent past, leaving room for optimism. All these factors will have an impact on foreign investors, who find that Sri Lanka has the most favorable policy environment for business among the South Asian countries.

The attitude of donors on governance issues may also affect the government's resolve to stay the course on reform. The government was under pressure in the early 1990s to improve its human rights record. Canada and several European donors were unwilling to provide assistance directly to the government. Instead, assistance was channelled increasingly through nongovernmental organizations (NGOs), albeit at reduced levels after 1991. Total aid flows have not been affected to date due to the dominance of Japan, the World Bank, the AsDB, and the United States in the aid group who have committed more than, or close to, what Sri Lanka could absorb each year. The issue is still open whether donor governments may instruct their representatives in the MDBs to withhold approval of loans to countries with questionable human rights records. The articles of agreement of these banks restrict them from interfering in the political affairs of member countries. However, the economic aspects of good governance can be pursued through policy dialogue and conditionalities imposed on adjustment operations. Public expenditure reviews, for example, could provide opportunities for the World Bank to question whether development expenditures are being crowded out by nondevelopment expenditures. In June 1992, Japan set out the principles governing its foreign assistance programs. These covered the pursuit of protection for the environment and development; avoidance of the use of official development assistance (ODA) for military purposes; and attention to the recipient's military expenditure, democratization, market economy, and human rights situations. The application of these principles has not had an impact on aid from Japan, which was the largest donor to Sri Lanka in both 1992 and 1993. Instead, the low rate of aid utilization has been of concern to the Japanese authorities, which may affect future commitments.

Lending for electric power development, to small- and medium-scale industries, and more recently for low-income housing through DFIs have been the most successful sectors of intervention in Sri Lanka. Support for the power sector began with two projects for hydropower generation, namely the Bowatenne and Canyon projects, both of which were judged to be generally successful when evaluated. It extended to rural electrification, distribution in secondary towns, and a sector loan for power systems expansion. A major project for the expansion of thermal power is awaiting implementation. Seven DFI loans have been approved to date, one of which is for low-income housing. These, along with similar operations from the World Bank and other donors, made it possible to reach small- and medium-scale industrialists who had no other source of long-term development finance. Three of these projects have been evaluated, of which two were generally successful and the other partially successful.

Development Impact

Growth of Subregions

In reviewing the role of the AsDB in the growth and investment performance of the Asia and Pacific region, it is necessary to recognize some basic facts. First, these countries accounted for 2.863 billion of the total population of 4.315 billion in all developing countries and 5.385 billion in the world in 1991. Second, the average growth in these countries outstripped that of all other developing regions of the world in the past two decades, except for the Middle East in the 1970s where it was marginally higher. As seen in Table 3.1, the difference from the other regions was greater during the 1980s when average growth in the Asian region was higher than in the earlier decade. Third, the performance of the region as a whole masks considerable differences among the various subregions of NIEs, North Asia, South Asia, Southeast Asia, and the Pacific Islands. Of the countries for which comparable growth statistics are available for both decades, five (including China and India) achieved increases while eleven registered declines in the 1980s. The growth in the NIEs declined marginally between the two periods except in Korea, which registered an increase. North Asia grew due to the predominant influence of China. South Asia grew as a subregion, with India, Nepal, and Pakistan achieving increases while the others declined between the two

Table 3.1   Average Real GDP Growth by Developing Region: 1972–1991 (in percentages)

Region	1972–1981	1982–1991
Africa	3.2	1.8
Asia	5.6	6.9
Europe	4.3	1.7
Middle East	6.0	—
Western hemisphere	5.1	1.4
All developing regions	5.0	3.6

Source: World Economic Outlook, IMF, October 1990 and October 1992.

periods. Growth rates declined in the 1980s in all countries of Southeast Asia and the Pacific Islands. The higher overall growth of the region in the 1980s was influenced by the significantly higher growth rates achieved by the largest developing countries of China and India. The average growth rates by subregion for the two decades are summarized in Table 3.2.

Table 3.2   Average Real GDP Growth by Subregion: 1970–1990 (in percentages)

Subregion	1970–1980	1980–1990
NIEs	9.0[a]	8.8
North Asia	7.9	10.1
Southeast Asia	7.4	5.2
South Asia	4.0	5.3
Pacific islands	4.3	1.2
Average	6.8	7.5

Source: Asian Development Outlook, AsDB, 1992.

The varying performances of the subregions and the countries within them reflect their human and natural resource endowments; development strategies adopted and the policy environment; economic relations with countries both within the region and without; political systems with varying degrees of stability (in the context of the rapid changes taking place elsewhere in the world that have influenced the inflow of resources, particularly private capital); and the extent of natural calamities. Infrastructure bottlenecks and labor shortages have been a problem in some countries, particularly in the NIEs and Southeast Asia. Further, progress made in structural and policy reforms leading to the deregulation and liberalization of the economies and the impact these had on foreign trade, domestic and foreign investment, the performance of public enterprises, and the financial systems in these countries contributed to different investment performances and consequent growth. Apart from financing new investment, the World Bank and AsDB, albeit sectorally, have assisted DMCs in formulating and implementing a range of policy reforms.

Investment Performance

Investment performance can be judged by its absolute level in relation to GDP, its changing pattern over the past two decades as reflected by the share of public investment, the mix between social overhead capital and directly productive activities, and the growth in FDI. Investment as a proportion of GDP declined on the average from 26.7 percent in the 1970s to 23.8 percent in the 1980s in all developing countries.[13] The ratio declined in all developing regions, except in Asia where it increased from 27.9 to 29.2 percent. Investment was buoyant in many Asian countries. Where comparable statistics are available for both decades, it is seen that the investment ratios increased, except in Hong Kong where it remained stable and in Fiji, the Philippines, and Taipei,China where it declined.[14] These averages also mask considerable differences between countries. The investment ratios were 30 percent or more in China, Hong Kong, Indonesia, Korea, Malaysia, Papua New Guinea, Singapore, and Thailand in 1991. It was under 15 percent in Bangladesh, Lao Peoples' Democratic Republic, Mongolia, Myanmar, and Vietnam, with the other countries falling in between. The long-term viability of the economies at the bottom end of the investment ladder requires a major attempt to increase these levels to at least those achieved by the countries in the intermediate category.

The share of the public sector in total investment in the Asian countries has been largely a function of the prevailing political ideology of the time and the strength of the private sector. At one end of the spectrum has been the laissez-faire system in Hong Kong, where the role of the government is restricted to the provision of public goods and services with the rest of the economy subject to minimum supervision or regulation. At the other extreme are the centrally planned systems operating in China, Lao Peoples' Democratic Republic, and Vietnam where, apart from some agricultural activities, the state has been the dominant producer of goods and services with both the factor and product markets being highly regulated. The expanding role of the public sector in economic activities in the past was based on the premise that the surpluses generated through the operation of public enterprises would be available to finance development expenditures. These expectations did not materialize, and public investments were financed largely from borrowings, both external and internal, leading to high levels of debt, heavy interest payments, and unsustainable budget deficits.

During the 1980s many developing countries in all regions reviewed their development strategies, which had given such a dominant position to central planning and the public sector. This led to policy changes that resulted in greater emphasis being placed on the operations of the market and the private sector for promoting development. Concomitant with this was the reduced role being assigned to the state in directly productive activities with emphasis on the provision of infrastructure and social services, technology development, environment management, and selective investments. In addition, government was identified more closely with the establishment of a policy framework that would lead to a favorable business environment for the private sector. Accordingly, its role was seen as providing the resources and incentives necessary for the development of infrastructure, human resources, and technology to facilitate private investment. Table 3.3 illustrates the changes in the private-public mix in investment in some of the Asian countries. The declining importance of the private sector in the subregions is seen as we move from the NIEs through Southeast Asia and South Asia to the centrally planned economies. The situations in some Southeast Asian countries differed from this pattern. High levels of public investment had to be maintained to remove infrastructure defiencies as, for example, in Taipei,China to remove bottlenecks in social overhead capital and to control environmental pollution. In addition, governments made selective policy interventions to foster development of the private sectors and for the development of specific industries in the NIEs and some Southeast Asian countries.

Table 3.3   Share of Public and Private Sectors in Total Investment: 1975–1990
(in percentages)

	Private Sector			Public Sector		
	1975–1980	1980–1985	1985–1990	1975–1980	1980–1985	1985–1990
NIEs						
Hong Kong	83	81	87	17	19	13
Taipei,China	50	53	58	50	47	42
Southeast Asia						
Malaysia	62	51	59	38	49	41
Thailand	71	65	76	29	35	24
South Asia						
Bangladesh	45	55	21	55	45	79
Pakistan	33	45	47	67	55	53
Sri Lanka	69	82	76	31	18	24
China	16	33	37	84	67	63

Source: Asian Development Outlook, AsDB, 1992.

While adopting policies geared to increasing investment levels and promoting the development of the private sector, the question has been raised whether structural change should be left entirely to market forces. At the macroeconomic level, exchange rate and trade policies influence the allocation of resources between traded and nontraded goods. At the sectoral level, various taxes, incentives, and subsidies could influence investment decisions. In addition, promotional incentives and direct government intervention in the form of preferential interest rates, credit guarantees, direct lending by state development banks, and directives on lending to specific industries have been successfully adopted in the NIEs and some Southeast Asian countries.[15] Interventionists who support policies of influencing resource allocation at the sectoral and microeconomic levels point to the successful industrial policies adopted in Japan, Korea, and Taipei,China. Noninterventionists on the other hand point to the experience of Hong Kong. The Asian experience tends to support a selective approach in promoting private sector development. The policy stance of many Asian developing countries has changed from support for import substitution to export promotion both at the macroeconomic and sectoral levels. Countries that had a better performance in the 1980s adopted the export-oriented policies similar to those of the NIEs. This indicates a definite role for the state for the provision of adequate physical infrastructure and human resources, access to new technology, and protecting the environment.

Foreign Direct Investment

FDI has become a major component of net resource flows[16] to developing countries during the 1980s. Net resource flows declined in absolute terms from $388 billion to $325 billion between 1981–1985 and 1986–1990. During these periods, FDI increased in absolute terms by 80 percent from $52 billion to $92 billion while it more than doubled as a proportion of net flows. Asia has been the major beneficiary of these flows and received 59 percent of the total during 1985–1990 and 65 percent during 1990. Among all developing countries, China was the largest recipient[17] during this period. Malaysia and Thailand were fourth and sixth respectively. Indonesia, Korea, and the Philippines were among the twenty largest recipients. FDI increased by over 50 percent in these six countries during 1991. The inflow of FDI to the Asian countries during 1985–1990 is summarized in Table 3.4.

The sharp increase in FDI during the 1980s took place mainly in the countries of East Asia and the Pacific. It is seen from Table 3.5 that its share of net resource flows increased from 11 percent in 1980 to 41 percent in 1991 while there was a corresponding decline in long-term debt from 84 to 54 percent. The share of private sources in total lending declined by 6 percent during this period while the share of unguaranteed lending from private sources increased from 20 to 57 percent. Overall, the share of FDI and unguaranteed lending in net resource flows increased nearly threefold during this period to more than 60 percent. In South Asia, the share of official sources (grants and long-term loans) in net resource flows was high, in the range of 85–89 percent. FDI was small and increased marginally from 2 to 4

Table 3.4   Foreign Direct Investment: 1985–1990 (in billions of dollars)

NIEs	
Korea	3.614
Singapore	18.260
Southeast Asia	
Indonesia	3.175
Malaysia	6.896
Philippines	2.475
Thailand	6.036
South Asia	
Bangladesh	0.001
India	1.439
Pakistan	1.010
Sri Lanka	0.213
Pacific islands	
Papua New Guinea	0.623
Others	0.205
China	15.924
Total Asian developing countries	59.871
Total all developing countries	102.069

Sources: Asian Development Outlook, AsDB, 1992, and World Debt Tables 1991–1992, vol. 1, World Bank.

Table 3.5   Net Resource Flows (in billions of dollars; percentage of total in parentheses)

	1980	1985	1991
East Asia and the Pacific:			
Grants	0.643	1.828	1.709
	(5.2)	(11.5)	(5.4)
FDI (net)	1.318	3.183	13.021
	(10.7)	(20.0)	(41.0)
Long-term debt	10.405	10.927	17.055
	(84.1)	(68.6)	(53.7)
Official loans	2.834	3.287	5.620
	(22.9)	(20.6)	(17.7)
Private loans	7.570	7.641	11.435
	(61.2)	(47.9)	(36.0)
Unguaranteed portion	1.517	0.470	6.478
	(12.3)	(2.9)	(20.4)
Total	12.365	15.939	31.785
South Asia:			
Grants	2.441	1.581	2.751
	(42.4)	(27.5)	(30.3)
FDI (net)	0.106	0.157	0.356
	(1.8)	(2.7)	(3.9)
Long-term debt	3.216	4.003	5.966
	(55.8)	(69.7)	(65.8)
Official loans	2.432	3.019	5.334
	(42.2)	(52.6)	(58.8)
Private loans	0.784	0.983	0.631
	(13.6)	(17.1)	(7.0)
Unguaranteed portion	0.199	0.186	0.014
	(3.5)	(3.2)	(0.2)
Total	5.763	5.740	9.072

Source: World Debt Tables 1992–1993, vol. 1, the World Bank.

percent. At the same time, the share of private sources in long-term loans halved to 7 percent by 1991, most of it being public and publicly guaranteed debt. Unlike the case of East Asia and the Pacific, the share of FDI and unguaranteed lending in net resource flows was small. It was 4 percent in 1991 compared to 5 percent in 1980.

Adoption of policies to promote the private sector was accompanied by the liberalization of the regulatory framework governing foreign investment. The success of the NIEs in attracting FDI to promote economic development through export-oriented industrialization has removed the fears that some Asian countries had about compromising their sovereignty. Another aspect of FDI was the emergence of the NIEs as a source of intraregional investment. These countries are seeking low-cost hosts in China and Southeast and South Asia leading to the development of a sophisticated regional division of labor. The relocation of industries from one tier of economies to the next in response to changing comparative advantage is referred to as the "flying geese" pattern of industrial development in Asia.

It is a truism that FDI requires a favorable policy environment, a friendly and stable tax regime, and political stability. This environment ensures that agreements concluded will be honored and political commitment exists to promote its inflow through the availability of physical infrastructure and labor skills to support such investments. Statistics for 1986–1990 show that South Asia accounted for less than 5 percent of FDI flows to the region. In spite of the introduction of new policies for its promotion, this poor performance reflects the lack of strong commitment to private enterprise, the dominance of the public sector in their economies, and the existence of bureaucratic regulations that impede private investment. Overall, the investment climate in South Asia is unfavorable in comparison to the countries in Southeast Asia that have benefited from FDI from the NIEs.

Net Transfer on Loans

Aggregate net transfers indicate the overall financial balance between inflows and outflows from all sources. Table 3.6 shows the aggregate position regarding the net transfers on loans to the Asian region during 1986–1991. Except in 1990 and 1991 there were outward transfers from the region. These net figures are the result of different trends for South Asia as opposed to East Asia and the Pacific and for different categories of creditors. South Asia received positive net transfers in each of the years in the range of $2.0–3.0 billion annually with the exception of 1990 when it was only $0.8 billion. In East Asia and the Pacific the transfers were negative during 1986–1989.

Table 3.6   Net Transfers on Loans to Asian Region (in millions of dollars)

	1986	1987	1988	1989	1990	1991
Public and publicly guaranteed debt						
Multilateral	1,486	2,083	2,203	2,624	2,716	2,959
World Bank	1,071	1,644	1,355	1,636	981	1,302
IDA	1,421	1,791	1,634	1,415	1,820	1,942
IBRD	−350	−147	−279	221	−-839	−640
AsDB	238	130	565	879	1,470	1,633
ADF	366	480	618	804	962	918
OCR	−128	−350	−53	75	508	715
Other	177	309	283	109	265	24
Bilateral	125	−202	1,044	2,427	2,429	1,489
Private	−609	−8,471	−4,928	−6,095	−6,699	−1,498
Subtotal	1,002	−6,590	−1,681	−1,044	−1,554	2,950
Private unguaranteed debt						
Subtotal	−2,013	−2,339	−2,104	938	2,913	3,708
Total	−1,011	−8,929	−3,785	−106	1,359	6,658

Source: AsDB and the World Debt tables.
Note: AsDB statistics include Afghanistan, Cambodia, Kiribati, Vietnam, Hong Kong, Singapore, and Taipei,China, which are not included in the World Debt tables.

This outward flow declined annually from a peak of $11.0 billion in 1987. It was reversed in both 1990 and 1991, when positive net transfers of $1.9 and $4.3 billion respectively were recorded. These were virtually double the levels achieved in South Asia.

The multilateral channel was a significant source of net transfers to Asia during 1986–1991. It was larger than the bilateral channel, except in 1990 when it was about 10 percent lower. Positive transfers from both sources during this period (except for 1987 when the bilateral transfers were negative) partly compensated for the outward transfers due to private credits both guaranteed and unguaranteed, the latter during 1986–1988. The World Bank has made significantly larger net transfers than the AsDB in each of the years except 1990 and 1991 when it was only 66 and 80 percent of the level of the AsDB respectively. Both concessional windows, in other words, the ADF and International Development Association (IDA), had positive net transfers during 1986–1991. Total IDA net transfers during this period were more than double those of the ADF though the divergence was less in the second half of the period. Transfers from the OCR were positive in 1989–1991 while IBRD transfers were positive only in 1989. The negative transfers were entirely due to nonconcessional borrowings by the East Asian and Pacific countries from both the World Bank and the AsDB, some of which were prepaid during this period. Guaranteed private credits led to negative net transfers in both South Asia and East Asia and the Pacific, the only exception being South Asia in 1986 and 1987. The outflows were more than twice as large during 1988–1990 in East Asia and the Pacific. Negative net transfers also took place in the South Asian countries for unguaranteed private credits in each of the years from 1986 to 1991, although they were significantly smaller than the outflows from East Asia and the Pacific during 1986–1988. The latter outflows were reversed during 1989–1991. This led to the reversal of the negative trend for private unguaranteed debt for the Asian region in 1989–1991.

Contribution to Sectoral Development

The Bank's contribution to the DMCs can only be assessed by assigning a share equivalent to its contribution to net resource flows to the region, both in overall terms and sectorally. Even such an analysis would not take account of the contribution made by domestic resources and qualitative differences in resource flows by type and lender. In any event, net flows from the Bank to the region have been small and in the range of 4.4 to 5.5 percent of aggregate net resource flows during 1987–1991, although in some DMCs the Bank is a large provider of ODA. FDI and private lending has exceeded 55 percent of overall resource flows to the region since the mid–1980s. Thus the direct impact of Bank lending has been small on the average, though other benefits have accrued to DMCs by the mobilization of cofinancing resources and technical assistance for institution building. Another benefit that could be attributed to Bank operations is the inflow of FDI and private lending that took place as a result of the policy reforms that DMCs introduced with Bank assistance, although these were sectoral in nature. A closer look should therefore be taken at Bank activities in the main sectors of intervention.

Of the $42.5 billion committed to the region by the end of 1992, the largest share—26.4 percent—has gone to agriculture and agro-industry. The second-largest share, which was allocated to energy, accounted for 24.7 percent. Physical infrastructure projects, mainly in transport and communications, accounted for a further 17.4 percent, while social infrastructure covering water supply and sanitation, urban development and housing, education, health, and population control accounted for 14.7 percent. Lending to the financial sector, mostly to DFIs, was the fifth major sector, to which 10.8 percent of the lending was channelled.

The agriculture sector in Bank terminology also includes forestry, livestock, and fisheries. The special features of Asian agriculture that had an impact on the Bank's lending program are that rice is the major food crop; that most DMCs are affected by heavy monsoon rains for only part of the year, thereby requiring irrigation water for year-round cultivation; and that small-scale subsistence farming predominates.[18] There were lessons from the experience of Japan, Korea, and Taipei,China that provided guidance for increasing productivity of rice cultivation. These were the need for adequate irrigation, the use of high-yielding seed varieties, fertilizers and pesticides, and institutions capable of formulating agricultural policies and providing extension services. Apart from these factors, land reform and market-determined prices for agricultural products were also important.

The first Asian Agricultural Survey was undertaken by the Bank in 1967. It coincided with major breakthroughs in the green revolution, which led to the development of improved high-yielding varieties of wheat and maize by the International Center for Wheat and Maize in Mexico and rice by the International Rice Research Institute in the Philippines. Similar achievements were made in the major plantation crops where improved clonal and hybrid planting materials raised the yields of rubber, oil palm, tea, and coconut. The survey optimistically expected the transformation of Asian agriculture through the dissemination of these new technologies. While these were adopted by large-scale farmers, and plantations, they did not benefit the majority of small-scale farmers who could not be reached by the support systems available to the agriculture sector. Further, the rise in oil prices that began in 1973 had an impact on fertilizer prices that led to a decline in consumption. Accordingly, the lending program turned to the supply of irrigation water and inputs for agriculture and research on a regional basis.

The Bank undertook a second Asian Agricultural Survey in 1976. At that time the outlook for the sector was pessimistic because of the possibility of food deficits increasing in the region, the prevalence of widespread rural unemployment, and deteriorating conditions in the environment. The survey recommended action to accelerate the growth in agricultural production and programs to reach a large number of small-scale farmers. Without these measures it argued that production increases on the scale required could not be achieved. The Bank committed itself to increasing its lending to the agriculture and rural development sector by 20 percent annually during 1979–1982 and exceeded this target. It also addressed the issues of institutional development, irrigation systems, operations and maintenance, and cost recovery. As well, from the second half of the 1970s there was a diversification of lending in the sector to aquaculture, livestock, and forestry.

A third Asian Agricultural Survey was conducted in the mid-1980s, which, unlike the earlier surveys, was prepared entirely by Bank staff without outside consultancy inputs. It recommended a continuation of the same broad policies while making them more flexible in response to the worsening energy situation, deteriorating environmental conditions, and the need to pay greater attention to equity issues and employment to reduce the widening poverty gap.

The loans made to DMCs in the agricultural sector covered irrigation, rural development, industrial crops, agro-industry, fisheries, livestock, forestry, support services (covering research, extension, training, marketing, storage, and credit), fertilizer production, and program loans. A substantial share of this lending was for irrigation and rural development (165 of the 374 projects financed to the end of 1992), which was central to the development of Asian agriculture. Operational difficulties brought about by weak institutional arrangements and distribution systems often prevented the full benefits of these projects from being realized. In addition, eighty-seven livestock, fisheries, and forestry projects were financed, with the balance of 122 projects being spread among the other areas listed above.

Expansion of agricultural production enabled most DMCs to achieve self-sufficiency in the food staples, mainly rice, and substantially reduce their dependence on imports. The goal of achieving self-sufficiency in rice was taken for granted in many DMCs, which made it a target of their agricultural development policy. Although this could not always have been justified on grounds of comparative advantage, the reasoning that food shortages might cause social unrest made it strategically important for some DMCs to adopt this policy. Overall, the Bank has been supportive of the agricultural development efforts of DMCs, and the investments it financed made a significant contribution to achieving food self-sufficiency in the region.

Cumulative lending to the energy sector exceeded $10 billion by the end of 1992, accounting for 24.5 percent of total Bank lending. Half this sum was lent in the five-year period of 1988–1992 when there was a considerable acceleration of the program, particularly in 1991 and 1992. When the Bank was established at the end of 1966, Asia was responding to the availability of cheap oil and substituting it for coal in industry and local fuel for domestic use. The energy crises of 1973–1974 and 1979–1980 changed these attitudes. Since that time, the primary objective of energy planning has been to reduce the dependence on oil and the import content of energy consumption. This led to accelerated efforts to increase the production of indigenous energy supplies and the development of nonoil resources. Accordingly, projects were financed for the production and distribution of natural gas, development of hydropower, production of coal, expansion of transmission and distribution facilities for power, and the improvement of energy utilization. Projects supported by the Bank made significant contributions in DMCs to meeting the needs of consumers and industry whose growth was impeded by the lack of adequate power supplies. Lending for rural electrification, the development of wood fuels, minihydropower, and biogas has augmented energy supplies in rural areas.

The Bank carried out a Regional Energy Survey in 1979–1980 that endorsed its focus on the development of indigenous energy resources and improvement of the efficiency of energy utilization. The survey recommended that the Bank should increase lending to this sector and mobilize cofinancing resources for its projects, which it did. It also recommended that resources should be allocated for energy master-planning, preparation of energy conservation programs, development of renewable energy resources, and training of staff and managers who could implement these programs. Several studies and related activities have been undertaken with regional technical assistance funds to assist in the development of the lending program since the mid–1980s. These included studies on improving the efficiency of power system operations, the analysis of regional electricity demand, power plant maintenance and management, electric power system expansion planning, increased utilization of natural gas resources, energy conservation, and a regional study on solar power. These studies assisted the Bank in expanding lending to the sector during 1988–1992.

The Bank has assisted industrial development projects that earn or save foreign exchange, use local resources efficiently, increase employment, enhance local skills, and promote development in the less-developed areas in DMCs. Most of the assistance to the industrial sector has been channelled indirectly to small- and medium-scale industries through lines of credit to DFIs. Where the Bank has provided direct assistance, it has generally been in support of large projects such as cement, petrochemicals, and fertilizer production. In addition, assistance has been provided to develop industrial infrastructure designed to help small- and medium-scale industries to improve their technology and productivity. Up to the end of 1992, the Bank has supported sixty-two industry and nonfuel mineral projects and provided loan funds totalling $1.82 billion, which accounted for 4.29 percent of total Bank lending.

Lending to the financial sector accounted for 11.35 percent of total Bank lending and amounted to $4.82 billion. Of this amount, eight program loans accounted for $1 billion and the balance of $3.82 billion was lent through 118 credit lines to fifty-nine DFIs in twenty-three DMCs. These credit lines were then on-lent in secondary loans to small- and medium-scale enterprises through 21,100 subloans. This lending was often coupled with technical assistance for institutional development to upgrade staff skills and enhance capacities to broaden services offered to clients. The assistance also included the establishment of new institutions, particularly in the smaller DMCs, the build-up of existing institutions, and rehabilitation of weak ones in other countries. Individual credit lines to DFIs for on-lending enabled the AsDB to assist a range of borrowers, both small- and medium-sized enterprises, that would have otherwise remained outside the scope of its operations.

The review of DFI operations conducted in 1987 concluded that, while the AsDB should continue to support these institutions and their activities, future credit lines should be channelled through a broader range of financial intermediaries to improve the functioning of the financial sector as a whole. Accordingly, "Apex" loans were introduced whereby an institution like a central bank was the recipient of AsDB lines of credit that were distributed among participating DFIs on a predetermined or "first-come-first-served" basis. In addition, "umbrella" credit lines, where a group of participating DFIs and/or commercial banks are allocated the proceeds of an AsDB line of credit for on-lending to subprojects, was also introduced. The latter enabled the use of private sector financial intermediaries for channelling funds.

The review of AsDB program lending policies in 1987 enabled the addition of another indirect instrument for the development of the financial sector by the provision of fast-disbursing loans linked to policy reforms in the sector and capital markets of the DMCs. The reforms were designed to improve the overall business environment through changes in the policy and regulatory framework necessary for the functioning of an effective financial sector. The AsDB has pursued such an agenda through program and large DFI loans in a few DMCs such as India, Indonesia, Lao Peoples' Democratic Republic, Pakistan, and Sri Lanka. In addition, technical assistance for financial sector and capital market studies was also provided. These changes expanded the scope of DFI lending by the AsDB.

The bulk of the credit lines to DFIs and financial intermediaries were on-lent to private industrial enterprises. They accounted for over 10 percent of total AsDB lending to the end of 1991. Further, financial sector and capital market development accounted for less than 1 percent of the total. The AsDB also provided financial assistance to food crop farmers, farmers' cooperatives, fishermen, and agro-processing projects through agricultural and agriculture-related credit lines to financial intermediaries serving this sector. These constituted a further 3.7 percent of AsDB lending through 1991. More recently, the AsDB has begun lending to the housing sector through financial intermediaries. Thus, AsDB support to the private sector through these intermediaries and financial sector program loans was nearly $5.6 billion or 15 percent of total lending in 1968–1991. This wholesale indirect approach has enabled the AsDB to reach a larger group of investors than would have been possible through the direct approach, as it is not cost-effective to process small loan and equity requests from small- to medium-sized investors. However, this approach did not support selective government interventions through directed and subsidized credit, which proved successful in a few Asian economies, mainly in East Asia.[19]

The AsDB used a similar approach with some of the new modalities introduced after 1983 for assisting the private sector directly. These made a developmental impact by contributing to the growth of financial institutions and, indirectly, to their beneficiary enterprises. Loans provided to leasing companies, when on-lent, enabled small- and medium-scale enterprises to purchase machinery to which they would not otherwise have access. Similarly, equity positions taken in venture capital companies have been distributed among new ventures enabling them to stimulate the entrepreneurial spirit among investors who contributed to their success. Lines of equity provided to DFIs made it possible for them to make equity financing available for small- and medium-sized enterprises that have limited access to institutional equity funds. In spite of the diversity of these facilities, they remained small in value terms.

Physical infrastructure, classified as transport and communications in Bank terminology, accounted for 17.4 percent of total lending to the end of 1992. It was made up of forty-six projects for the construction, rehabilitation, modernization, and expansion of port facilities; eighty-nine for the rehabilitation, maintenance, and construction of primary, secondary, and feeder roads; sixteen telecommunications projects to improve and extend services; and eight railway projects to increase freight capacity. Total lending to the sector reached $7.4 billion at the end of 1992, of which more than 50 percent was committed during 1988–1992. The share of lending to this sector was around 20 percent since the mid–1980s, which took it back to the levels that prevailed in the early 1970s, from which it declined for the rest of the decade. The OPP Study for the 1980s envisaged a decline in this sector and suggested that greater emphasis be placed instead on social infrastructure, as did the expert panel for the 1990s.

Lending to social infrastructure increased from 10–11 percent in the early 1970s to over 19 percent during 1979–1981, leading to an average of 15.3 percent during 1970–1981. Its share declined to a little under 15 percent during the 1980s, close to the long-term average. Bank interventions to date have financed

a) seventy-five water supply and sanitation projects benefiting more than 94 million people;

b) sixty-three education projects involving the rehabilitation, expansion and establishment of primary, secondary, and tertiary level education and training institutions, which have benefited millions of children and about 175,000 teaching and administrative staff to date;

c) twenty-nine projects providing physical and institutional support for housing and a variety of urban infrastructure facilities; and

d) twenty-four health and population projects covering the establishment or upgrading of rural health facilities and referral hospitals, health manpower development, production of essential drugs, and improvement of storage and distribution of medical and family planning supplies.

Total lending for social infrastructure projects was $6.24 billion by the end of 1992 and accounted for 14.7 percent of total Bank lending. As the project numbers would indicate, health and population accounted for the smallest component (1.56 percent) of social infrastructure lending.

There were good reasons for the marginal decline in the share of social infrastructure and for the increase in the share of physical infrastructure that was observed in the 1980s in comparison to the 1970s. Two new large borrowers, namely China and India, emerged that were restricted to using only the OCR. They chose not to borrow for social infrastructure but borrowed heavily for energy and physical infrastructure. Other DMCs such as Indonesia, Thailand, and some South Asian countries began to experience physical infrastructure bottlenecks, which led to an increase in borrowing. Further, the Bank appears to be facing difficulties in expanding its lending for health and population projects due to the need in many DMCs to consolidate and strengthen basic health services instead of to expand them.

Many DMCs suffer frequently from natural disasters such as hurricanes, earthquakes, and floods, which destroy some of their capital stock, including physical and social infrastructure. The Bank has been actively involved in the rehabilitation process after such events to assist DMCs in resuming their development activities. This has been an important feature of AsDB operations since the mid–1980s, particularly in Bangladesh, the Philippines, and Western Samoa.

From among the sectoral contributions made by the Bank in the region, several stand out in relation to others. Irrigation and rural development projects made a significant contribution to achieving food self-sufficiency in many DMCs. The focus is now changing from major irrigation projects to those concentrating on rehabilitation and maintenance. Projects for hydropower and thermal generation, transmission, and distribution facilities extending in some cases to rural areas have eased bottlenecks that were impeding industrial development, and consequently growth, in some DMCs. The extension of supplies to a larger number of consumers in the region has improved the quality of life. A number of roads and ports projects have improved access of goods and services to markets and, in many cases, opened up new areas. Lending to intermediary DFIs, though some of them have been weak institutions, has made it possible for the Bank to reach a large number of small- and medium-scale industrialists that would not have been possible through direct lending. Education and water supply and sanitation projects supported by the Bank have reached millions of beneficiaries in the region. The direct contribution made by the Bank in each of these sectors is again difficult to estimate. What can be said is that the Bank has become a major development partner in one or more of these sectors in each DMC where it has an active lending program.

The World Bank/AsDB Interface

The issue of coordination between the AsDB and World Bank is important for the DMCs because both are large donors in most of them, lending and offering policy advice often in the same sectors. The World Bank was already lending in many DMCs before the AsDB was established in 1966. Further, it chairs consultative groups that exist for DMCs to consider the foreign assistance requirements of the country in coordination with other donors. The exceptions are the DMCs for which round table meetings are organized by the UNDP, mostly for the smaller countries in the region. It is clear that the World Bank assists countries in formulating their macroeconomic framework while both banks assist in sectoral policies. Unless there is an allocation of responsibility for different sectors to the two banks—and there are very few examples of this—coordination is necessary at the sectoral levels. Decisions have to be made on which bank's sector plans the coordination will be based, recognizing that the World Bank does more economic and sector work. How are these decisions actually implemented by staff at the field level in DMCs? The coordination issue is complex and has to be dealt with separately for each DMC.

There is a general commitment to collaboration at the management levels of the AsDB and World Bank. Senior management from both institutions have held annual coordination meetings since the late 1970s. The purpose of these meetings is to share views and experiences on global and regional developments that have operational implications and pose major development policy issues for the two institutions. Project or program-specific issues that require resolution by management are also sometimes discussed, although these are normally left to operations staff. At this level, collaboration covers exchange of information on work programs, lending allocations, planned missions, and policy papers; visits between the staff of both institutions (which take place more frequently by World Bank staff visiting Manila during field missions); contacts between resident missions and project staff in the field; and increasing collaboration in areas of special emphasis such as the environment and gender issues.

Coordination with both the World Bank and IMF takes place through Bank resident missions, where they exist. In the absence of such missions, coordination takes place in DMCs during field visits for programming or project-specific purposes. Additional consultations take place when World Bank staff visit Manila during their field missions. The AsDB also consults with other donors in capitals of DMCs during programming missions. Thereafter, additional consultations take place in the context of project-specific loan proposals with donors providing assistance to the sector or implementing agency. The AsDB maintains that its coordination efforts have been most effective in its support to public utilities such as the water and electricity authorities that receive assistance from a number of sources. In Sri Lanka, the AsDB, U.S. Agency for International Development (USAID), and the World Bank assist the National Water Supply and Drainage Board. The AsDB financed a sector project for the rehabilitation of water supply to secondary towns. USAID was concerned with institutional strengthening of the Board while World Bank assistance concentrated on the area around the capital city of Colombo. The three donors closely coordinated their activities to address various institutional issues affecting the Board such as water tariffs, cost recovery, accounts receivable, and the debt/equity ratio. These consultations were facilitated by a covenant in the AsDB sector loan that made six-monthly coordination meetings mandatory. In addition, reports of loan review missions were exchanged regularly.

Similarly, in Indonesia, both the Bank and the World Bank are financing the National Electricity Corporation, an electric power utility. The Bank's support has focused on projects in the outer islands, with the World Bank assisting the corporation's system in Java. However, both institutions have coordinated the manner in which they addressed issues related to the power utility's financial performance, including capital structure, revaluation of assets, rate of return on equity, and tariff increases. These issues were addressed as a result of sustained coordination. In the process the corporation has benefited from the active dialogue between its two major lenders.

While these examples do not lead to the conclusion that coordination is perfect, the AsDB does what it can within the limits imposed on it by the other donors. The coordination with the World Bank could be more effective if there were opportunities for AsDB staff to visit Washington, D.C., which is important due to the absence of a Bank office there. Unfortunately, visits do not occur unless they are linked to specific events. This lack of reciprocity is a weakness in coordination arrangements that would provide the World Bank with greater opportunities to assist and influence the policy agenda of DMCs, making it necessary for other donors to operate within those parameters.

The AsDB's program lending began in 1978 and was initially used for financing imports of production inputs for the agricultural sector. Following a performance review in 1987, sector operations encompassing policies, investments, and institutional development were approved. Certain guidelines were introduced with the new policy. First, the AsDB was expected to use World Bank analyses of sectoral issues in program-lending operations, but an in-house capacity for this was to be established. Second, the AsDB was not expected to engage in program lending that would encompass macroeconomic policy issues because these were perceived to be the responsibility of the World Bank and IMF. This division of functions has certainly been maintained in the program loans that have been extended to the agriculture, industry, and financial sectors. Third, sector and investment lending are dependent on an appropriate macroeconomic framework. This makes it imperative for the AsDB to coordinate with the World Bank and IMF to ensure compatibility of its programs. It is not clear what the AsDB would do in the absence of an appropriate framework being adopted in the context of an adjustment program supported by the World Bank and IMF. Such situations do not seem to have arisen in the recent past.

The expert panel for the 1990s suggested that the AsDB should strengthen its analytical capability in the macroeconomic field, while drawing on the knowledge of the World Bank and IMF. The panel further suggested that the AsDB broaden its policy dialogue with DMCs by establishing a multilateral policy forum to review the macroeconomic and sectoral policies of these countries with other members. This proposal was in keeping with the recommendations made in the OPP Study that the AsDB's capability as a development resource center be fostered. An internal World Bank working paper prepared in 1989 on "Future AsDB–World Bank Relations" urges caution in moving into this area, as the AsDB does not have the skills to undertake these tasks. It is, nevertheless, an issue that AsDB management must tackle as it moves into the preparation of a new generation of country operational-strategy studies. Staff are now required to describe the framework for assessing the macroeconomic and social performance of DMCs in these strategy studies. It is not clear whether these assessments are to be independent of World Bank/IMF programs, but they are required under the agreement reached with donors at the fifth replenishment of the ADF. Further, the AsDB sees a role for itself in assisting DMCs to formulate the policy environment necessary for the development of the private sector.

These developments and an increased role for the Bank in policy-based lending to sectors compound the need for closer collaboration with the World Bank. However, until the AsDB develops a capacity to assess macroeconomic policies, which is central to any lending program be it policy-based or investment, it will find that it is functioning under a policy agenda formulated with World Bank assistance. Accordingly, the DMCs will pay more attention to the World Bank in setting its policy and priorities for its borrowing program. This has certainly been the case in the countries where Bank operations have been reviewed in this study. The AsDB should shake off its early "family doctor" image and become a full-fledged consultant in the development business. The small number of economists with analytical capability in the AsDB cannot coordinate macroeconomic policy with World Bank staff effectively, reinforcing the DMCs' perception that the AsDB has little to offer in this area.

In December 1988, the Bank agreed with the government of Papua New Guinea and the World Bank to take the lead agency[20] role in six sectors in Papua New Guinea: agriculture and livestock, fisheries and marine resources, roads, ports, urban water supply and sewerage, and health. This role primarily meant assisting in policy formulation, conducting sector studies, and increasing lending and technical assistance when required. The Bank also agreed to assist the government in securing cofinancing, where necessary, and to be more active in donor coordination in these sectors. It was decided at the time that the Bank could provide support on a selective basis in other sectors as well. Accordingly, a complementary, or supporting, role was proposed in industrial development, urban infrastructure and housing, and the DFIs.

The lead role implied that greater technical assistance will be given to sector policy studies and institutional development and relative priority accorded to supporting projects in these sectors. It did not imply that the Bank would be the only lender, the largest lender, or a lender at all to these sectors. No undertaking was given that studies would be done to offer policy advice to the government on macroeconomic issues, which was left to the World Bank and IMF. Sectoral strategies and policies were to be developed consistent with the broad macroeconomic policies and targets of the adjustment program. Those that were relevant for sectoral policies at the time were the high level of minimum wages relative to the skills and productivity of the labor force, the exchange rate policy, taxation, investment regulation, and subsidies. Apart from the agriculture and possibly the transportation sector, the loan and technical assistance operations undertaken after the assumption of the lead agency role do not indicate that the Bank has been very active in assisting the government in policy formulation in these sectors. In agriculture, where the Bank has undertaken more operations than in any other sector, its lead role was undermined by the government requesting the World Bank to conduct a study on revitalizing agriculture without consultation with or any information being conveyed to the Bank. It was gathered from Bank staff that the World Bank took no action to inform the AsDB of the study until a draft report was sent.[21]

The formal coordination of foreign assistance to the Philippines takes place through the annual consultative group meetings chaired by the World Bank. The AsDB is a member of this group and is among the four largest donors along with the World Bank, Japan, and the United States. During recent meetings, many of the discussions tended to focus on stabilization and adjustment programs that are being implemented by the government. Since the policy dialogue with the government on these issues is the responsibility of the World Bank and the IMF, the AsDB's role in such discussions can only be marginal. Policy discussions relating to AsDB lending have focused entirely on sectoral issues without any conditionalities being attached to those of a macroeconomic nature. It was perhaps for this reason that the Bank was initially left out of the core group, namely, the World Bank, IMF, Japan, and the United States, which held regular consultations on assistance to the Philippines, although the Bank was subsequently invited to join. This treatment did not provide adequate recognition of the Bank's role in assisting the Philippines over the past five years. It committed $1,631 million during 1988–1992, of which $550 million was from the ADF, and $632 million during 1991–1992, of which $200 million was from the ADF. Further, it took the lead role in assisting the government to assess the damage caused by the July 1990 earthquake, and it coordinated the rehabilitation assistance from the donor community. Similarly, the Bank was invited to join the donors funding the Philippines' commercial debt reduction agreement only after all the negotiations were completed.

The only region where coordination has been a two-way process is the South Pacific (excluding Papua New Guinea), where the AsDB, in agreement with the World Bank, assumed the lead role in 1980. In these countries the World Bank tended to cofinance AsDB loans based on project appraisals undertaken by Bank staff instead of undertaking their own appraisals. The World Bank strategy in recent years has been to produce a series of regional reports on economic and sectoral issues, while the AsDB has produced country economic reports to be used in conjunction with these. The Bank aims to prepare such reports for each South Pacific DMC every two years. These will be used for roundtable meetings that will be organized for these countries. As in the past, the UNDP will assist governments in preparing their own submissions, including project proposals to these meetings. It is understood from the World Bank that it is contemplating discontinuing the arrangement with the Bank following a review of it by the Operations Evaluation Department.[22] No action appears to have been taken as yet. In the meanwhile, the DMCs have expressed a wish to deal directly with both the AsDB and the World Bank. Similar coordination by the Bank appears to have been undertaken among all donors, sometimes through local meetings of the consultative group, in Bangladesh in the railway, energy, and DFI sectors.

Consultations appear to be sporadic and less frequent with the IMF, although the AsDB Operations Manual states that program lending for sectors should be compatible with IMF operations in the country.[23] An example of collaboration with the IMF was the approval of technical assistance of $2.41 million for Cambodia in April 1992. This was cofinanced with the UNDP, and the Bank assisted in formulating and implementing an IMF stabilization program. The Bank also undertook legal and economic work in Cambodia before other multilateral agencies, which proved useful to their subsequent operations. It is understood that there are staff exchanges between the Bank and IMF. If these are judged to be useful, there may be a case for similar exchanges between the staff of the World Bank and the RDBs.

Coordination between the AsDB and the World Bank needs to be improved in the interests of the DMCs. The World Bank has the staff capability and mandate to assist governments to formulate their macroeconomic policy agenda. While accepting this position, the Bank can play a strong supporting role in its program, sector, and investment lending. This would, nevertheless, require a capability to dialogue with governments on macroeconomic issues to the extent that they impinge on the Bank's lending program. Unless this is achieved—and there are staffing implications here—due recognition may not be given by the DMCs and World Bank to the size and quality of the Bank's lending program. It is inevitable that there would be healthy rivalry between the two institutions over the funding of projects, with frequent allegations of pirating. One hopes that this would work towards the long-term benefit of the DMCs and not to their detriment. The relationship between the two institutions should be based on respect for the quality of each other's lending program, fully recognizing the dominant role of the World Bank in all DMCs except the Pacific. This is often related to its role as chair of the consultative group. The Bank should not be apologetic about its program and should participate actively with other major donors in assisting DMCs in their policy formulation and the provision of capital and technical assistance for projects and programs.

Experience recommends the need for better coordination between the AsDB and World Bank in the interests of DMCs. Projections of available resources from both banks indicate that the increase in lending levels of the past decade, particularly of concessional funds, cannot be maintained. With this background, DMCs wish to avoid any overlap and consequent wastage that may result in a suboptimal use of resources. Given that the World Bank chairs consultative groups (where these exist) and assists DMCs to formulate their macroeconomic policies, coordination efforts are needed at the sectoral level. DMCs should take the initiative in bringing about coordination by discussing the issues with the World Bank and AsDB and possibly the largest bilateral donor in the country, which in most cases is Japan. A sectoral division of responsibility between donors should be attempted, based on comparative advantage and past performance in the sector, as well as the capacity to undertake economic and sector analysis. The lead agency role in the assigned sector does not exclude other donors from being active in it, but it should be with the concurrence of the DMC and lead agency for that sector. Strict guidelines should be drawn for donors undertaking lead agency responsibilities. The lead agencies and guidelines should be reviewed at periodic intervals in each DMC to improve their effectiveness. This can only happen if the concerned DMC takes an interest in making them work.

Notes

1. "Economic Review and Bank Operations: Indonesia," February 1993, AsDB.

2. The Netherlands chaired the intergovernmental group on Indonesia from its inception up to 1991. It was the principal forum for aid coordination and consultation. Following the termination of the aid relationship between Indonesia and the Netherlands, the government invited the World Bank to chair the consultative group in 1992. Total commitments in 1991 were $4.75 billion.

3. Brian K. Parkinson, *The Eastern Islands of Indonesia: An Overview of Development Needs and Potential,* AsDB Occasional Papers no. 2, January 1993.

4. A postevaluation is conducted by the Post-Evaluation Office of the

Bank after project completion and the report of its findings is presented as a Project Performance Audit Report.

5. "Country Operation Program Paper for Indonesia: 1993–1996," AsDB, April 1993.

6. An example of effective donor action was the case of Kenya where bilateral donors in the consultative group exerted pressure to hold elections in 1993.

7. "Country Operational Program Paper for Pakistan: 1993–1996," AsDB, May 1993.

8. The budget for the FY/1994 and the elections held in October 1993 showed progress in both these areas.

9. The Bank approved a loan of $29 million for agricultural inputs in 1986 under its earlier program-lending policy.

10. This loan was not drawn fully due to noncompliance of some of the conditionalities.

11. "Country Operational Strategy for Sri Lanka," AsDB, August 1993, page 20.

12. Please see the section entitled "Evaluation Criteria" Chapter 4 for definitions of these classifications.

13. *World Economic Outlook,* IMF, October 1992.

14. *Asian Development Outlook,* AsDB, 1992.

15. *East Asian Miracle: Economic Growth and Public Policy,* the World Bank, 1993.

16. Defined to include grants and FDI on a net basis.

17. Singapore was the largest recipient of FDI during this period, but it is no longer classified as a developing country.

18. Dick Wilson, *A Bank for Half the World,* AsDB, 1987.

19. *The East Asian Miracle: Economic Growth and Public Policy,* the World Bank, 1993.

20. *Lead Agency Role in Papua New Guinea,* AsDB, May 1989.

21. The World Bank disputes this.

22. "The World Bank and the Pacific Island Countries: An OED Review," the World Bank, May 1992.

23. It is not known how this may be achieved.

PART 2

DEVELOPMENT AGENDA

4

LOAN PERFORMANCE AND INSTITUTIONAL GOVERNANCE

Loan Quality and Evaluation

Trends and Issues

Concerns regarding loan quality surfaced in the MDBs when borrowers began to accrue arrears in their loan repayments and were subjected to varying sanctions. The AsDB did not experience these problems and did not feel it necessary until April 1993 to adopt policies on sanctions as comprehensive as those in other MDBs. Major concerns were expressed in the donor community with the release of the report of the Portfolio Management Task Force[1] (the Wapenhans Report) by the World Bank in September 1992. The portfolio of the World Bank had undergone a steady deterioration in performance during the 1980s when the share of projects with major problems experienced during implementation increased from 11 percent in FY 1981 to 20 percent in FY 1991. Projects judged to be unsatisfactory upon completion increased from 15 to 37 percent during the same period. Worldwide, it was estimated that some 39 percent of the borrowing countries had problems of implementation in more than 25 percent of their projects. Cancellations of World Bank loans had also increased by about 50 percent in the past three years.

The initial response to the report of the management of the World Bank was to recognize that tension existed in the staff because of the emphasis placed on making new commitments and achieving lending targets as opposed to the importance of giving adequate attention to effective implementation. It was considered appropriate for the focus of World Bank operations to shift to providing more and better implementation assistance and additional support for institutional development for loans already committed, rather than new lending. Further, all parties accepted that improving project quality at the time of approval requires the active participation and commitment of the borrower to the project. Only with the participation of implementing agencies and beneficiaries will the process be strengthened. More time will be spent on project preparation, intensive supervision in the field, and consultations with implementation agencies. They also agreed that there should be scope to shift responsibility for project identification and preparation to the borrower in countries with a reasonable institutional capacity.

The report of the World Bank task force had an impact on the RDBs. Since they were experiencing similar problems, the AfDB, AsDB, and the IDB subsequently commissioned similar reviews, though not all in the same depth. In the case of Asia, the Central Projects Services Office of the Bank had already drawn the attention of management to the deteriorating health of the Bank's portfolio. The AsDB conducted its study during the second half of 1993, following agreement to set up a task force around the time of the 1993 annual meeting. It was primarily an internal review with staff input provided by about eighty staff members at different levels. Two former executive directors of the Bank served as external consultants to the task force.

The work of the AsDB task force dealt principally with project quality. It established four working groups[2] covering quality at entry, project implementation, feedback mechanism, organization, staffing, and budget implications. The quality-at-entry working group dealt with project identification, preparation, appraisal and negotiation, and loan approval. The project implementation working group dealt essentially with project supervision. The effectiveness of feedback mechanisms was dealt with by that working group while the fourth dealt with the organization and resource requirements of the changes proposed by the three other groups. The report of the task force was released in Manila in early February 1994.

It is useful to examine the recent trend in the share of successful projects that have been completed both by the AsDB and World Bank in Asia and compare them with their respective long-term averages. Table 4.1 shows that there was a decline in the quality of the World

Table 4.1   Ratio of Successful Projects in Asia (in percentages)

	1987	1988	1989	1990	1991	1992	1988–1990	1974–1991
World Bank	84	87	67	70	80	86	72	81
AsDB	50	77	56	30	52	39	44[a]	62[a]

Sources: Annual Reviews of Evaluation Results, World Bank, and Reports of Post-Evaluation Activities, AsDB.
Note: a. The three-year and long-term averages for the AsDB were for 1989–1991 and 1973–1991.

Bank portfolio in the Asian region in recent years. The AsDB portfolio appears to have been similarly affected. Apart from the decline in project quality, these trends reflect

a) the numbers of projects evaluated by the World Bank and AsDB in the region. The long-term averages were based on the results of 371 and 872 evaluations, and the three-year averages were based on eighty-eight and 276 evaluations for the AsDB and World Bank, respectively;

b) the sectoral composition of the projects evaluated by the two banks each year;

c) the IBRD/IDA mix of projects in the case of the World Bank and the OCR/ADF mix of projects in the case of the AsDB;

d) whether the projects evaluated were the first undertaken in the sector and by the implementing agencies with financing from the banks;

e) the periods during which the projects were implemented indicating different policy environments and the experience gained by the Bank in lending to the country concerned; and

f) different classification criteria used by the two institutions with the Bank relying more heavily on the economic internal rate of return (EIRR).

The EIRR is the interest rate that equates the present value of the future stream of net benefits (financial and other) with the initial investment.

Evaluation Criteria

The evolution of the AsDB evaluation methodology led to a change in its system in 1988. Three categories were introduced for measuring success: generally successful, partially successful, and unsuccessful. (Only those in the generally successful category are included as successful projects in Table 4.1. It should be noted that the World Bank had, until recently, only two categories, successful and unsuccessful.) Investment loans were subject to audit on a more selective basis, unlike in the past when it was done for all completed projects. This led to the selection of investment loans that were more complex and had problems and lessons for Bank operations. All sector and program loans were evaluated after 1987. The Bank was concerned about the biased nature of the sample that was selected and consequently revised the basis for selecting completed investment loans in 1992. All first loans to a DMC or a subsector were evaluated, and a random selection adopted for the rest. As before, all completed sector and program loans continue to be evaluated. The change in sampling methodology would have influenced the decline in the ratio of successful projects, the extent of which cannot be assessed.

The Bank adopted three broad performance categories in 1988.[3] Judgment on project success is based on the actual costs and benefits at the time of evaluation, whether they were intended or unforeseen at appraisal, and the likely scenario of future performance when critical variables and the uncertainties associated with them are taken into consideration. The factors used for assessing performance include

a) the reestimated EIRR based on quantifiable benefits that are considered to be reliable;
b) the achievement of a least-cost or cost-effective design;
c) the sustainability of future operations;
d) unquantified though perceived economic benefits and costs, which cannot be included in the EIRR computation;
e) socioeconomic impact that does not enter into the EIRR computation; and
f) the extent to which the major purposes and goals, set out at appraisal or modified and subsequently accepted, have been achieved and are commensurate with the costs actually incurred.

The most important criteria are the reestimated EIRR, confirmation of the least-cost approach, and project sustainability.[4] Some benefits, such as those from education, health, utilities, technology transfer, and improvements in the policy framework and institutions, are difficult to quantify. Similarly, the costs of adverse environmental, distributional, and sociocultural impact are not easy to estimate. In view of this, qualitative assessments are made of (b) through (f) where there are problems of data and for projects (or project components) where the EIRR is not normally estimated, such as in education and health and program loans.

A project is judged to be generally successful if the EIRR at evaluation calculated for most or all of the project is 10 percent or more for the most quantifiable components taken together or separately, if the project has been implemented by the least-cost approach, if no major part of it has failed, and if it meets the sustainability test. The project would also be classified as generally successful if items (b) to (f) in the preceding paragraph are satisfied, the EIRR is in the range of 8–10 percent, and there are substantial unquantified economic benefits or prospects of improvement if remedial action is taken. A project or component for which the EIRR cannot be reestimated will be judged to be generally successful if most of the project objectives have been or are expected to be achieved with no major shortfalls, there are no significant cost overruns that are not commensurate with the benefits, the project has been implemented by the least-cost approach, and it meets the sustainability test.

A project is categorized as partially successful if the EIRR is reestimated to be 4 percent or more for most components for which benefits and costs can be quantified and in the range of 6 to 7 percent for the overall project, the costs associated with failed components are more than compensated for by benefits from other parts of the project, the least-cost test is substantially met, and the project is sustainable at a reduced level of benefits. The project will be similarly rated if the EIRR is in the range of 4 to 5 percent, the items (b) to (f) are satisfied, and the project is considered to have substantial unquantifiable economic benefits that could be realized if appropriate remedial steps are taken. If the EIRR cannot be reestimated, the project could be similarly classified if it is expected to yield worthwhile benefits in relation to actual costs despite shortcomings in the achievement of objectives and if the conditions set out in (b) through (f) are met. Any project whose EIRR at the time of evaluation is expected to be below 4 percent is categorized as unsuccessful and is perceived to be a technical and economic failure with project facilities operating at a low level of installed capacity with little prospect of improvement.

The criteria adopted for evaluations by the Bank have evolved over time. They became comprehensive as experience was gained and advances took place in the methodology. There appears to be an excessive reliance on the EIRR for judging the success of projects. Consequently, the weaknesses in the studies are those factors that do not lend themselves to quantification and require judgments to be made. Examples of these are the socioeconomic impact and the sustainability of future operations, which are often jeopardized due to the lack of funds being allocated for operations and maintenance.

The EIRR cutoff for a successful project at the World Bank is the same as that at the Bank. An EIRR of 10 percent or more for a major portion of the total investment, or some other significant benefits where the EIRR is less than 10 percent, is necessary to meet the minimal requirement for a satisfactory project. Such a project may yet be classified as unsatisfactory if major institutional and policy objectives are not met or significant external costs are omitted. Where EIRRs are not estimated, the overall performance rating is made on the basis of cost-effectiveness in achieving project objectives. The World Bank has recently broadened its classifications to four groups: highly satisfactory, satisfactory, unsatisfactory, and highly unsatisfactory.

Feedback of Evaluations

The effectiveness of an evaluation system depends largely on the methodology adopted and the extent to which the studies are used as guidance in future operations. The Bank has gathered a wealth of information in the 399 Post-Evaluation Reports that were completed by the end of 1992. They were circulated to staff within the Bank and member governments. Summaries of the reports and the lessons for sectors are included in the computerized postevaluation information system of the Bank. In addition to the reports, the Post-Evaluation Office has undertaken reviews of postevaluation studies in some DMCs, impact evaluations of assistance to particular sectors or sub-sectors in some or all DMCs, and the reevaluation of some projects for which Post-Evaluation Reports were prepared earlier. The Post-Evaluation Office has also prepared annual reports highlighting the major findings of the reports and studies, and an annual report of postevaluation abstracts from the information system.

The findings and recommendations of the annual reports are discussed on an interdepartmental basis. Discussions with the audit committee and with the Board follow. Operational departments have to include a discussion of postevaluation experience in the sector and country in project/program briefs, appraisal reports, and reports and recommendations of the president on projects to ensure that the feedback from evaluations are effective. Further, a management committee on postevaluation findings was set up in 1991 to discuss issues raised in the Post-Evaluation Reports and annual reviews and to follow-up action taken by Bank staff. The president chairs this committee, which consists of the three vice presidents and the heads of all operational departments. Feedback workshops are held on postevaluation findings and the lessons learned. Staff make presentations on evaluation findings at seminars organized by the Bank for staff of agencies that implement Bank-financed projects.

There are, however, no systematic arrangements to follow up the recommendations made on completed projects, in spite of the internal mechanisms established to ensure a feedback from evaluated projects. The annual report for 1991 reported that an examination of unsuccessful projects evaluated during 1989–1991 indicated that follow-up was minimal except where there was a follow-on project. A review of the success rates of postevaluated projects during 1973–1990 shows that they were lower for initial projects of the implementing agency and sector in Group A and B countries. It did not appear to influence project success in Group C countries.[5] This supports the view that the Bank's leverage with the borrower and implementing agency for acting on outstanding recommendations is diminished when a project is completed and there is no succeeding project. It appears that implementing agencies do not even advise the Bank of action taken or improvements made in such cases. Any follow-up of partly successful and unsuccessful projects would have major staffing and budgetary implications if the Bank were to undertake review missions and provide advisory technical assistance. Since 38 percent of postevaluated projects during 1973–1991 are in this category, the Bank could begin by making a selective but systematic approach to prevent these investments from becoming nonproductive and a financial burden on the DMCs.

It is encouraging that the Bank has recently made efforts to strengthen the postevaluation capability of DMCs by providing technical assistance. So far, five countries—Bangladesh, Nepal, Papua New Guinea, the Philippines, and Thailand—have received such help.

Lessons of Evaluations

In reviewing the Bank's experience in postevaluation, one should take account of the following factors when interpreting the annual success rates:

a) many of the projects that have been evaluated were approved in the 1970s when the external environment was unfavorable due to escalating oil prices and high inflation, making project implementation more difficult;
b) there was a larger proportion of projects in Group A countries, which have weaker institutional capacities and limited budgetary resources, thereby reducing the success rate;
c) the number of first-time projects in the sample evaluated; and
d) the mix of sectors and subsectors in the projects evaluated. It is noted that the subsectors in agriculture and agro-industry have the lowest success rates historically, mainly due to weaker institutional capacity in this sector in many DMCs.

Project and program selection is critical for the success of the Bank's assistance to any DMC. The number of postevaluations that have been completed are large enough to draw lessons for improving project quality. These were summarized in a paper prepared during the ADF VI negotiations.[6] The lessons point to the need for

a) more technical assistance for preparing feasibility studies followed by detailed engineering design that takes into account sociocultural aspects, where appropriate;

b) increased technical assistance to implementing agencies for project supervision and institution building over the long term;

c) adequate account taken of the capacity of the implementing agency in the project design to avoid overestimating benefits and underestimating costs;

d) flexibility to approve changes in project design, scope, and cost allocation among different items due to technical considerations or changes in the economic environment;

e) the introduction of effective monitoring of benefits from the project and appropriate corrective action to ensure expected benefits;

f) formal midterm reviews for complex projects with scope for making changes;

g) more attention to sustaining satisfactory financial and operational performance of implementing agencies in maintaining project facilities during their lifetime; and

h) the participation of beneficiaries as an integral part of project preparation and implementation, as well as operation and maintenance. These need to be built into the project design and implementation arrangements.

These are critical issues for project preparation and implementation, whose adoption will improve the quality of projects financed by the Bank. They were discussed by the working groups on quality at entry and project quality in implementation during the deliberations of the task force, and the need for them was agreed on. There are implications for the project cycle, staff, and budget, including the availability of technical assistance in support of loan operations. They are being examined by the steering committee for a review of the Bank's organization appointed by the president of the Bank following the release of the task force report in February 1994. The committee is expected to submit its report later in the year.

Country Strategies and Programming

The Planning Process and Role of the Board

The Bank was in a transitional phase in its loan operations and organization in 1992 and 1993. Much of the impulse for these changes came from the nonregional members. The establishment of the Strategic Planning Unit in 1991, which reported directly to the president, served as the focal point for bringing about many of the changes within the Bank. Donors took the initiative in urging the

Bank to set up the unit. The AsDB was the first RDB to establish a strategic planning process. Following the preparation of the Bank's medium-term strategic framework for 1992–1995 and the country operational strategies for a few DMCs in 1992, the Strategic Planning Unit worked with management to modify the planning cycle within the Bank, in order to take account of the changes and enable the Board to participate in the process more formally, with 1993 marking the first year in which the new planning cycle was implemented. It was introduced when the operational strategies for most of the DMCs had not been revised on the basis of the Bank's strategic framework. Thus, the process should be viewed incrementally and revised, based on experience gained.

The planning cycle that was introduced in 1993 began with a discussion in January of the Bank's Medium-Term Strategic Framework (a rolling three-year document that is revised annually). Accordingly, the 1992–1995 strategic framework was revised and a new document produced for 1993–1996, which was further refined in the 1994–1997 strategic framework. The new generation of operational strategies based on the strategic framework will be on a multiyear cycle, produced continuously, and submitted to the Board for informal comment. They will have greater analytical content than before and reflect both the strategic objectives of the DMC and the Bank's strategic framework and recommend the most effective intervention that could be made by the Bank in the DMC. These strategies will also establish a framework for measuring country performance.

Country programming missions will take place after the discussion of position papers for each DMC with management. These papers set out the issues, focus, and scope of these missions. They lead to the preparation of country operational program papers[7] for each DMC covering a four-year time frame (including the current year) but containing a detailed lending and technical assistance program only for the first year. The country operational programs will also contain the performance reviews conducted on the basis of the framework set out in the country operational strategy for the DMC. They will be used to prepare Country Program Notes that will be more extensive than the country section contained in the Bank's operational program that was previously prepared. These notes are expected to relate the lending program to the operational strategy and include a discussion of performance.[8] An informal board discussion of the Compendium of Country Notes is expected to take place at the end of the first quarter of each year. Thereafter, management will issue planning directions to programs and projects departments and estimates of country assistance work plans for the next year; indicative plans for the two subsequent years will be prepared around midyear. The next stage in the planning cycle will be the preparation of the three-year rolling work plan and budget framework, which will be discussed informally by the Board around September each year. This will enable the Board to determine whether the priorities identified by the Bank's shareholders are being reflected in the allocation of resources. Finally, the budget for the following year will be considered in November or December, first by the budget review committee and then by the full Board. The annual planning cycle is summarized in Table 4.2.

Table 4.2   Annual Planning Cycle

1. Preparation of country operational program papers (COPPs)	January
2. Update of bank's Medium-Term Strategic Framework	February
3. Preparation of Compendium of Country Program Notes	February–March
4. Development of country assistance work plans for following year and indicative plans for two subsequent years	June–July
5. Preparation of three-year rolling work plan and budget framework	August–September
6. Approval of budget	December

Source: AsDB's Medium-Term Strategic Framework, 1949–1997.
Notes: Country operational strategy studies (COSSs) are prepared on a multiyear cycle, and economic and social work (ESW) is undertaken when required; both feed into the country programming process. Also, timing set out is based on 1994 planning cycle.

The changes introduced over the past two years have increased the role of the Board somewhat in the preparation of operational strategies and the country lending programs, specifically in steps 1, 3, 5, and 6 of the annual planning cycle. The former are made available to the Board informally after they are sent to the concerned DMC for comment. The views of the Board could be taken into account by Bank staff when finalizing the operational strategy. The discussion of the update of the strategic framework provides the context for the planning cycle in the subsequent year. Board input on the lending program is less certain. The Compendium of Country Program Notes is seen by the Board only when the country programming mission is completed and the lending program for the year decided on. Thus, a discussion of performance is unlikely to impinge on the lending level for the current year. Possibilities exist for making some changes, perhaps marginally, during the second half of the year. Board views are more likely to influence the lending program in the succeeding year. This is an aspect that has to be kept under review as the new planning cycle is implemented fully and changes made based on experience gained. Since the planning process is evolving, any comments here on its effectiveness would be premature.

The Board continues to approve loans as in the past. Authority for the approval of technical assistance grants up to $600,000 has been given to the president, without review by the Board, under a delegation of authority. This has led to an anomaly in the new planning process, in that most project preparation activities are not subject to Board review, although they influence the project pipeline for subsequent years, the loans for which the Board approves. The Bank undertook a review of technical assistance activities after concerns had been expressed that advisory and regional activities lacked focus and funds were becoming tight. The report recommended that technical assistance be integrated into the Bank's strategic planning, regional activities be subject to a clearer setting of priorities, and all of them be brought within the Bank's evaluation system. The second strategic framework took action on the first of these recommendations.

Following the introduction of the new planning process, it is seen that the role of the Board in the preparation of country operational strategies and country operational programs has increased somewhat. The Board, representing the entire membership, should have a greater input in their preparation because they are documents critical to the lending program of each DMC. The DMCs, fearing donor domination of the process, are apprehensive about such a shift and prefer to see greater management and staff freedom in the conduct of Bank operations. Nevertheless, such a move is desirable in the interests of achieving better governance in the Bank. There could be a trade-off with a lesser involvement of the Board in the approval of individual loans, as in the case of technical assistance grants.

Strategic Framework and Operational Strategies

The Bank's first medium-term strategic framework (1992–1995)[9] identified five strategic development objectives. These were to achieve

a) economic growth, with the private sector as the main engine of growth due to the contribution that competition, market mechanisms, and individual incentives make to the productive and efficient use of resources. Governments should concentrate their interventions in areas where the markets are inadequate and require legal and regulatory frameworks that only they can provide;

b) poverty reduction, since it is recognized that economic growth by itself is not adequate to raise the living standards of the poor, women, and other disadvantaged groups;

c) a reduction in the burden of poverty that has fallen disproportionately on women. There is the need to create employment opportunities and access to credit, education, and health services for women if they are to play a more productive role in employment;

d) progress in population planning to ensure that the success in attaining other development objectives will be mutually reinforced; and

e) protection of the environment from the pressures of development and population growth and remedies for the past degradation of the environment and depletion of natural resources.

The identification of these five objectives came about through Bank operations beginning in the early 1980s. They were partly identified in the *Report of the Expert Panel* published in 1989. More recently, the donors who participated in the ADF VI replenishment considered that poverty reduction, economic growth, environmental improvement, the role of women, and population issues should be the focus of the Bank's ADF lending, as they should equally be the focus of operations from the OCR. In the second medium-term strategic framework for 1993–1996, the Bank's strategic objectives were confirmed. In addition to pursuing these objectives, four thematic priorities were highlighted. These were private sector development, public sector management, human resource development, and natural resource management, which would be relevant for all the sectors in which the Bank operated. The framework stated that these development objectives should apply to all Bank lending, technical assistance, and economic and sector work in each DMC depending on conditions in each country.

The country operational strategies provide an opportunity for the Bank to set out the basis for its loan and technical assistance operations in the medium term (normally three to five years). These describe how the Bank can contribute to the economic growth of each DMC, taking into account the country's plans, priorities, constraints, and policy environment and the AsDB's own broad concerns as reflected in the medium-term strategic framework. Beginning in 1983, country operational strategies were prepared for each DMC as a follow-up of recommendations made in the OPP Study for the

1980s. It specifically stated that country programming should be a two-way process involving the Bank's perception of the strategic orientation of its role in a DMC as well as the country's own plans and priorities. The first generation of operational strategies did not achieve the intended purpose as they were too diffuse in nature and permitted the Bank to make any sectoral choices within its current areas of intervention. As the donors report for ADF VI[10] stated, the Bank should attempt to make the operational strategies more analytical, with clearer priorities, and more prescriptive in nature and use them as key determinants of its sectoral priorities in each DMC. It was anticipated that, if the operational strategies were focused, the Bank's programming would be more responsive to shifts in the policy and economic environment in the DMCs.

The preparation of the second generation of operational strategies within the Bank's medium-term strategic framework began in 1992 and has continued through 1993 and 1994. The Strategic Planning Unit provided guidance to the programs departments in the preparation of these documents. They found difficulties in ensuring that the operational strategies provide guidance and the sectoral justifications for the preparation of country programs, thereby making them consistent with the Bank's strategy. Unless this is achieved, there will be no change from previous strategies. They should enable the Bank to make choices for its intervention in each DMC, since resources are not unlimited. Otherwise, it will offer a range of choices in its areas of sector specialization, as it did in the past. Based on the guidelines provided by the Strategic Planning Unit, the new operational strategies are expected to contain the following:

a) a summary of recent performance and developments;
b) a summary of development outlook and issues;
c) development assistance experience and outlook;
d) the future role of the Bank; and
e) instruments of Bank support and implications of the proposed role and strategy.

Item (d) should analyze the main options for Bank involvement, government priorities and preferences, and the activities of other donors, while (e) should examine the main sectors for future support and the modalities to be used, justification of the sectors chosen, criteria for the selection of projects, and the need for more sector work, where necessary. The operational strategies are likely to be short documents that provide the link between the Bank's strategic framework and the DMC's priorities and plans and the country program. They will probably be revised every three to five years, unless there has been a major policy shift by the DMCs affecting their investment programs and thereby the choice of projects that the Bank could make for country programs. Close liaison with other major donors is an essential aspect of this process, and it is important that the Bank does what it can to ensure that this is achieved. Bank staff should, for purposes of coordination, keep abreast of the country assistance strategies that are being prepared by the World Bank. These are done annually for all the IDA-only or "blend" countries with annual IDA lending of $200 million or more, and IBRD or "blend" countries with annual lending of $350 million or more.[11] For other borrowers, the strategies are prepared every two years and for those with infrequent operations, every three or more years.

Country Programming

The first step in the country programming process is the decision made by the Bank's management on country allocations from both the OCR and ADF. The programming cycle is three years, although the missions that go out, following decisions being made on country allocations and the framework of the lending program, use a four-year period as a time frame. The missions review the status of projects in the current year and discuss project and technical assistance possibilities for the next three years with the ministries of finance and planning and other development ministries. A tentative country program for the next three years is drawn up that contains profiles of project and technical assistance proposals for each of the three years. Understandably, the program for the first year is based on firmer proposals than those for subsequent years. The project proposals for subsequent years may be firmed up based on technical assistance in project preparation that has yet to be carried out. The proposals for each DMC are aggregated on the basis of lending modes and sectoral shares and revised according to the Bank's current guidelines and targets for these. This process was strengthened in 1983 by the preparation of country operational strategies, the purpose of which was to improve the focus of the annual lending program for each DMC. As stated earlier, these were too diffuse to serve the intended purpose. One hopes that the new strategies that are being produced within the Bank's strategic framework will provide the country programming process with the much needed guidance and direction that the earlier ones did not.

The weaknesses in the country programming process were recognized in the OPP Study for the 1980s. First, although it follows a three-year cycle, the annual lending targets and other ceilings such as those on total program lending are major constraints. This rigidity in the system, which also exists in the World Bank, creates pressure on both the DMC and the Bank to commit loans up to the programmed levels. It often leads to the premature commitment of loan obligations by the borrower, an unnecessary bunching of loan approvals in the second half (most often in the last quarter) of each year, and the tendency to select projects in sectors that have greater absorptive capacities. In addition, if Bank-wide sectoral and lending modality targets have to be met on an annual basis, DMC priorities are also likely to be further distorted and projects, which may be neither of high priority nor ready for implementation, may be included in the annual lending programs. The remedy for this shortcoming is for the Bank to move to a genuine rolling three-year lending program while de-emphasizing the annual levels.[12] Fulfillment of lending targets would then be measured on a three-year basis. This could reduce the bunching problem and also improve the quality of projects financed, since they could be adequately prepared. Where targets exist for sectors and lending modalities, adherence to them should also be measured over a multiyear framework as suggested for country-lending levels.

A second problem has been weak project preparation and advisory and operational technical assistance proposals that are included in the country programs. The lessons drawn from Post-Evaluation Reports indicate the need for more technical assistance for preparing feasibility studies, followed by detailed engineering design, where needed, and increased participation by beneficiaries in the process. The OPP Study stated that advisory and operational technical assistance was, for the most part, directly related to loan projects and there was little consideration given to providing assistance for institution building in a systematic, broadbased, and sustained manner. This same criticism has been made in the Post-Evaluation Reports, which pointed to the need for increased technical assistance to implementing agencies for project supervision and institution building over the long term.[13] The decision taken to include these programs within the Bank's strategic framework may help to overcome the problems. However, performance of technical assistance projects needs to be kept under review and any necessary corrective action taken.

Effective country programming, leading to the preparation of a projects pipeline that could have an impact on the development efforts of DMCs, requires detailed economic and sector work by staff or consultants using the Bank's technical assistance funds. The Bank needs to undertake a number of regional development, sectoral, and issue-related studies that would assist in its sectoral programming and capacity to identify priority DMC project needs. This would enable it to build up a knowledge base of the sectors to assist staff in conducting an effective policy dialogue with DMCs. Staff may be able to benefit from the economic and sector work of the World Bank and other donors that would require effective coordination with these agencies in the concerned DMC. This is an aspect to which the Bank needs to pay attention as it seeks to improve country programming in the context of the strategic framework and the country operational strategies that are being prepared. The latter will benefit from the preparation of detailed sectoral studies and issues on a regional or country basis as proposed. However, the Bank needs additional staff resources with the requisite skills for effective country programming and to implement lending programs that meet the critical needs of DMCs.

The Compendium of Country Program Notes that is prepared under the new planning process will include sections on country performance and outstanding development issues, the link between the Bank's strategic concerns and the country operational strategy, priorities of the strategy and key policy issues, other donor activities and cofinancing, the economic and sector work program, and the loan/ technical assistance pipeline. This coverage will be a considerable improvement over the section on each DMC included in the previous operational program. It should enable the Board to have useful discussions on each country program and increase its input in the planning process.

Allocation of Bank Resources

The operating principles of the Bank, as set out in the Articles of Agreement, have not provided any guidance on the allocation of resources to individual DMCs. However, special attention should be paid to the needs of the smaller and less-developed DMCs to avoid a disproportionate amount of its resources being used for lending to any one DMC. Subject to these broad guidelines, indicative country lending figures have been based on per capita GNP, debt service capacity, population, absorptive capacity, and performance. These provide a basis for conducting the Bank's annual country programming exercise, which is consolidated into a three-year rolling plan and adjusted for other ceilings, such as those applicable for program lending (both of total Bank and ADF lending) and private sector operations. In spite of these planning figures for individual DMCs, the actual lending is influenced by the availability of viable projects and programs in the country and the pace at which the Bank and DMC can process loans and begin implementation, subject to the overall availability of Bank resources for that year.

GNP per capita is an important benchmark for Bank lending. The upper limit for a country's eligibility for ADF credits is $850 in 1990 prices. Within this ceiling, 90 percent of the ADF has been allocated during ADF IV and V to low-income DMCs that had a per capita GNP below $610 at 1990 prices. There is no similar ceiling for OCR lending, although the DMCs currently borrowing OCR are low-income and lower-middle-income countries with a per capita GNP not exceeding $2,320 at 1990 prices. The Bank works on the principle that, with increasing per capita GNP, DMCs will first reduce the need for ADF and then OCR, following which they should seek access to capital markets. The South Pacific and other small DMCs (for example, Bhutan and the Maldive Islands) with comparatively high GNP per capita are exceptions to this principle and to the cutoff for access to ADF resources.

The Articles require the Bank to be satisfied that a borrower can meet its obligations under the loan agreement. The debt-service ratio is one indicator of a DMC's capacity to repay loans, but it has to be judged along with other debt indicators such as total debt/GNP, total debt/exports of goods and services, and interest/exports of goods and services in the context of the balance-of-payments situation and outlook. If a country is judged to be creditworthy in the opinion of the Bank, the Bank will lend from its OCR. If it is not, the DMC has a strong case for seeking access to the ADF because of its inability to service loans borrowed at market or near-market terms.

Subject to the limitations placed by the Articles, larger DMCs can expect to borrow more resources from the Bank if they need the funds. Thus, countries with larger populations could receive larger amounts of lending, both in absolute terms and as a share of total lending. Considerations of minimum project size and the need for a continuing lending program have introduced a well-recognized small country bias in Bank operations measured in terms of lending per capita. During 1987–1991, Indonesia received 30.5 percent of OCR lending compared to 0.4 percent for Fiji; in per capita lending terms, however, Indonesia received $20.30 compared to $58.80 for Fiji.

The absorptive capacity of a DMC refers to the effectiveness with which it puts capital to use at the project level. There is little merit in allocating Bank resources to countries beyond their capacity to absorb them effectively, thereby preempting more responsive DMCs from receiving them. Accordingly, countries that have demonstrated a higher absorptive capacity tend to receive a larger share of Bank resources than would be warranted by other criteria alone. This is not a static situation, as the AsDB attempts to improve absorptive capacity by providing technical assistance for institutional development.

The last (but not the least) criterion for deciding on resource allocation is performance. This assessment has to be made in conjunction with the other criteria and factors. Weak performance by itself is not a justification for reducing lending. The Bank's mandate would require it to support the efforts of DMCs that are willing to take steps to improve performance. Good performance tends to improve credit-worthiness and increase absorptive capacity. Performance criteria will be discussed in the next section, as its importance has been high-lighted in the agreement reached with donors during the ADF VI negotiations to base ADF allocations on country performance.

Assessment of Country Performance

During the negotiations for ADF VI, donors urged the Bank to base access to the ADF on development performance and give priority to this criterion, as is being done increasingly by the IDA. It was agreed that the assessment of performance would be based on three major criteria. These are

  a) sound economic management;
  b) efforts towards growth with equity and poverty reduction; and
  c) efforts towards sustainable economic and social development.

The Bank was urged by donors to establish program targets for the social sectors and address the crosscutting themes that had been identified as priorities in its strategic framework. It was asked to reduce ADF allocations to DMCs that revealed weak performance at annual reviews and limit the program to those activities that promised the most productive use of concessional funds. In such cir-cumstances, lending is to be reduced to a core program that would be the minimum necessary to maintain dialogue with the borrower, with the focus of Bank operations being on nonlending activities such as economic and sector work that is geared to improving perfor-mance.

Such procedures would bring Bank allocation criteria in line with those used by the IDA. During the negotiations for IDA 10, it was agreed that access to resources should, as in the case of the previous replenishment, be based on annual assessments of performance. Allocations are to be related to the country's commitment to the cen-tral objectives of the IDA, which are poverty reduction, economic adjustment and growth, and environmental sustainability. Countries whose performances did not meet these criteria are to be limited to a core program to maintain a dialogue and a level of economic and sec-tor work necessary to restore lending in the future. It is understood that some donor countries wished to include political sustainability indicators to measure performance, but there was no consensus on this issue.

The Bank proposes[14] to review performance in two parts. Economic management is to be assessed by performance in short-term macroeconomic stabilization, medium-term structural adjustment, and economic growth. Several indicators have been selected whose performance will be used in this assessment. Equitable and sustainable development are subsumed in the review of crosscutting issues covering poverty, gender, population, and the environment. Once again, several indicators have been selected for review. Unlike the ones included under economic management, those under crosscutting issues might not show any significant change from year to year. Instead, changes in the indicators should be monitored every three to five years, and only changes in policy should be monitored in the annual review of country performance. It will be possible for Bank staff to make use of material on social indicators that are available and the poverty studies done by the World Bank for an increasing number of borrowing countries to assist in the assessments of these issues.

The indicators chosen for review under economic management are normally the subject of policy dialogue that the IMF and World Bank conduct with the DMC during the implementation of stabilization and structural adjustment programs respectively. Where the countries have programs that are being monitored by the IMF and World Bank, it will be easy for the Bank to monitor these reviews and make the assessment on economic management. Where no such programs are being implemented, it is not clear how this assessment will be done, given the Bank's position that it does not engage DMCs in a dialogue on macroeconomic policy issues.

Country assessments will be done on the basis of the framework proposed by the Bank in September 1992. Their introduction will have an impact on the size, scope, and quality of the lending program of the Bank. The country operational strategies will establish the framework by which individual country assessments will be carried out during the annual programming missions. The conclusions will be included in the Compendium of Country Program Notes, which will be submitted to the Board for informal discussion. The comments made in the preceding paragraphs regarding the crosscutting issues should be taken into account in the annual assessments.

While performance evaluation procedures were introduced at the World Bank principally for recipients from the IDA, it is also one of the factors affecting IBRD lending levels. Similarly, the Bank will make regular performance assessments of OCR borrowers. These, along with other relevant allocation criteria and the willingness of DMCs to borrow from the OCR, will influence country-lending levels to borrowers from the OCR.

The introduction of the new planning process and its various components and the various processes designed to incorporate cross-cutting issues in Bank operations are to ensure that the quality of the Bank's lending program improves. Many of the changes have been introduced due to pressure from donors, but the Bank has taken them on board and needs to demonstrate that it has the capacity to deliver. A period of consolidation appears to be necessary as the new process-es are absorbed in Bank operations. Modifications will be required based on experience, and staff with the necessary skills need to be recruited. The role of the Board could be enhanced further in the planning activities, but there may be tension here between the inter-ests of donors and DMCs who may prefer to see management and staff retain their traditional role.

Notes

1. "Effective Implementation: Key to Development Impact, Report of the Portfolio Management Task Force," World Bank, September 1992.

2. "Task Force on Improving Project Quality," AsDB, July 6, 1993.

3. "Report on Post Evaluation Activities During 1991," AsDB, April 1992.

4. Project sustainability was not addressed in two project performance audit reports reviewed. These were the Third Tea Development Project and the Agricultural Inputs Program in Sri Lanka.

5. Group A (DMCs with full eligibility for ADF): Afghanistan, Bangladesh, Bhutan, Cambodia, China, Cook Islands, India, Kiribati, Lao PDR, Maldive Islands, Marshall Islands, Micronesia, Mongolia, Myanmar, Nepal, Pakistan, Solomon Islands, Sri Lanka, Tonga, Vanuatu, Vietnam, and Western Samoa.

Group B (DMCs with eligibility for ADF receiving a blend of ADF/OCR): Indonesia, Papua New Guinea, the Philippines, and Thailand.

Group C (DMCs not eligible for ADF): Fiji, Hong Kong, Korea, Malaysia, Singapore, and Taipei,China.

6. "Project Quality," AsDB, November 1990 (mimeo).

7. The latest developments in the planning process described in the Bank's "Medium-Term Strategic Framework" (1994–1997), the President's Office, AsDB, February 1994.

8. The Bank has stated that it does not intend to use performance reviews for determining a specific level of assistance to each DMC or making intercountry allocations of ADF resources, although the donors' report on ADF VI leads one to believe otherwise.

9. *The Bank's Medium-Term Strategic Framework 1992–1995*, AsDB, March 1992.

10. "Replenishment of the ADF and Technical Assistance Special Fund," AsDB, December 1991.

11. The World Bank strategies are presented to the Board with the first IDA Credit or IBRD Loan for the financial year. It is included in the report and recommendation of the president to the Board with respect to the credit or loan.

12. The task force on improving project quality recommended the adoption of three-year rolling lending targets in place of annual targets.

13. The Bank is concentrating on advisory technical assistance to build up institutional capacity in DMCs.

14. "Bank Operations and Country Performance," AsDB, September 1992 (mimeo).

5

RESOURCE MOBILIZATION

Replenishment of the Asian Development Fund

Agreement for the sixth replenishment of the ADF for an amount of
$4.2 billion, or special-drawing-rights (SDR) 2.97 billion, for 1992–
1995 was reached in December 1991. This compared with an ADF V
replenishment of $3.6 billion, or SDR 3.2 billion, at the exchange rates
applicable at the time. The period covered by ADF VI was four years,
as were the three previous replenishments. ADF I and II only covered
three-year periods. Unlike the IDA, in which lending is committed
against particular replenishments, all available ADF resources are
pooled and used in accordance with the policies applicable at the
time. Accordingly, any ADF resources available at the end of a replenishment period are automatically available for commitment in the
succeeding period, along with the new replenishment.

ADF V was intended to cover the four-year period from 1987 to
1990. In early 1991, it was estimated that $2.9 billion was available for
commitment. Accordingly, ADF V was extended by one year and the
period of ADF VI changed to 1992–1995. During 1991, only $1.35 bil-
lion was committed from ADF V leaving the balance to spill over into
1992. This was partly due to delays on the part of the United States in
releasing the third and fourth tranches, which was done by the end
of 1992. Thus, the balance of ADF V became available for commitment during ADF VI, making the total of $6.024 billion during
1992–1995. The latest replenishment became effective in August 1992,
when the Bank received commitments exceeding the minimum trigger figure of 50 percent.

In accordance with the agreements reached during ADF VI, available resources are to be allocated to the following categories of recipients:

a) the traditional ADF recipients, namely Group A countries and

Papua New Guinea, which received allocations during ADF V;

b) currently nonactive ADF countries, which can borrow if loan operations are resumed;

c) eligible DMCs that joined the Bank after January 1, 1990, or Marshall Islands, Micronesia, Mongolia, and Tuvalu;[1] and

d) Indonesia and the Philippines, depending on resource availability and the need for external support on concessional terms.

China and India will not receive concessional funds during ADF VI. The Bank will allocate the largest share of ADF VI to the traditional ADF recipients as a group. Priority will be given next to categories (b) and (c) above. Both Indonesia and the Philippines could receive limited (and reduced) access to the ADF for projects directed at poverty reduction, the primary social sector, and protection of the environment. Within these broad guidelines, the Bank will regulate access to the ADF, based on need and development performance.

A review of ADF V during 1987–1991 shows that a total of $6,232.1 million was lent during this period. The annual average of $1,246 million compares with that of $665 million during ADF IV, an increase of 87 percent. Group A countries accounted for only 80 percent of ADF V, compared to 96 percent during ADF IV. This was mainly due to the renewed access provided to Indonesia and the Philippines, which received a total of $1.1 billion to assist them with their restructuring efforts during this period. As can be seen from Table 5.1, annual loan commitments increased during 1987–1990 and declined in both 1991 and 1992 by 9.0 and 14.3 percent respectively. Therefore, the annual availability of ADF resources during the remaining period of ADF VI, 1993–1995, would be of the order of $1.5 billion annually, subject to exchange rate fluctuations and timely contributions by the United States (which has not been a usual occurrence). Since resources have to be allocated to previously nonactive

Table 5.1   ADF Loan Commitments: 1987–1995 (in millions of dollars)

1987	957.6
1988	1,083.5
1989	1,363.3
1990	1,480.5
1991	1,347.2
1992	1,155.0
1993–1995	4,869.0[a]

Source: AsDB Annual Report, various years.
Notes: a. Estimated.

and new borrowers, it is likely that traditional recipients will collectively receive less during ADF VI than they did during ADF V.

Following the midterm review of ADF VI, which was held at the time of the 1994 annual meeting of the Bank, it is likely that preliminary discussions will begin on the next replenishment due in 1996. With the availability of concessional funds becoming tighter, it is likely that the period of ADF VI may be extended or the size of the next replenishment reduced in comparison to ADF VI. This needs to be taken into account in projections of resource needs of the region.

General Capital Increases

In addition to the four GCIs that the Bank negotiated in 1971, 1976, 1983, and 1994, there have been capital subscriptions by new members and special increases to accommodate the needs of some members. The authorized capital of the Bank at the end of 1992 was $23,223.7 million, of which $23,100.1 million was subscribed and $2,787.0 million of the subscribed amount was paid in. Although GCI III was intended to cover only 1983–1987, the capital has been adequate to meet the Bank's lending needs up to the end of 1993.

In terms of the Articles, the total amount outstanding of loans, equity investments, and guarantees made by the Bank in its ordinary operations shall not at any time exceed the total amount of its unimpaired subscribed capital (not pledged against borrowings by the Bank), reserves, and surplus included in its OCR (referred to as the Bank's lending authority). This gearing ratio is similar to that of the World Bank. However, total loans outstanding have been interpreted in the World Bank to mean total disbursed and outstanding loans while the AsDB has interpreted it more conservatively to include the undisbursed portion of approved loans as well. Thus, in comparison to the World Bank, the AsDB requires a greater amount of share capital to sustain the same level of lending.[2]

In addition to the conservative gearing ratio that is limited by statute, the Bank has restricted its borrowings by the adoption of certain covenants in bond issues that provided assurances to its holders. The Bank's current policy stipulates that any new borrowing or guarantee chargeable to the OCR, when added to the total outstanding borrowings and guarantees, should not exceed the callable capital subscribed by member countries with convertible currencies. Within this constraint, the Bank had restricted its borrowing further to 85 percent of the permitted level. This was increased to 95 percent in 1990. The policy on borrowing once again differs significantly from that of the World Bank, which places no such limitations. Accordingly, in 1991, the Bank's gross debt as a percentage of callable capital was substantially lower than the similar ratio for the World Bank. The last outstanding bond issue by the Bank with these restrictive covenants on borrowings expired in June 1993. This should ease the constraints on the Bank and enable it to borrow up to the limit of the callable capital of members with Triple-A and Double-A ratings and liquid assets.

The growth in OCR lending during 1983–1992, as illustrated in Table 5.2, was 14.5 percent. Beginning with a lending level of $4.5 billion in 1993, an annual growth in OCR lending of 10 percent was estimated to require a capital increase on the order of 100 percent over five years. At the time of writing, the Bank had obtained approval from its membership for a capital increase of 100 percent with a paid-in share of 2 percent.

Table 5.2   OCR Loan Operations: 1983–1992 (in millions of dollars)

1983	1,189.8
1984	1,550.6
1985	1,171.2
1986	1,368.1
1987	1,480.9
1988	2,062.2
1989	2,260.3
1990	2,491.7
1991	3,433.5
1992	3,954.4

Source: AsDB Annual Report, various years.

There was no agreement among shareholders about the timing and size of GCI IV during most of 1993. Many wished to conclude the negotiations as early as possible in 1993, to enable the capital increase to be in place for 1994. However, several fundamental issues were raised in relation to the capital increase. A basic concern was the size of the institution that shareholders wished to support, which should reflect the needs of DMCs for borrowing from the OCR and the Bank's contribution to the overall resource needs of the region. The Bank has only nine borrowers from the OCR, of which five (China, India, Indonesia, Pakistan, and the Philippines) account for the bulk. Nevertheless, it expects the traditional borrowers to generate a higher demand for OCR due to the deepening of reforms and the need for greater modernization in the concerned DMCs. Additional demands may be made by new and currently nonactive members and by those borrowing from the ADF, due to reduced availability of concessional funds.

The second issue that followed from the first is the ability of the Bank to produce a quality portfolio that reflects the members' geographical, sectoral, and operational priorities without too large an increase in staffing or the budget. These matters could have been dealt with as a follow-up of the implementation of the ADF VI negotiations set out in the donors' report, leaving only residual issues for the GCI IV negotiations. The third issue was the financial policies that were reviewed in a working paper[3] in November 1992. It addressed the policies on exposure limits; delinquency, including the possibility of rescheduling private sector debt to avoid default; liquidity; the accrual of interest; and provisioning against potential loan losses and key financial ratios.

The fourth issue was the choice between a GCI that would either be adequate to cover all loan commitments as in the past, or one proposed by the United States where the Bank would make commitments in excess of its capital but manage its exposure to ensure that loan reflows and existing headroom (net lending authority minus actual commitments) would be adequate to meet projected disbursements. The latter approach would have been assisted by a reinterpretation of "loans outstanding" in the Articles to mean only disbursed and outstanding loans. Based on either approach, a sustainable level of lending is that which can be maintained indefinitely from loan reflows and available headroom based on the last or another specified year in the period of the capital increase. Thus, the size of the GCI IV would depend on whether it is based on commitments or disbursements, the growth in OCR lending agreed for the GCI IV period that takes into account both supply and demand factors, and the choice of the year at which the lending level is to be sustained. This approach was not pursued during the negotiations.

The earlier U.S. position on GCI IV (taken during the Bush administration) appeared to have been that the AsDB should reinterpret the Articles without seeking an immediate capital increase. This would have postponed the negotiations and enabled the Bank to increase its OCR lending well into 1995, although it would not have addressed the long-term capital needs of the Bank. The last GCI was ten years ago. If the immediate capital requirements were met by reinterpreting the Articles without agreement on the GCI, it could have sent a wrong signal to the capital markets, adversely affecting the terms on which the Bank is able to borrow from them. Market confidence is also based on continuing shareholder support. This will be provided by a contribution to the paid-in portion of a capital increase, although this could be a lower share than in past GCIs as agreed in the negotiations. In practice, the paid-in portion could be zero but for the sentiments that this would generate in the market.

An issue that held up the finalization of GCI IV was the need for a report on negotiations as an informal contract between the Bank and shareholders. This was done in the case of ADF VI, between the donors and the Bank, since it was essentially a donors' report. Since GCI IV involves the entire membership, its usefulness for Bank operations was questioned. The issue was resolved by the preparation of a paper on "The Bank's Future Direction and Operational Agenda for the 1990s," which included commitments by the management on the Bank's future operational agenda.

Issues Affecting Resource Needs

Nonactive DMCs

Afghanistan, Cambodia, Myanmar, and Vietnam have not been active borrowers for most of the past ten years. Cambodia had no loan operations for over twenty years. Before the recent resumption of Bank operations, it had a loan approved from the special funds resources in 1970 and technical assistance in 1973. Bank operations were resumed with the approval of technical assistance for macroeconomic management in April 1992. It was funded by grants of $2.41 million from the AsDB and $1.44 million from the UNDP, both of which are being executed jointly by the Bank and the IMF. Following the clearance of arrears to the Bank in November 1992, Cambodia ceased to be in nonaccrual status. Shortly thereafter, a loan from the ADF of $67.7 million for rehabilitation assistance to the transport, power, agriculture, and education sectors was approved. This loan has become effective and several technical assistance projects in the agriculture, transportation, and education sectors have since been approved.

Vietnam had its last OCR and ADF operations approved in 1973 and 1974 respectively. Resumption of Bank operations in the country had been held up for a long time due to the embargo placed by the United States, which consistently opposed any action to clear arrears to the international financial institutions (including the Bank) and the approval of technical assistance proposals by the Bank.[4] Action has been taken on both issues after a change in U.S. policy in the second half of 1993. The first technical assistance project since 1978 was approved in October 1993 for $568,000 to assist in the development of small-scale rural credit. Although the Articles provide for it, the Bank does not normally conduct its loan and technical assistance operations by a majority vote of the Board. Otherwise, Bank operations in Vietnam would have resumed long before 1993.

The last loan to Afghanistan from the ADF was made in 1979. No loan disbursements took place after 1981. The Bank had begun gathering economic data on the country and attended several donor meetings held in Islamabad to assess sectoral rehabilitation needs in November 1992, following the approval of technical assistance to assess the priority for transport and communications rehabilitation. Since then, the political and security situations have deteriorated, leading to a suspension of further activities. When normalcy returns, the claims on the international community for concessional assistance for rehabilitation of the economy and resettlement of refugees will be considerable. The Bank will be expected to participate fully in these assistance programs and possibly to take the lead in some, as it did in Cambodia. Afghanistan has continued to service its debt to the AsDB during the period of suspension of loan operations without any accrual of arrears.

The Bank approved its last ADF loan to Myanmar in 1986. Although loan supervision missions were resumed in 1989 and disbursements continued after a temporary suspension, no new loans are planned. It is unlikely that there will be a resumption of operations until steps are taken to restore democratic government in the country. Although the Bank has no explicit policy in this regard, this is another instance where major developed-member countries have succeeded in preventing loan and technical assistance operations from resuming. Since no technical assistance activities have been approved after 1987, the building of a pipeline of projects for the country program will require an extended start-up period. Myanmar has serviced its debt to the AsDB without any accrual of arrears.

New Members

Tuvalu (formerly the Ellice Islands, with a population of 8,000), an independent country in the Commonwealth, became the fifty-third member in May 1993. This brought the number of regional members to thirty-seven and the DMCs to thirty-three. Tuvalu had chosen to separate from the Gilbert Islands, which became Kiribati at independence.

Unlike other MDBs, the AsDB allowed nonsovereign entities like Hong Kong and the Cook Islands and several other South Pacific countries to become members before they gained independence. Applications for membership of these countries were presented by the member responsible for the applicant's international relations. This method is still applicable to the Pacific island countries that are in this political category. Palau and the Marianas Islands, both U.S. trust territories facing the prospect of a phasing out of payments due to them under the compact with the United States, are likely future applicants. New Caledonia and Tahiti may have their applications presented by France, but their status as French territories may make separate membership impossible. Niue, a self-governing territory with New Zealand responsible for its defense and international affairs, may also be a future applicant. While these countries would be eligible for full or associate membership based on the criteria set out in the Articles, the AsDB would need to review the assistance that it could realistically provide to these microstates, beyond occasional technical assistance. The international donor community should consider the possibility of meeting the special needs of these territories through mechanisms other than a development bank.

An important membership issue in 1993 was that of the Central Asian Republics of the former Soviet Union. These are Azerbaijan, Kazakhstan, Tadzhikistan, the Kirgiz Republic, Turkmenistan, and Uzbekistan, who became eligible for membership by joining ESCAP in 1992. They also joined the World Bank and European Bank for Reconstruction and Development (EBRD). While the consensus among members favored membership, the conditions under which these six countries can borrow from both the AsDB and EBRD were initially left unresolved. Both the United States and Japan appeared to favor a demarcation of responsibility between the two. It had been hoped that this would be resolved by the AsDB concentrating on public sector projects and programs and the EBRD supporting mainly those in the private sector in accordance with its mandate to utilize up to 60 percent of the resources available to it for the private sector. This division was not agreed to because of the weak and, in some cases, nonexistent private sectors in these countries. In view of this, the EBRD felt that such a demarcation would inhibit their funding activities to a great extent. The two banks subsequently resolved the matter in a Memorandum of Understanding. Meanwhile, the Bank admitted Kazakhstan, the Kirgiz Republic, and Uzbekistan to membership in August 1993 as regional members, subject to their completion of procedures. Kazakhstan completed these procedures in January 1994, followed by Kirgiz Republic in April.

A related membership issue is the application made by Iran, which has always been eligible to join the AsDB in view of its membership in ESCAP. It did not take up the shares that were initially allocated when it lost the bid for Tehran to become the headquarters site of the Bank. Consequently, Iran did not become a member. Recently, the first full session of the expanded Economic Cooperation Organization, made up originally of Afghanistan, Iran, Pakistan, and Turkey and now including the six Central Asian Republics, met to discuss export growth strategies and measures necessary for attracting FDI, particularly investments in infrastructure. Iran's main motive in wanting membership in the AsDB, apart from seeking solidarity with other Islamic countries, is to position itself as a market for goods and services for Bank-funded projects in these republics as they begin to develop their infrastructure and other sectors. Thus, the enlargement of the Economic Cooperation Organization will make it a significant subregional grouping among the DMCs, together with the South Asian Association for Regional Cooperation, the Association of Southeast Asian Nations (ASEAN), and to a lesser extent, the Pacific DMCs. Concurrence of all members[5] has not been obtained for the admission of Iran. The United States has indicated strong opposition.

The only other membership issue for the AsDB is that of North Korea. No formal approach has been made, but it is understood that informal channels have been used to sound out the Bank on the possibility of membership. As a member of ESCAP, North Korea is eligible for membership, but it is likely to face opposition from some members, including the United States. Russian membership has also been mentioned as a possibility, but it can only be admitted as a developed nonregional member, not eligible to borrow from the AsDB.

Graduating DMCs

The process of maturation of DMCs has been described in the OPP Study for the 1980s. This is a transition from borrowing only ADF resources (Group A countries receiving only ADF resources), to a "soft blend" in which small amounts of OCR are combined with larger amounts of ADF (no DMCs are in this category), to a "hard blend" in which the proportion of OCR is larger (Pakistan and Papua New Guinea, with Indonesia and the Philippines being provided temporary access to the ADF), to a denial of access to the ADF (all OCR-only countries). This process can be varied to ration the available ADF resources among the low-income and lower-middle-income countries.

It is equally important to define the process by which a higher-middle-income DMC can phase out or receive only occasional allocations from the OCR. This transition requires a benchmark that would trigger the process of graduation activities by the Bank. The World Bank uses a GNP per capita level of $4,300 in 1990 prices. When this level is reached, it leads to a phasing down of activities, which could be completed within a period of five years, depending on the country's creditworthiness and access to capital markets, institutional capacity, and sustainability of development. Graduation from the

IBRD does not automatically lead to graduation from the International Finance Corporation (IFC). Technical assistance can be continued by the World Bank on a reimbursable basis with services being provided for one year without charge. Disbursements of on-going projects continues after the countries have graduated.

The Bank has no graduation policy and needs to formulate one. The advisory group to the OPP Study for the 1980s recognized the importance of the process. It envisaged that the DMCs approaching graduation will receive reduced lending during a transition period with loans being made available from time to time, perhaps on harder terms, to increasingly take on the role of donor members of the Bank. The activities envisaged are providing grant funds and expertise for technical assistance, participating in Bank procurement, and making adjustments in their trade policies to assist less-developed DMCs.

Four countries, Hong Kong, Korea, Singapore, and Taipei,China, have voluntarily graduated from receiving OCR loans and technical assistance as seen in Table 5.3. Both disbursements and debt service payments to the AsDB continued after new lending ceased. Although no definitive policy has been adopted by the Bank on activities in which graduated DMCs could engage, proposals made have included the following:

a) receiving technical assistance from the Bank for project preparation, institution building, capital market development, and staff training on a reimbursable basis. This would be without prejudice to the participation of graduated country nationals in regional technical assistance activities;

b) opening up financial and capital markets in graduated DMCs to foreign portfolio investment, encouraging financiers in these countries to invest in low-income DMCs (evidence of which already exists), in some instances with Bank participation;

c) entering into cofinancing arrangements with the Bank for projects in borrowing DMCs with funds from commercial and official sources in graduated DMCs;[6]

d) raising funds in graduated DMCs where their capital markets have developed adequately;

e) making contributions to ADF replenishments; and

f) transferring technology from graduated DMCs that have established a comparative advantage.

As members, graduated DMCs continue to be eligible for procurements. It has to be an interactive process involving this group of

Table 5.3   Last Year of Bank Operations in Nonborrowing Countries

	Loans	Technical Assistance
Hong Kong	1980	—a
Korea	1988	1988
Singapore	1980	1981
Taipei,China	1971	1968

Source: Loan Technical Assistance and Private Sector Operations Approvals, December 1992.
Note: a. Never received technical assistance from the Bank.

countries, the borrowing DMCs, and the Bank for their mutual benefit. The activities have to be defined precisely and the graduated DMCs encouraged to participate fully in the interests of regional cooperation, which the Bank has a mandate to promote. With the exception of Korea, it does not appear that other graduated DMCs have taken much interest in the activities of the Bank after becoming nonborrowers. Korea ceased to borrow only in 1988 while the others stopped much earlier.

Changes in Financial Policies

The AsDB has enjoyed a reputation for unusually conservative financial policies among the MDBs, including a conservative gearing ratio, low leverage, and high liquidity targets. Underlying the Bank's financial performance has been the region's economic performance, which has been better than that of the other developing regions. A recent study[7] that compared highly indebted countries with Asian countries (among which there are none in this category), concluded that success in managing debt is closely linked to macroeconomic management, and that macroeconomic stability and prudent economic policies are the most important factors influencing the debt situation. If the policies are sound, it is possible for a country to withstand temporary debt service difficulties. One DMC in Asia, the Philippines, has rescheduled its external debt. Only a small number of DMCs have been in nonaccrual status. Even then the amounts involved were small. The latter have been entirely due to adverse political developments. It is significant that a country such as Afghanistan, which has been in a state of war for more than ten years, has continued to service its debt to the Bank. Another indicator of the economic strength of the region has been the inflow of FDI to most DMCs. Further, member states with investment-grade debt ratings and above accounted for 84.9 percent of the callable capital of the

AsDB at the end of 1991, which was much higher than that of the AfDB (33.6 percent), IDB (49.4 percent), and the World Bank (72.6 percent). The Bank's preferred creditor status and prudent lending policies have enabled it to avoid any loan-losses in its twenty-eight-year history. Nevertheless, there are some warning signals. Loan concentration in the AsDB is the highest among the MDBs. Some of the large borrowers are moderately indebted, and some of their debt indicators are above critical levels. These factors suggest the need for the Bank to review and adopt explicit policies, where necessary, on arrears and sanctions, loans in nonaccrual status, loan-loss provisioning, and loan concentration.

Sanctions and Nonaccrual Policies

The policies of MDBs that have an immediate impact on arrears are the sanctions imposed following their accumulation and the accounting treatment of loans placed in nonaccrual status. When arrears of principal, interest, and other charges begin to accumulate and are not settled within a given period of time, consideration of new loans is suspended. Following the lapse of a further time period, disbursements on existing loans are suspended. If arrears of interest and other charges continue for a further period, all loans are placed in nonaccrual status. Accrued interest and other charges remaining unpaid are deducted from income for the current period and recorded thereafter only when payments are received. The period for each of the three stages varies for the different MDBs.

In the case of IBRD and IDA loans, the sanctions policy was strengthened in 1990. When the period of arrears exceeds thirty days, no loans to that borrower will be proposed to the Board or signed. If the borrower is not the government but a public sector or other agency, the government will be informed at the end of thirty days that if payment is not received within forty-five days of the due date, no loans to or guaranteed by the government will be proposed to the Board or signed. The next level of sanctions begins at the end of forty-five days when the government and borrower (if they are different) are informed that disbursements on the loans in arrears will be suspended at the end of sixty days unless payment is received. Cofinanciers and the relevant RDB will be informed of the suspension a few days before it goes into effect. If the arrears are not cleared in 180 days, the country is automatically placed in nonaccrual status. There is a simultaneous suspension of disbursements to countries receiving loans from both IBRD and IDA sources when the country is placed in nonaccrual status. A case-by-case approach is adopted for IFC operations.

Although the loan regulations provide for sanctions in the event of loan arrears, there was no explicit policy adopted by the AsDB for suspending new loan commitments and disbursements until 1993. The policy adopted provides for the suspension of new loans to or guaranteed by the DMC being presented to the Board or signed if interest or principal on a public sector loan is overdue by sixty days, following notification to the country at the end of thirty days. If arrears continue beyond sixty days, disbursements on all loans are suspended at the end of ninety days following notification to the country at the end of the sixty days. Since 1988, Bank policy placed loans in nonaccrual status when principal or interest is overdue by one year. In June 1992, the Bank adopted a different trigger period for private sector loans, which are placed in nonaccrual status when principal or interest is overdue by six months. This was extended to both public and private sector loans in 1993. These changes brought Bank policy in line with that of the World Bank.

Loan-Loss Provisioning

Loan-loss provisions are amounts that are specifically charged against current income and accumulated as loan-loss reserves. If loan write-offs become necessary, they are first charged to the loan-loss reserve. If this proves to be inadequate, they are charged against income in the year that the loss occurs. The shareholders' protection against capital impairment depends on whether loan-losses exceed the loan-loss and ordinary reserves that receive allocations from net income. While the World Bank begins provisioning as soon as a country is placed in a nonaccrual status, or 180 days after arrears begin to accrue, the other MDBs appear to follow a more liberal timetable. The World Bank initiated provisioning in 1986. Under policies adopted in 1988, provisions were calculated for all countries in nonaccrual status on a consolidated basis. The policy was amended in 1991 to take account of other risks in the portfolio. Further, provisioning levels were converted from absolute amounts to a share of the World Bank's total loan portfolio, including the present value of callable guarantees outstanding. The provisioning level under the new policy was originally set at 2.5 percent of the value of the portfolio and subsequently increased to 3 percent in 1993.

The Bank adopted a policy on loan-loss provisioning in 1993. In terms of this policy, the Bank will make specific loan-loss provisions on both OCR and ADF public sector loans when the borrower's interest or principal payments have been in arrears for one year. Similar provisions will be made for private sector loans when they have been in arrears for six months. In addition, the Bank will continue to make loss provisions on equity investments on a case-by-case basis when values have decreased significantly due to continuing income losses, declining or negative net worth, or other financial indicators. The Bank also decided to make general provisions for investment losses on its private sector portfolio at a rate of 8 percent by 1995, moving to that level from 4 in 1993 and 6 percent in 1994. With the introduction of these new policies, the Board will decide annually the amount of loss provisions to be charged against net income.

Loan Concentration

As shown in Table 5.4, the AsDB had the highest country concentration in its loan commitments among the RDBs in 1991. Eighty-two percent of the loan commitments from the OCR were made to the five largest borrowers, Indonesia, the Philippines, India, Pakistan, and Malaysia, in that order. The ratio had increased from 73 percent in 1986. The AsDB is perhaps unique among the RDBs in that one borrower, Indonesia, has consistently received over 30 percent of the OCR commitments in each of the years 1986–1991. It is a moderately indebted low-income country, along with India and Pakistan. Further, the Philippines, which is among the major borrowers, is also moderately indebted, although a middle-income country. It has had eight reschedulings since 1984, although it met all its debt-service payments to the AsDB. Indonesia is the third-largest borrower from the IBRD with loan commitments amounting to 10 percent of its portfolio. Its total debt outstanding of $87.8 billion at the end of 1992 makes it the largest debtor among the DMCs (and the third largest among the borrowers from the World Bank). Commitments to India are 17.5 percent of the AsDB portfolio with the percentage higher in recent years due to the fact that it began borrowing from the Bank only in 1986. Further, loans to India are 11 percent[8] of total commitments by the IBRD, and thereby its largest borrower. Its total debt outstanding was $79.0 billion at the end of 1992, the second-largest

Table 5.4 **Loan Portfolio Concentration of Selected MDBs**

	AsDB	IBRD	IDB	AfDB
Total number of borrowers	15[a]	91	24	46
Largest borrower	36%	12%[b]	18%	14%
Five largest borrowers	82%	46%	66%	49%
Seven largest borrowers	95%	52%	75%	59%

Source: "Review of the Bank's Major Financial Policies," November 1992, AsDB.
Notes: a. At present, there are only nine active OCR borrowers.
b. Percentage of loan commitment.

among the DMCs. It sought emergency assistance from the World Bank and IMF in 1991 to avoid a breakdown in external payments. The present situation in the AsDB is that the four largest borrowers from the OCR are moderately indebted, and the outstanding debts of two of them are large.

The existing concentration in the loan portfolio reflects the lending pattern of the past. Changes to the existing shares can be made only over a period of time. In addition, any attempt to diversify the present range of borrowers and dilute the shares of the largest OCR borrowers may lead to a downward revision of the resources needed and hence of future capital increases. Bank projections show that the long-term share of the four largest borrowers, China, Indonesia, India, and the Philippines, will remain around three-quarters of outstanding OCR loans, with the shares of China and India declining due to increasing demands from other DMCs brought about by the likely curtailment of concessional funds.

China and India have chosen not to borrow from the OCR for social sector and poverty reduction investments, for the reason that financial returns are too low to provide for the repayment of loans. Instead, they have repeatedly requested access to ADF resources, for which both countries are eligible. At the World Bank, however, concessional IDA funds are available for investments in these sectors. If the availability of these funds is reduced in the future, along with replenishments of the ADF, it is likely that China and India will reconsider their positions. This will have an impact on the future demand for the OCR. At the same time, with a small number of active borrowers, a high degree of loan concentration appears to be unavoidable, although a ceiling of 25 percent for a single country may be a reasonable target in the long term.

Notes

1. Since Tuvalu joined after ADF VI became effective, eligibility had to await the mid-term review.

2. The IDB uses a definition of loans outstanding similar to that of the World Bank, while the AfDB uses the more conservative definition of the AsDB.

3. "Review of the Bank's Major Financial Policies," AsDB, November 1992.

4. The Bank had taken the position that arrears need not stand in the way of project preparation and advisory technical assistance.

5. The Articles provide for the admission of new members by an affirmative vote of two-thirds of the number of member countries representing not less than three-fourths of the total voting power of the members. In practice, new members have been admitted by consensus.

6. A general framework for cofinancing projects in the Asia-Pacific region was agreed to with Korea's Economic Development Cooperation Fund in April 1993.

7. Ishrat Hussain, *How Did Asian Countries Avoid the Debt Crisis?* the World Bank, October 1991.

8. The IBRD enforces a portfolio share guideline of 10 percent per country, although this could be exceeded in certain circumstances.

6

LOOMING DEVELOPMENT CHALLENGES FOR THE BANK

Overview of Needs

The countries in the region fall into four groups based on their socio-economic indicators. These economic groups are distinct in size, resource endowments, socioeconomic achievements, and policy environment. These are the NIEs; the countries that are better endowed with natural resources in Southeast Asia (Brunei,[1] Indonesia, Malaysia, the Philippines, and Thailand); the low-income South Asian countries (Afghanistan, Bangladesh, Bhutan, India, Maldives, Myanmar, Nepal, Pakistan, and Sri Lanka), as well as China, Mongolia, and the countries of Indochina (Cambodia, Lao Peoples' Democratic Republic, and Vietnam); and the Pacific countries.

The same pattern is observed in financing the resource gap that has emerged during the past two decades. The NIEs were most dependent on private foreign capital while the Pacific countries (excluding Fiji and Papua New Guinea) were dependent entirely on official development assistance (bilateral and multilateral) that was concessional in nature. Two other economic groups were dependent on both sources of funds, the Southeast Asian countries, Fiji, and Papua New Guinea being more dependent on private foreign capital than those in low-income Asian countries.

The *Asian Development Outlook* for 1990[2] stated: "Openness and market orientation are more characteristic of the NIEs and the South East Asian countries than of South Asia and the centrally planned economies, though even the two latter groups have been moving, more or less cautiously, in that direction." Most Asian economies have been characterized by policy reforms of different scope and depth over the past decade. These changes need to be consolidated and the program of reforms completed. Improvements are still required in the efficiency and effectiveness of state enterprises that remain a significant segment in many economies in the region. The liberalization of the trade and foreign exchange regimes must be sustained and deepened. Incentives for foreign investments and the institutional framework for promoting, approving, and monitoring them also need to be improved. So does the efficiency with which the financial sector functions to serve the needs of the private sector, because it has provided the impetus for growth in many economies. The agenda for reforms in DMCs is therefore substantial. The Bank needs to continue supporting the sectoral policy reforms in coordination with other donors, particularly the World Bank.

In carving out a role for itself in providing financial resources to the region for the rest of the decade, the AsDB could adopt a different agenda for each of the four economic groups, recognizing that FDI is playing an increasing role in many DMCs. The NIEs need to be persuaded to contribute to the development of the region by cofinancing projects and programs, providing technical expertise that they have acquired in reaching this stage of development, and undertaking foreign investments in less-developed DMCs where the policy environment for foreign capital has improved. A very recent example of such a cofinancing arrangement is the framework agreement signed between the AsDB and Korea for using development assistance from the Korea Economic Development Cooperation Fund. In the countries of Southeast Asia, which are better endowed with natural resources, the Bank's role should be to assist in financing physical and social infrastructure projects that have become bottlenecks to their further development and consolidate the policy improvements that have been achieved. As these countries move up the technology ladder, they should be encouraged to invest in the low-income DMCs, particularly those in South Asia and Indochina. The Bank could serve as a promoter or a catalyst in this process, which is already taking place. Accordingly, the Bank's primary financing role should be concentrated in the low-income Asian countries, where it could assist in a range of sectors. It should also support World Bank and IMF assistance to improve the policy environment and enable these countries to attract foreign investment that could replace borrowings in many sectors. In the microstates, the Bank should work with the international donor community to determine the most effective means of providing foreign assistance. The provision of technical assistance should be a priority for these countries. The AsDB should also play a leading role in coordinating assistance for the rehabilitation of countries emerging from war situations such as Cambodia and Afghanistan and those affected by natural calamities, which occur frequently in some DMCs.

A broad agenda of this type has to be set within the strategic framework that has been adopted by the Bank. Priority is being given to promoting growth, protecting the environment, incorporating the social dimensions of development, assisting the vulnerable groups in society, identifying opportunities for supporting the private sector, and introducing human rights and governance issues in the Bank's loan and technical assistance operations. These are fundamental changes to Bank operations, which were carried out primarily through project financing during the first twenty years with a diversification into nonproject lending modes thereafter. Though the AsDB has agreed with its membership, primarily the donors, to make these changes, there are major budgetary and staffing implications in the medium term. These changes have to be supported by a human resources strategy for the Bank to meet emerging needs of the DMCs.

Role of the Bank in the Pacific DMCs

The Bank and other donors have been grappling with the problems of the Pacific DMCs for many years to determine the most effective process by which their development efforts can be supported. The small size of these countries, their scattered geographical locations, and other intractable development problems have made it necessary to question whether the traditional assistance provided by institutions like the Bank, which have difficulties in processing microloans, are best suited for this purpose. The World Bank has for the most part cofinanced projects with the Bank. These have been mainly to DFIs. The AsDB had taken the lead role vis-à-vis the World Bank in these activities in the past. In regard to technical assistance, however, the UNDP is also a major source of funds. It also had responsibility for assisting governments prepare for roundtable meetings where the donors have collectively considered the foreign assistance needs of each of these DMCs.

A recent World Bank report[3] set out the "Pacific Paradox" that, during the past decade, "virtually no growth occurred in average real per capita income despite a favourable natural and human resource endowment, high levels of aid, and reasonably prudent economic management." The policy work undertaken by the World Bank and the Development Assistance Committee of the Organization for Economic Cooperation and Development (OECD) assessed the development challenges and major problems faced by the Pacific DMCs. These showed that the lack of external resources was not the critical bottleneck facing these countries. Instead, severe human resource constraints that led to an almost colonial dependence on expatriates, oversized administrations and a bias towards the public sector, low levels of institutional absorptive capacity, weak incentive systems and policy environments, and inadequate aid coordination were the main impediments to the efficient use of resources. This led to poor economic performance in the 1980s in spite of large investments financed by external assistance, which was over 20 percent of GDP in these countries. The economies are high cost, inefficient, and unable to compete internationally. These issues have been discussed at various meetings held between the Pacific DMCs and the donor community. It has been accepted that concerted action was necessary in planning and policy formulation, human resource development, aid coordination, and private sector promotion to correct this situation.

The Bank increased its presence in the South Pacific in 1984 by opening the South Pacific Regional Office in Vanuatu with a view to increasing its operational efficiency in the region. Its role and mandate were circumscribed by the requirement to seek head office approval on many issues, which limited its effectiveness. The office covered all South Pacific DMCs with the exception of Papua New Guinea whose operations were handled directly from Manila. A similar situation prevails in the Northern Pacific with the accession to membership of the Marshall Islands and the Federated States of Micronesia. A task force in 1989 and an ad hoc working group in 1990 on Bank operations in the South Pacific recommended the establishment of a broadly defined, omnibus, technical assistance grant fund to finance both temporary and permanent staff positions, training, assessment of rehabilitation needs after natural disasters, project implementation assistance, and seed capital for indigenous entrepreneurs. They further recommended strengthening the regional office by giving it responsibility for country strategy studies, economic work, and country programming; processing and administration of stand-alone advisory and operational project implementation and regional technical assistance projects; collaboration with concerned departments at the Bank in processing projects; and the administration of loans, including the preparation of project completion reports.

After studying the report of the working group, the Bank management transferred responsibility for work on country programming, economic analysis, and operational strategy in the South Pacific DMCs to the regional office. In addition, they transferred to Vanuatu the processing of some, and administration of most, loan and technical assistance projects, including the preparation of project completion reports; communications with the DMCs in the region; and responsibilities for aid coordination. The South Pacific regional office prepares an economic report every two years for each South Pacific DMC. These provide guidance for government policy formulation and planning. The aid coordination process in these countries is facilitated by the policy dialogue that is promoted through these reports. The process for roundtable meetings is also enhanced by the analyses in these reports, which provide macroeconomic, sectoral, and other types of analysis such as on public expenditure.

As proposed by the task force and working group, these changes required the staff strength at the Vanuatu regional office to increase to fourteen. By June 1993 it had reached a level of ten. Another development that took place in 1990 was the formalization of a special conference between the governors of the Pacific DMCs and the president of the Bank as an adjunct to the Bank's annual meetings. This served a political need in the region because the Bank was perceived as catering primarily to the needs of the larger countries without adequate attention being given to the microstates.

Bank lending to the Pacific DMCs as a share of the total during ADF VI is expected to double in comparison to the totals during ADF V and ADF IV. Further, the technical assistance program is projected to be of the order of over 9 percent of total lending. This may not be achieved due to problems of absorptive capacity and human resource constraints. The Bank has also begun to address the main problem areas that impede efficiency. Efforts are under way to enhance the planning and policy formulation capacities. Priority is being given to human resource development; and aid coordination is being improved through the active participation of the regional office in the roundtable meeting process for these countries and in development meetings between the Pacific DMCs and the donor community.

Stimulating the private sector is a major problem in these countries. The constraint appears to be the small size of projects, for which the loan processing costs are high. In addition, the project proposals are not well developed; the local entrepreneurs do not have ready access to appropriate professional advice and lack training in technical and business management skills. The Bank's wholesale approach through DFIs has highlighted the problems of reaching these small entrepreneurs. Of the eleven DFI projects that were evaluated, two were judged to be successful, seven partially successful, and two unsuccessful. In response to the needs of the small-scale private sector, the IFC set up the South Pacific Project Facility, modelled on the lines of similar funds in Africa and the Caribbean, to assist in the development of small- and medium-scale industries with the funds provided by various bilateral and multilateral donors. Two-thirds of the funds are earmarked for Papua New Guinea and Fiji for projects in the range of $0.25–4.0 million for an initial period of five years. The lower limit is a problem for the other Pacific DMCs for whom such projects are major enterprises, as are the lack of extension services for small-scale private sector operations.

The World Bank report on Pacific Island economies in March

1993 analyzed the reasons for the low levels of efficiency with which aid resources have been used by the Pacific DMCs. Among these are the lack of a clear and consistent statement of government policies, strategy, and sector investment priorities; limited capacity to plan and oversee development assistance leading to a high degree of reliance on donors to define, design, and implement aid projects; the high unit costs of aid projects resulting from the geographical remoteness of the country, the lack of consulting and construction capacity, and a shortage of skills in government; frequent natural disasters leading to costly repair and rehabilitation programs; and the shortage of local funds for recurrent and maintenance costs that have led to short life spans for aid-financed investments. These problems could well be a catalog of reasons for low aid effectiveness in other DMCs, but they apply with great validity to the Pacific DMCs.

Most of the small island economies have no demonstrable long-term viability, and the difficulties experienced by the Bank in assisting them show that other institutional arrangements have to be sought and pursued with vigor. Various proposals have been made, including the creation of a Pacific Islands Development Bank for providing capital assistance. These were not pursued, due to the lack of donor support. Nevertheless, technical assistance for financing long-term experts (with the possible danger of a long-term dependency relationship developing, often with particular foreign nationals); short-term and, where necessary, long-term training abroad; and short-term advisory services through facilities established in the Pacific region such as the UNDP's Pacific Region Advisory Services and the Short Term Advisory Services of the South Pacific Forum Secretariat should be provided to the limit of the region's absorptive capacity. Other external resource needs of these countries are being provided by the donor community as a whole, though not necessarily in a coordinated manner, and through remittances received from nationals living abroad, mostly in Australia and New Zealand. If these sources are in danger of being reduced drastically in the future, the donor community as a whole needs to consider how the external resource requirements of these countries can be mobilized. In the meanwhile, the focus should be on improving the effectiveness of using resource transfers received from abroad. The World Bank report[4] suggested that steps be taken such as the clear and concise articulation of government development policies and sectoral priorities; an improved management approach to the selection and use of available sources and forms of aid; the more extensive use of non-governmental organizations; the better coordination of foreign assistance at the country/donor level; and the more appropriate design of aid activities.

There are no easy solutions for enhancing the effectiveness of AsDB operations in the Pacific. The coordination arrangements with the World Bank need to be reviewed and its concerns addressed, keeping in mind the wishes of the DMCs to deal directly with the World Bank. Otherwise, given that the financing requirements of these countries are small, there will be duplication and wastage between the two large donors, the World Bank and AsDB, which are not well set up to handle the needs of small economies. It is also necessary to take into account the role of the UNDP in mobilizing resources for these countries through the roundtable meetings that it organizes. The South Pacific forum could be asked to take the leadership in suggesting the most effective coordinating mechanism with the assistance of the three agencies.

Assistance to the Private Sector

The Bank traditionally focused on the public sector as the primary recipient of its assistance in fostering economic development in the DMCs. While doing this, it did not ignore the private sector. It channelled assistance to private enterprises through intermediary DFIs as early as 1968, the first year of its lending operations. In the uncertain economic environment of the 1970s and 1980s, the DMCs that had open economies and more developed private sectors were better able to respond to the adverse changes of that period. Many DMCs shifted their development strategies from those based on a growing government role to one that sought to support the private sector. In addition due to resource constraints, some DMCs opened to private sectors such areas as power and transportation that had been the preserve of the public sector. This provided the background to the change in Bank policies in the early 1980s leading to direct support for the private sector. This change was made, it should be added, with a push from the donors, in particular the United States.

Direct Assistance

The major component of Bank assistance to the private sector to date has been provided indirectly through credit lines to selected DFIs. The Bank began direct assistance in 1983 by introducing an equity investment facility. This led to equity participation in enterprises either directly or through lines of equity to selected financial institutions, which was a variation of the DFI credit line approach. An additional feature of the Bank's equity operations has been the underwriting of country and regional investment funds. Further developments in direct support to the sector were the introduction of unguaranteed loans in 1985 and the mobilization of complementary loans from other financial institutions that were channelled through the Bank. These funds thereby obtained the preferred creditor status of the AsDB.

When the AsDB began providing direct assistance to the private sector, its developmental role was reinforced by the catalytic and demonstrational nature of the activities it financed. The exposure limit of 25 percent in the equity capital of a single enterprise was designed to ensure that other financing sources were not displaced by the Bank. Its catalytic nature has been justified on the grounds of being an initiator of investment, a source of confidence rather than of funds, a link between domestic and foreign entrepreneurs and financial intermediaries, and an agency capable of developing indigenous competence in capital market operations. Its demonstrational role needs to take into account the requirement stated in Article 14 (v)[5] that it is a lender of last resort. This role leads to assistance being channeled to pioneering activities such as support for leasing and venture capital businesses. At the same time, the Bank's role as a catalyst for mobilizing resources would ensure that it does not crowd out other lending institutions from financing particular projects.

The role of the AsDB in direct financing operations has to be closely monitored because it functions in a highly competitive environment where domestic and foreign financial institutions seek business opportunities. In view of this, its assistance has to be relevant to the needs of the DMCs and able to respond to them in a timely manner on competitive terms without crowding out other lenders. The rationale for a private sector borrower seeking AsDB assistance has to be that the funds are cheaper and that the Bank's participation will attract cofinanciers on competitive terms. These advantages have to outweigh the costs of a longer processing time of a loan application by the AsDB than that of a commercial bank.

Bank staff should be able to operate with credibility in a private sector environment and would benefit by undertaking detailed assessments of the capacities of the sector in its DMCs. Five[6] assessments have been undertaken in the Asian region by the World Bank in collaboration with the IFC. In addition, the Foreign Investment Advisory Service of the Multilateral Investment Guarantee Agency has conducted a range of studies in fourteen DMCs during the past two years. These should be used by the AsDB in consultation with the World Bank to assist in the preparation of strategies for the private sector in the country operational strategies. When preparing these strategies, special capacity studies should be undertaken for the other DMCs without which definitive statements of needs cannot be made.

The private sector plays a dominant role in the countries of ASEAN-4 and the NIEs. These countries may find it easier and less cumbersome to mobilize domestic and foreign private capital for private sector projects. It may yet be helpful to involve the AsDB in cofinancing large projects in view of the likely catalytic impact it will have on other lenders. There is an a priori case for limiting direct assistance to countries where the private sector is not dominant. It is therefore likely that the share of direct assistance to the private sector in Bank operations will increase only gradually. As shown in Table 6.1, private sector investment facilities as a share of total Bank operations were marginally in excess of 2 percent to the end of 1992.

Table 6.1 Summary of Private Sector Investment Facilities (cumulative up to December 31, 1992; in millions of dollars)

Equity facilities	
Line of equity	31.000
Investment	143.824
Underwriting	45.754
Unguaranteed loans	
OCR	481.810
ADF	14.500
Total bank funds	716.888
Complementary financing loans	161.600
Total	878.488
Total bank operations	42,458.900

Source: Loan, Technical Assistance and Private Sector Operations Approvals, AsDB, December 1992.

Policy Environment and Technical Assistance

In many cases, AsDB assistance to DFIs and other financial intermediaries through credit and equity lines has been coupled with technical assistance for institution building. This tended to focus on enhancing the appraisal and supervision capabilities of these institutions. In addition, technical assistance has been provided with financial sector program loans for upgrading the staff skills in institutions involved in the securities markets and for offering training opportunities to venture capital and fund management companies. The technical assistance funds available to assist borrowers in developing their institutions provided it with a comparative advantage over the IBRD and IFC in similar operations designed to assist the private sector in the past. In addition, the Bank can provide technical assistance for project preparation activities, although its use for private sector projects is discouraged because opportunities for cost recovery are less than in the public sector. A review of this policy is necessary, particularly in the less-developed member countries to which direct assistance by the AsDB should be primarily directed to promote viable private initiatives.

In addition to project-specific technical assistance, Bank support could be used for formulating the policy framework for developing the private sector. Technical assistance funds could be used to undertake sector and subsector studies; formulate and implement policy reforms necessary to assist the private sector; design the restructuring of public enterprises, including the privatization of some; formulate the tax, regulatory, and legal regime necessary for promoting private investment; train private sector staff; and promote institutional development. Given the overall responsibility of the World Bank and IMF for assisting countries to formulate their macroeconomic framework and supporting policy reforms with adjustment operations, the Bank must identify a niche for itself in undertaking these technical assistance activities to develop the private sector. The staff should have the capacity to undertake a policy dialogue with DMC governments on the recommendations made in these studies and assist them to implement the findings. It would not be adequate merely to finance studies and make them available to the concerned government without engaging in a constructive policy dialogue.

The AsDB has undertaken a number of studies on capital markets, mutual funds, venture capital, and leasing companies and the business environment for the private sector in selected DMCs. Some of these led to the implementation of policy reforms in the financial sector in the context of program loans in India, Indonesia, Lao Peoples' Democratic Republic, Pakistan, and Sri Lanka. These studies tended to focus on institutional and regulatory reforms and research required for formulating policy, especially in the financial sector and securities markets. The Bank has the ability to allocate technical assistance funds for policy studies more readily than the World Bank. However, both the Bank and the World Bank are engaged in assisting DMCs in policy development for the private sector. In view of this, technical assistance funds should be channelled where the Bank has a comparative advantage and a capacity to undertake a policy dialogue. The reforms brought about in the financial sector and capital markets in Indonesia are examples.

Institutional Changes

The expert panel, which assessed the distinctive role that the AsDB could play in responding to the emerging needs of the DMCs in the 1990s, examined the contribution that the Bank could make in the development of the private sector. The panel recommended an expanded role for the AsDB in view of the growth potential of this sector in many Asian economies, particularly in industry, trade, and employment. It proposed that the policy dialogue should be expanded and technical assistance used to promote policies and an institutional environment conducive to growth. A role for the AsDB was also envisaged in expanded direct financing of the private sector with a view to attracting additional outside resources. Assistance for privatization, lending to public enterprises run on commercial lines without government guarantees, and innovative mechanisms for supporting NGOs were further proposals. It also recommended the establishment of an Asian Finance and Investment Corporation (AFIC) as an affiliate similar to the IFC to complement the efforts of private banks and direct investors by providing funds of a catalytic nature. The panel recommended the establishment of a separate department for private sector operations, as an alternative to direct and indirect assistance, to play an advisory and operational role in the development of capital markets.

There was little support within the AsDB management for transferring the growing private sector activities to an affiliate similar to the IFC. Instead, it proceeded to establish a Private Sector Department and the AFIC as a separate private financial institution. The latter is a joint venture between the AsDB (the largest shareholder with 30 percent of its paid-up capital) and 25 financial institutions (which are mostly private) from nine countries in Asia, Europe, and North America, with the largest share held by Japanese banks. Its primary purpose is to contribute to the development of private enterprise in the DMCs by providing additional financial flows and complementing local funding. It functions as an autonomous commercial institution and attempts to maintain both profitability and developmental concerns in its operations. It has a mandate to pay particular attention to the low- and middle-income DMCs.

The AsDB's objective was to establish the AFIC as an organization that would be a source of cofinancing for private sector operations and would play a developmental role while maintaining a quick response capability. Although initially the AFIC was heavily dependent on the AsDB for identifying project opportunities, this dependence has declined over the first three years of its operations.[7] It is necessary to decide on a division of labor between the two institutions. Projects involving long gestation periods, extensive project analysis, and longer investment horizons would be more relevant for AsDB operations, while the AFIC could focus on projects with quicker payback periods. Similarly, for reasons of managing country risk, the AFIC could focus on countries where the private sector is in a more advanced stage of development. At the same time, it could ful-fill its developmental role by financing projects in the less advanced DMCs, protecting itself where necessary under the AsDB's comple-mentary financing scheme.[8] Whatever guidelines are adopted for the AFIC and AsDB operations, it is likely that there will be overlap and possibilities for joint endeavors in many countries. Close consulta-tions will therefore be necessary between them. These are best under-taken in the context of private sector assessments and other studies prepared by the World Bank, IFC and Foreign Investment Advisory Service, and the AsDB's country operational strategies.

The private sector task force set up in 1991 had a mandate to assess the experience of the Bank's private sector operations and rec-ommend appropriate changes, including the further integration of such activities in all its operations. The task force reported in December 1991. The major organizational change proposed was the assimilation and integration of the AsDB's private sector planning, development, and assistance efforts into its mainstream support for the public sector in DMCs. It was judged that a separate Private Sector Department would not support the strategic objective of inte-grating private sector operations into the AsDB's lending program. Accordingly, the task force recommended that every projects depart-ment take responsibility for both public and private sector opera-tions, and that a small Private Sector Support Unit be established to provide skill-based technical support needed in projects depart-ments. The support unit was established in the last quarter of 1992 and the other organizational changes have been deferred. The inter-action between the staff of the support unit and those in projects departments needs to be kept under review.

Build, Operate, and Transfer (BOT) Projects

In line with the proposed integration of the private and public sector operations, the upgrading of the physical infrastructure of the DMCs provides opportunities for collaboration between the AsDB and pri-vate sector in BOT projects. It enables the private sector—domestic, foreign, or joint venture—to participate in the formulation, imple-mentation, and operation of new capital-intensive infrastructure pro-jects. Collaboration could also take place for rehabilitating similar existing projects. These infrastructure projects have long gestation periods and were previously undertaken only by the public sector. An integral feature of these is that private enterprise owns and oper-ates them for an agreed period (the cooperation period), at the end of which time ownership and management are transferred to the public sector. If the economic life of the project exceeds the cooperation period, the BOT enterprise could be asked to continue operations under the same conditions or through a lease arrangement. It could be transferred to a new private enterprise during the extended period or during the original cooperation period. These projects could also be operated on a build, operate, and own basis.

The development of BOT projects has come about due to two main factors. There has been a growing reliance worldwide on the private sector for the provision of physical infrastructure. This has been reinforced by the privatization of many similar public enterprises. The second factor is the budgetary constraints faced by governments that make it difficult to maintain existing facilities and undertake new investments. These projects are of recent origin in the AsDB. The first examples were a private power generation project at Navotas in the Philippines by the Hopewell Energy Corporation (for which an unguaranteed loan of $10 million and a direct equity investment of $1.1 million were made) and the Bangkok Expressway project (for which an unguaranteed loan of $30 million and a direct equity investment of $10 million were made).

A Framework for Assistance for Private Sector Development

The thrust of the strategy proposed by the private sector task force was that operations should be directed primarily at developing a policy environment that would encourage private sector growth in all DMCs, with the expectation that this would accelerate economic growth. The form and extent of private sector development will vary across countries depending on their level of development, the commitment of the government, and the effectiveness of policies that encourage the operation of market forces. It is recognized that private sector operations need to be integrated with programs supporting the public sector since they relate to all sectors of a DMC economy. It is necessary to undertake studies of the structure, characteristics, and capacity of the private sector in pursuing this approach. In addition, sector analysis and investment studies should be carried out to develop a country-specific strategy for the private sector. These should form an integral part of the AsDB's and the World Bank's operational strategy for each country. A close liaison should be maintained between the relevant divisions and departments of the two banks while these studies and assessments are being conducted. The AsDB could benefit from studies already undertaken by the World Bank group.

The primary aim of Bank operations should be to improve the existing policy framework in DMCs, remove constraints to the growth of the private sector, and harness and foster its development.

The need for direct Bank intervention in support of private sector projects and programs does not exist in all DMCs. The NIEs and ASEAN-4 countries do not appear to need any general Bank support for mobilizing long-term resources for private sector investment. Direct support to the private sector should focus primarily on the countries of Indochina, the Pacific, and South Asia and China. Even in these countries, support should be concentrated on financing social and physical infrastructure projects supportive of private sector development (including BOT-type projects), DFI lines of credit, and financial sector loans instead of direct private sector operations. DFI lines of credit should, however, be made available only on a selective basis to avoid successive credits to institutions that do not appear to respond to a series of technical assistance projects for institutional development.

Bank technical assistance funds should be used for carrying out sector studies for formulating and implementing policy reforms, public enterprise restructuring including privatization, institutional development, and training. In many countries, the private sector is small, and it is necessary to foster the spirit of entrepreneurship and to teach modern management practices to small businesses. It may be possible for the Economic Development Institute of the World Bank to undertake such training in the region after asking the Bank to identify needs and by using the Bank's regional technical assistance funds. While this work could be piggybacked on AsDB loan and equity operations, they should complement activities undertaken through adjustment operations supported by the World Bank for private sector development. A similar complementary role should be played by the AsDB to foster the development of the financial sector and capital markets for resource mobilization, building on the experience gained from traditional DFI credit lines and the more recent financial sector loans.

A final issue that should be considered is the extent of direct private sector financing that could be made using the range of financial instruments available without having an adverse effect on the AsDB's triple-A rating. These instruments bear comparison only to those used to finance IFC operations. Projects selected for financing should be commercially viable under prevailing market conditions while having a developmental impact. Further, to safeguard the interests of the Bank's credit rating, it is important that such financing should not become volume-driven like its other lending. It would be advisable to prescribe a share of overall AsDB operations for both equity investment and unguaranteed loans. Perhaps, a ceiling of 5 percent or an equivalent amount in absolute terms based on current lending levels could be made applicable over the medium term (possibly three years) instead of annually as in the case of other operational ceilings. In setting such a ceiling, it should be recognized that direct support would not become the most important aspect of AsDB support for private sector development and that direct support should only be made available to countries whose needs are greatest.

Protecting the Environment

Numerous environmental issues are of concern to the DMCs. Rapid economic growth, the use of technology-intensive production methods, and population increase (often leading to rapid urbanization) are among the factors that will place a tremendous demand on the natural resources of a region. Without careful planning and remedial action, drastic environmental conditions can result, such as the loss of current forest cover on the order of 10 percent over the next ten years; salinization and waterlogging of irrigated land; the destruction of near-shore fisheries, coral reefs, and mangroves of importance to island economies; and the expected five- to tenfold increase in air and water pollution in the next decade. Environmental concerns have also been raised in the case of specific large projects such as the Sardar Sarovar Dam in the Narmada Valley in India (which was supported by the World Bank) and other major irrigation projects in the region. Recognizing the extent of these problems, many DMCs introduced environmental legislation and established institutions to protect the environment. Unfortunately in many cases, due to the lack of trained personnel, of inadequate funding and insufficient data, and of weak coordination between concerned government agencies, their impact has been less than desired.

Proposals for incorporating environmental issues in Bank operations were first made in 1979. They evolved during the 1980s, and the Bank's environmental policy framework was endorsed by the Board in 1986. This policy requires the country operational strategies prepared for each DMC to deal with environmental issues relevant for overall economic development and individual sectors. These should assist country programming missions to design projects and programs that address environmental and natural resource issues, particularly in the resource-based sectors such as agriculture, fisheries, forestry, and energy. The Office of the Environment has prepared Environment and Natural Resource Briefing Profiles and/or Environmental Strategy Reports in selected DMCs to assist programming missions. These strategy reports set out the country's major environmental and natural resource problems; legislative and institutional solutions; environment policy; major initiatives taken by the government, donors and nongovernmental organizations in the field of environment; and gaps in environment work, planning, and management needs of the sector. Where such reports have not been prepared, staff should seek access to studies such as the Country Environment Profiles that have been prepared by other donors such as the USAID.

At the country level, the Bank is assisting in integrating environmental considerations into national development plans through the formulation of a national conservation strategy. Another intervention has been the integration of these into the formulation of national economic policies. At the project level, the Bank ensures that the preparatory stage includes an initial environmental examination and impact assessment for projects and programs where they have been judged to be necessary. The section of the Operational Manual covering the integration of environmental considerations in Bank operations states that the Office of the Environment categorizes loan and technical assistance projects listed in the country operational program for each DMC according to their anticipated environmental impact. This is based on its type, location, sensitivity, scale, and the nature and magnitude of its potential impact and availability of cost-effective measures to mitigate the adverse effects. These categories are the following:

- Category A: Projects where an Environmental Impact Assessment (EIA) is required;
- Category B: Projects where an EIA is not required, though an Initial Environmental Examination (IEE) is required; and
- Category C: No EIA or IEE is normally required.

Those in category A and some selected projects in category B are classified as environmentally sensitive, requiring special attention during design to address adequately environmental issues or to adopt mitigating measures.

Where the Bank assists in the preparation of environmentally sensitive projects, staff carries out IEEs in accordance with the environmental guidelines for the sector when fact-finding missions for technical assistance are mounted. Such guidelines are available for the agriculture and natural resources, industry, power, and infrastructure sectors. Following a review of the IEE, the terms of reference for an EIA are prepared with the assistance of the Office of the Environment. These assessments normally contain details of the project and its environment, anticipated environmental impact and mitigating measures, alternatives, cost-benefit analysis, institutional requirements and environmental monitoring programs, and public involvement. Once the EIA/IEEs for environmentally sensitive projects are completed and reviewed by the Office of the Environment, summaries are released to the Board with the agreement of the borrower. This is done at least 120 days before Board consideration of the project. In addition to these summary reports, the full EIA or, where appropriate, the IEE will also be made available, upon request, to Board members.

Arrangements made on appropriate environmental management measures in environmentally sensitive projects is normally included in the Memorandum of Understanding agreed between the Bank and borrower during project appraisal. These will then be incorporated as loan covenants in agreements or the minutes of negotiations, in addition to the standard environmental provisions contained in Bank loan documents. The costs of implementing appropriate environmental safeguards should be estimated at the appraisal stage and financed under the loan or by the borrower. In the latter case, the appraisal mission should determine that adequate budgetary resources are available to meet the costs. Once project implementation begins, review missions will evaluate operations and maintenance arrangements, institutional commitments, and loan covenants covering environmental planning and management requirements. The implementation of mitigating measures will also be reviewed during these missions.

Program loans do not normally require the preparation of EIAs or IEEs. If there are environmental implications arising from the policy and institutional reforms introduced with the loan, appropriate covenants should be included in the agreement. Not all subprojects in sector loans (whether they are a time slice or segment of an investment program) are identified at the time of loan processing. A few are identified to establish the broad parameters of the size of the loan. Feasibility studies including EIAs/IEEs are prepared for these during the formulation of the loan to demonstrate their preparation to the implementing agency. This is done in the interests of building up its institutional capability. The capacity of the implementing and environmental protection agencies to prepare IEEs/EIAs is determined at the appraisal stage and appropriate monitoring procedures established to satisfy the Bank's requirements.

It appears that the Bank has introduced comprehensive procedures for integrating environmental aspects into loan and technical assistance operations. These are being introduced at a time when other crosscutting issues are being integrated into Bank operations. This raises concerns that the projects and programs departments may not treat them with the same degree of attention that is required. In addition, there are staffing implications for introducing a Bank-wide environment program of this nature. The Office of the Environment has only 10 professionals.[9] Substantial work by consultants may be required to administer this program effectively, unless staff numbers are increased.

Incorporating Social Dimensions in Bank Operations

Concerns about integrating social dimensions in Bank operations arose when it was recognized that the DMCs, with more than half the world's poor, did not provide opportunities for all groups in the population to benefit from rapid growth. Special programs are needed for women and some ethnic and vulnerable groups to benefit from this growth, and safety nets are needed for the poor for reasons of equity and to preserve stability in the country. Further, population planning and human resources development are a priority in DMCs to sustain a balance between economic growth and the environment. The Bank has adopted a number of policies over the years to address these issues, although their consideration in an integrated manner has only taken place after pressure from donors.

Poverty reduction has been an implicit element in most Bank operations since its inception. Direct concern with poverty reduction stemmed from the recommendations of an internal task force on the Bank's role in poverty alleviation established in 1988. The policy was strengthened in 1990 in the context of the ADF VI negotiations. The integration of women in development in Bank operations began in the 1980s and an explicit policy on the role of women in development was adopted in 1985. Based on these policies, an action program was approved in the context of the ADF VI negotiations. Bank operations to address human resource development cover the subsectors of health and population, education, water supply and sanitation, and urban development. Health and population operations were guided by its policy paper on population prepared in 1979 and its sector paper on health, population, and development in Asia and the Pacific prepared in 1991. Similarly, activities in education are guided by a sector paper on education and development in Asia and the Pacific that was approved in 1989.

The social dimensions that have been identified for inclusion in Bank operations are

a) poverty reduction;
b) enhancing the role of women in development;

c) human resources development including population planning; and

d) avoiding or mitigating adverse effects on, and protecting, the vulnerable groups.

Poverty reduction[10] involves helping the poor, through direct assistance, to undertake production activities that generate employment and income; implementing development policies and investments that expand employment opportunities; and improving access to health, family planning, and related services. Women in development (WID) encompasses policies and activities that help all women to develop to their full potential, improve their productivity, contribute to the economy, and share in the rewards of development as equal partners with men. Human resources development, including population planning, comprises the provision of services such as health and population, education, water supply and sanitation, and urban development to improve the living standards and quality of life that contribute toward achieving sustained and accelerated economic growth. Vulnerable groups in society include women, children, indigenous and tribal people, ethnic minorities, illegal settlers and squatters, those at the bottom of the social ladder, disabled people, and new and old immigrants. These groups are often poor and unable to absorb economic, environmental, and social shocks, and their condition is expected to worsen due to policy reforms or program intervention. Safety nets and compensation mechanisms have to be provided to protect them from the adverse effects of reforms and other interventions, at least in the short term. The Bank is introducing certain processes in its operations to address the issues that cover three of its strategic objectives.

Social Dimensions in Country
Operational Strategies and Programs

According to the guidelines,[11] country operational strategies should address social dimensions to determine whether growth is being achieved with adequate attention being paid to equity, and whether the policies and social processes are contributing to equal opportunities for women and men in different regions and among different social groups to promote social harmony and political stability. Both qualitative and quantitative assessments can be made to determine the impact of development priorities on social dimensions in DMCs. A qualitative review can be done by examining

a) DMC policies and strategies relating to social dimensions;
b) laws, regulations, and administrative directives relating to the progress of the poor, women, and vulnerable groups;
c) social and political pressures favoring certain groups of the population and geographic areas;
d) the capacity of different social groups to mobilize, implement, and sustain development activities; and
e) institutional mechanisms for the participation of different segments of the population and the extent to which these can be used to express popular will.

A quantitative review can be based on data on

a) the allocation of resources to the social and other sectors in annual and five-year plans;
b) allocations within sectors to particular geographic and population groups;
c) the allocation of public sector personnel by sector or geographic area; and
d) tax revenues and domestic resource mobilization including their effect on different income groups and segments of the population.

The analysis in the country operational strategy should provide a basis for consultations between Bank staff and agencies in the government and outside such as in business, labor unions, women's associations, nongovernmental organizations, and other donors. These consultations should enable the AsDB to identify areas of agreement on social and economic development goals and to allocate resources in support of them. The dialogue should also assist the Bank in identifying areas for further economic and sector work. Support can be expected from other donors in pursuing the social objectives of the government and providing a basis for formulating a lending program consistent with its strategic objectives. The analysis made during the preparation of the country operational strategy should provide indications of the gaps in the country's efforts to address social dimensions and highlight the need to focus on specific social programs in future assistance. Project completion and audit reports prepared by the AsDB and similar reports prepared by other donors should also provide information on the areas where resources are likely to be most productive. Further, the economic and sector work of the Bank (and the World Bank) may provide guidance on areas of social concern that could benefit from receiving Bank assistance.

Social Dimensions in Project Preparation and Processing

Detailed guidelines are being drawn up to incorporate social dimensions in project preparation, beginning with profiles at the country programming stage. Some information will be required in the profile on the clientele, whether it is likely to have significant social effects and the extent to which social dimensions and associated processes will be important. The fact-finding/appraisal stage will follow when an initial social assessment is prepared to provide a comprehensive picture of the target groups and organizations that may be affected positively or negatively. The assessments will also rate the level of development of each subpopulation; assess the target population's needs and demands for the project, its absorptive capacity to participate in the design and implementation and utilize the project inputs, and ability to operate and manage the project facilities upon completion; and identify institutions that could be involved in the design, implementation, and evaluation. If the assessment concludes that social dimensions and associated processes are likely to be important elements of the project, a detailed analysis called the social design will be prepared and incorporated in the feasibility study. The necessity for this will be clear if the assessment reveals that there are limitations on the demands and needs of potential beneficiaries, deficiencies in the absorptive capacity of the target populations, potential negative impact for some subpopulations, and significant opposition to the project.

Where a social design needs to be incorporated in the feasibility study, the following associated social processes must be undertaken:

a) adopt participatory approaches to development. This provides opportunities for beneficiaries and adversely affected groups to take part in decisionmaking and instill a sense of ownership and commitment to the project;

b) undertake a gender analysis, to examine the different roles that can be played by men and women in the project and to identify constraints to women's participation in mainstream project activities;

c) introduce benefit monitoring and evaluation, to design simple indicators that can measure progress and assist in identifying adjustments required during implementation;

d) undertake social analyses to design a project that is socially responsive and sustainable; and

e) promote cooperation with nongovernmental organizations to foster partnerships with government agencies to complement and reinforce Bank assistance.

Classification of Projects in
Terms of the Bank's Strategic Objectives

A new classification system for projects was introduced to monitor the application of strategic objectives in the operational program for each DMC. Firm and pipeline projects are classified into traditional growth projects: those aimed directly at social concerns (poverty reduction, human resources development, and WID); those aimed directly at the environment; and growth-oriented projects that have secondary features in their design to address social and/or environmental concerns. The Bank has set itself a ceiling of not more than 50 percent in the traditional growth category. The target for 1992 was met (with 46 percent being in this category), although in value terms they accounted for 63 percent of the loan funds. The percentages for the other categories were eighteen for social, eight for environment, and twenty-eight for growth-oriented projects with secondary features addressing social and environmental concerns. The target was also met in 1993.[12]

The Bank does not intend to set such targets for each DMC. Due regard will be paid to each country's circumstances and access to other assistance. The 1992 loan approvals indicate that the AsDB's overall focus was on growth-oriented projects with the position being more pronounced in value terms. A large number of small projects in value terms reflecting nongrowth objectives would not satisfy the guidelines. Nevertheless, this categorization is a useful beginning as the Bank designs its portfolio to reflect its strategic objectives.

The incorporation of social dimensions in Bank operations would require considerable effort on the part of staff to fall in line with the new orientation. It also places a tremendous burden on the DMCs throughout the project cycle. Project preparation becomes more laborious when social dimensions are added to the other requirements that have been introduced, such as the preparation of environmental assessments. These changes are at the beginning of a transition phase that is taking place in the Bank. The proper institutional arrangements for managing them and the staff implications of these changes are in the process of being assessed. These should therefore be viewed as a beginning rather than something that has been accomplished. The will to institute changes has certainly been demonstrated by the AsDB.

Good Governance, Democratic
Development, and Human Rights

Good governance, democratic development, and human rights are controversial issues in the Asian region with governments apprehensive of their implications for development assistance. They have opposed the introduction of conditionalities attached to lending that are political in nature. The issues should nevertheless be addressed as they are on the agenda of the donor community and have been dealt with differently at the bilateral and multilateral levels. As stated earlier, the Articles of the Bank prohibit it from being influenced in loan and technical assistance decisions by the political character of the concerned DMC. Only economic considerations should be relevant to the decisions. Similar considerations prevail in the World Bank. Nevertheless, donor pressure led to the suspension of lending by the Bank to China after the Tiananmen massacre in 1989 and to Myanmar after the brutal suppression of political rights in 1988. Further, objections in the United States on political grounds prevented a resumption of lending to Vietnam until 1993.

These examples make it clear that the Articles have been breached through donor pressure, and it is perhaps time that the issues are confronted to avoid discriminatory treatment of some DMCs. At a bilateral level, several Asian countries such as China, Indonesia, Myanmar, and Sri Lanka had their assistance reduced or suspended due to violations of human rights or suppression of democratic institutions. The last major shareholder of the AsDB to make a policy statement on these issues was Japan, when it set out the principles governing foreign assistance in June 1992. These covered, among other issues, attention to levels of military expenditure, democratic development, respect for human rights, and protection of the environment. If Japan applies the principles in this statement to its allocation of bilateral assistance, some Asian countries to whom Japan is a major donor will be adversely affected.

It is useful to discuss the issues relating to good governance to determine the extent to which the Bank could take them into account in its policy dialogue with DMCs. The report of the IDA-10 negotiations identified four major dimensions of governance that are critical for the development process. These are

a) accountability, which includes financial accountability in terms of an effective system for expenditure control and cash management and an external audit system at the macro level and the accountability to government of implementing agencies and parastatals for their operational efficiency at the micro level;

b) transparency, which ensures public knowledge of government policies and creates confidence in its intentions, enabling private sector investment decisions to be made with complete knowledge of the policy environment and reduction of corruption and waste;

c) the rule of law, which will provide a stable and predictable legal framework for businesses and individuals to assess economic opportunities and act upon them without fear of arbitrary interference or expropriation; and

d) participation, which will enable communities and groups directly affected to participate in the design and implementation of programs and projects. This is essential to secure commitment and support for projects and improve the possibilities of successful implementation.

The World Bank was urged by the IDA donors to engage countries in the economic aspects of these governance issues in their policy dialogue. Some of these, such as improvements to public sector management through public expenditure reviews and civil service and parastatal reforms, are being addressed through lending for adjustment. Public expenditure reviews are particularly important in focusing government attention on priority investment and recurrent expenditures. They provide the means by which attention is drawn to social sector expenditures that are not protected during the adjustment process and to evidence of development activity being preempted by large nondevelopment expenditures such as for defense. Issues relating to democratic development and human rights fall outside the scope of these discussions, although it could be argued that they have long-term implications for the capacity of a country to initiate and sustain programs for effective poverty reduction and economic adjustment.

The *Asian Development Outlook* for 1992 presented the results of a study on the levels and growth of military expenditure in DMCs. Data on military expenditure, economic growth, and government expenditure on social sectors for selected DMCs from this study are presented in Table 6.2. In spite of problems of data reliability, some conclusions were drawn. First, in some DMCs the levels of military expenditure are high in relation to the levels and rates of economic growth. Second, no conclusions about the link between military expenditure and economic growth were possible, although it may appear that high economic growth allows a high rate of growth in military expenditure. Third, a reallocation of expenditure to the social sectors by reducing military expenditure may be possible, but whether this will take place will depend on the priorities of the government and the realization of the wasteful nature of military expenditure, particularly if it is used primarily to repress its own nationals.

The Bank's criteria for assessing development performance has avoided these issues due to their controversial nature. DMCs opposed the introduction of the concept of performance-based ADF

Table 6.2 Military Expenditure and Economic Development

	Military Expenditure				GDP Growth	Government in 1989[a]		
Country	Average ($m) 1988–1990	Average Per Capita ($) 1988–1990	% of GDP 1990	Average Growth (%) 1981–1990	(%) 1981 1990	(% of total) Defense	Education	Health
Bangladesh	312	2.8	1.5	4.9	4.1	10.0	10.6	4.9
China	6,400	5.8	1.6	–1.7	10.1	—	—	—
India	9,497	11.5	2.9	5.8	5.4	17.2	2.7	1.7
Indonesia	1,820	10.2	1.5	–4.5	5.5	8.3	10.0	1.8
Korea	7,916	186.8	3.9	4.9	9.9	24.9	18.5	2.0
Malaysia	1,732	99.8	4.6	0.5	5.2	—	—	—
Myanmar	322	8.1[b]	3.1	–4.7	0.0	18.7	13.7	5.0
Nepal	59	3.2	1.8	11.1	4.7	5.2	10.0	5.0
Pakistan	2,804	25.6	7.1	8.0	6.3	29.5	2.6	0.9
Philippines	633	10.4	1.6	--0.1	1.0	13.0	17.1	4.3
Singapore	1,378	511.5	4.8	6.9	6.3	21.2	19.0	5.2
Sri Lanka	201	12.0	2.3	18.8	3.9	5.4	10.7	6.2
Taipei,China	6,397	319.9	4.8	4.6	8.5	—	—	—
Thailand	2,233	40.3	3.2	3.3	7.8	17.8	19.3	6.3

Source: Asian Development Outlook 1992, AsDB.
Notes: a. Data for Bangladesh and Pakistan refers to 1985 and 1986, respectively.
b. Data refers to 1988.
— = not available.

lending. This opposition would have been more vehement if the criteria were expanded to include good governance, democratic development, and human rights. It is difficult to see the Bank expanding the policy dialogue with DMCs to include these issues, given its reluctance to engage in substantive discussions on macroeconomic policies. It will probably follow the lead of the World Bank in this regard, as will the other RDBs. This would tend to suggest that a collective and coordinated approach should be developed for the MDBs in dealing with DMCs on these issues.

Regional Activities

When the Bank was established, it was expected to become a focal point for regional cooperation and collective development of its DMCs. This objective has been pursued with varying degrees of enthusiasm over the years. In practice, however, regional activities have been undertaken primarily through technical assistance operations. They have included a range of activities encompassing regional surveys, seminars, and studies such as two Asian agricultural surveys, South Pacific agricultural survey, regional energy survey, regional cooperation in energy, regional seminar on transport policy, regional study on global environment issues, studies on subregional cooperation among the countries in Indochina, Myanmar, China, and Thailand, growth triangles for promoting development of selected regions in DMCs, and development roundtables held on a variety of topics. There have, in addition, been several contributions to regional research institutions such as the International Rice Research Institute in the Philippines, the Asian Vegetable Research and Development Center in Taipei,China, the International Irrigation Management Institute in Sri Lanka, and the International Crop Research Institute for the Semi-Arid Tropics in India. While these activities have contributed to the regional consideration of some development issues, they have not made a significant impact on regional cooperation mainly due to the lack of a political will among the DMCs.

There are five distinct subregional groupings in Asia and the Pacific. These are the ASEAN; the Economic Cooperation Organization, now expanded to include the Central Asian Republics; the Pacific DMCs; the South Asian Association for Regional Cooperation; and the former centrally planned economies. The membership of some and the prospective membership of the other Central Asian Republics; the implementation of adjustment programs and policies to promote private investment, including FDI in the former, centrally planned economies and South Asian countries; and the opening up of the economies of Cambodia and Lao PDR are providing a new impetus for exploring opportunities of regional cooperation, at least on a subregional basis. A number of initiatives have been taken by the Bank as a result of the momentum that has been generated in the region.

The Bank has recognized the benefits that can accrue from regional cooperation in areas of trade, investment, finance, technology, infrastructure, natural and human resource development, and environmental protection. It is proposing to adopt a phased approach in promoting regional cooperation, initially by increasing the understanding and awareness of its potential benefits to DMCs. It will take stock of research useful to promoting areas of regional cooperation, and it will provide regional technical assistance for studies aimed at quantifying the benefits of better cooperation or the economic costs of its absence. In the second phase, projects that have regional or subregional implications will be identified and the Bank will assist in undertaking studies, facilitating discussions on potential problems, and working out possible solutions. In the third phase, the Bank will finance selected regional pilot projects. It is often mentioned that some national projects could have regional implications: one example is soil conservation measures in Nepal that will benefit both India and Bangladesh.

The OPP Study for the 1980s dealt with the action required for the Bank to evolve as a regional institution and made various recommendations. These remain valid in spite of the new approach proposed by the Bank. The concept of developing the Bank as a regional resource center as proposed in the study was supported strongly by the advisory group. It was envisaged that the Bank would build up and participate in a series of interlocking information, research, analytical, and training networks and become a center for new thinking on development issues and strategies in the region. While the AsDB has launched a number of regional research studies, such as the recent work on urban and rural poverty, and has provided a forum for seminar discussions on a number of development issues, it is still seeking the intellectual leadership that was the long-term goal in undertaking these activities. The Bank was urged to remain alert to fresh possibilities for assisting joint development projects and other endeavors among contiguous subgroups of its DMCs. ASEAN was the only viable subregional grouping in the early 1980s. Much progress has been made in this regard although the political will in the other groupings may not be as strong as it has been in ASEAN. Nevertheless, there are opportunities for the Bank to be a catalyst in promoting the formulation of projects that cut across national boundaries that can only be implemented successfully by multilateral agencies.

The Bank has taken a number of initiatives recently. Growth triangles have emerged as a solution to the problems of regional integration among countries with different socioeconomic systems and levels of development. These triangles cover areas in each country, and economic cooperation is localized to them. Among the existing growth triangles in Asia are Singapore, the southern part of the State of Johore in Malaysia and the islands of the Riau Province in Indonesia and Hong Kong, Taipei,China, and the southern region of the Peoples' Republic of China, mainly in the Pearl River delta of Guangdong and the Xiamen area of Fujian. An emerging growth triangle covers the area of the Tumen Basin that includes the northern provinces of the Peoples' Republic of China, a part of Siberia in the Russian Federation, and North Korea. Japan, the Republic of Korea, and Mongolia are expected to be included in this development and to provide capital and natural resources. The experience of these growth triangles was discussed at a regional workshop held by the

Bank in early 1993. The assessments made supported the view that these were superior to existing forms of cooperation because of low political and economic risk. This was primarily due to the small areas covered and the export-oriented, nonexclusive nature of their activities. These triangles generate benefits to countries that are not part of them due to the spillover of foreign investment and the provision of market access. This regional workshop was followed with another study that undertook the preparatory work on a new growth triangle covering the four northwestern states of Malaysia, the five southern provinces of Thailand, and the two northern provinces of Sumatra in Indonesia.

A Bank report on subregional economic cooperation published in February 1993 identified the transport sector for cooperation between two or more countries in the group studied that comprised Cambodia, Lao PDR, Myanmar, Thailand, Vietnam, and the Yunnan Province of the Peoples' Republic of China. These countries share borders and natural resources, and the Mekong River passes through or borders them. The report mentioned several projects, such as the improvement of the road linking Ho Chi Minh City, Phnom Penh, and Bangkok; repairing border bridges between the Peoples' Republic of China and Vietnam; and constructing a new port at Vinh in Vietnam as the ocean terminus to Highway 8 in the Lao Peoples' Democratic Republic. In addition, energy projects are well suited to subregional cooperation. The Lao PDR, the Yunnan Province, and Myanmar are interested in developing a hydropower project and exporting electricity to Thailand, Cambodia, and southern Vietnam. Myanmar and Vietnam are developing offshore petroleum resources, which Thailand is interested in tapping through a pipeline. Environmental and water resources management and telecommunications are other possible areas for cooperation. These will promote trade and investment within the subregion and provide opportunities for the Bank to finance these projects through appropriate modalities that have to be determined.

Notes

1. Not a member of the Bank.
2. *Asian Development Outlook 1990,* AsDB, page 17.
3. "Pacific Island Economies: Toward Efficient and Sustainable Growth," World Bank, March 1993, page 1.
4. Ibid., page 11.
5. *Agreement Establishing the Asian Development Bank,* AsDB, 1965.
6. India, Indonesia, Pakistan, the Philippines, and Sri Lanka.
7. To the end of March 1992, loan, equity, guarantee, and underwriting

operations totalling $136.3 million had been approved by the AFIC for nine countries and one regional mutual fund.

8. Loans cofinancing projects with the Bank under this scheme are granted the preferred creditor status enjoyed by the Bank.

9. As of March 1993.

10. *Guidelines for Incorporation of Social Dimensions in Bank Operations,* AsDB, October 1993.

11. Ibid., note 6, page 199.

12. In the context of the GCI IV negotiations, the Bank has committed itself to increase the share of lending that addresses social and crosscutting concerns, including environmental projects to the extent they address poverty reduction and social equity. This should eventually account for 40 percent of the lending volume.

7

ACHIEVEMENTS OF THE BANK

A major achievement of the Bank has been the expansion in its lend-ing program. The commitment of $30 billion in loan funds in the decade since 1982 in comparison to $10 billion up to that time bears testimony to this. As a consequence, the Bank has become one of the top three lenders of ODA to most DMCs and in some cases the largest. Bank lending also mobilized cofinancing resources amount-ing to $13,997.34 billion by the end of 1992. There has also been an increase in membership to fifty-five (from the original thirty-one), of whom thirty-nine are classified as DMCs. The increasing resource needs of the members have been met by successful borrowings in international capital markets and succeeding replenishments of the ADF. The multiplier effect achieved by the AsDB, in translating a paid-in capital of $2,787.0 million (12.1 percent of the subscribed cap-ital) to lending of $28.894.6 million from the OCR by international capital market borrowings, is evidence of the success of the multilat-eral system in mobilizing resources.

In spite of the rapid increase in loan commitments over the past decade and in spite of the Bank's share of ODA being large in some countries, its contribution to aggregate net resource flows has been small and averaged 5 percent during 1987–1991. However, it has increased its impact by its success in raising cofinancing resources of the order of one-third of gross loan commitments up to the end of 1992. Further, the inflow of FDI and private loans may have been facilitated by the policy reforms that were introduced with Bank assistance. A cautionary note has to be added to this discussion on lending volume. All past reviews of the Bank and the Report of the Task Force on Improving Project Quality have criticized the empha-sis that had been given to lending volume rather than to quality. Thus, achievements related to volume have to be judged in the con-text of concerns about quality.

Leaving aside for the moment concerns of quality, however

important, the Bank's major achievement was its success in mobilizing resources and channelling them to the DMCs. No bilateral channel could have achieved this volume. Nor would the World Bank, even if these extra resources had been given to it. Further, it is unlikely that the Japanese government would have contributed so generously to a concessional fund at the World Bank (even if it had been earmarked for use in Asia and the Pacific), because it would not have the same influence there that it does in the AsDB. Thus the volume issue, in spite of the concerns expressed, is a major achievement. In addition, the existence of two large, active lenders in the region bring different perspectives and new ideas to the development problems of DMCs.

The Bank concentrated on becoming a sound lending institution for projects in the initial ten to fifteen years of its lending operations. Since the end of the 1970s, the Bank began to diversify its lending modalities into program and sector lending that required the Bank to engage DMC governments in policy discussions, albeit only sectorally. The use of these modalities increased over the 1980s. They accounted for an average of 27.9 percent of total lending during 1991–1992 compared to an average of 7.8 percent during 1979–1990. Concomitantly, the policy dialogue with DMC governments has increased during this period, in the context of both program and sector lending, for the preparation of country operational strategies and subsequent country operational programs when the country's socioeconomic performance is assessed in the context of the framework set out in the strategy. The focus has been on sector policies with the dialogue on macroeconomic policies remaining the responsibility of the World Bank and IMF.

Technical assistance funds have been deployed effectively in support of the Bank's lending operations. They have focused primarily on project preparation, project implementation, and institution building of executing agencies. The AsDB has a comparative advantage over the World Bank, which only recently was able to fund these activities on a grant basis and on a limited scale. Technical assistance grant funds were available to the Bank since its inception. The World Bank gained access to funds for project preparation from numerous consultant trust funds established at the World Bank by bilateral donors in the second half of the 1980s and from the Policy and Human Resources Development Fund in 1990. The Institutional Development Fund, set up in 1992, provided the World Bank with funds for institution building. In addition, regional technical assistance funds available to the Bank have been used for activities and studies of interest to DMCs as a whole such as those on urban and rural poverty, subregional cooperation, growth triangles, and transition from centrally planned economies.

Instruments for assisting the private sector directly were first introduced in 1983. These covered equity directly and through lines of credit, underwriting, unguaranteed loans, and complementary financing. As the Bank's financial involvement in private sector projects was expected to be catalytic in nature, direct Bank funding of private sector projects have remained small. It was around 2 percent of total lending on a cumulative basis at the end of 1992. The Bank believes that it should focus on the creation of physical, institutional, and legal infrastructure and a policy environment conducive to private sector growth. Technical assistance for policy development has made a significant contribution in some DMCs, particularly in the financial sector. A review of private sector operations in the Bank in 1991 led to the integration of direct private sector support with that provided to the public sector. In 1992, a Private Sector Support Unit was established to strengthen private sector initiatives in the mainstream of activities of projects departments.

The AsDB established a Strategic Planning Unit in July 1991 and formulated a medium-term strategic framework for its operations. A new generation of country operational strategies are being prepared based on this framework and the DMCs' development strategies. These have a greater analytical content than those in the past and, taking full account of implementation experience, select sectors for intervention in which the Bank has a comparative advantage in the country. The strategies provide the framework for conducting annual country programming missions and performance assessments. These changes in process led to the adoption of a new planning cycle that was fully implemented for the first time in 1993.

There has been a closer integration of environmental considerations in Bank operations beginning in 1986. This was followed by the establishment of a full-fledged Office of the Environment in 1990. Clear guidelines have been set out to ensure that environmental issues are dealt with adequately in project preparation and implementation. These have included the adoption of comprehensive environmental review and impact assessment procedures and the integration of environmental considerations in all phases of Bank operations. There has been a significant increase in the number of environment-related technical assistance activities and environmental components in some projects.

The integration of social issues in Bank operations, including gender, poverty alleviation, human resources development, and greater cooperation with NGOs, began in the second half of the 1980s and was consolidated by the establishment of the Social Dimensions Unit in 1992. With these developments, the AsDB began classifying projects into traditional growth projects—those directly concerned with the environment, poverty reduction, human resource development, and gender issues—and growth-oriented projects, which have secondary features in their project design that address the crosscutting issues. The ceiling for traditional growth projects was set at 50 percent, which was met in both 1992 and 1993, although the percentage was higher in value terms. The Bank agreed at the GCI IV negotiations to work toward a target of lending volume of 40 percent for projects concerned with the environment, poverty reduction, and social issues.

Although the Bank has a mandate to promote regional cooperation among its DMCs, past efforts have consisted of seminars, workshops, and training involving nationals from more than one DMC in subjects of common interest. Recent political changes in the region, whereby DMCs are identifying themselves with subregional blocs, has provided opportunities to take major initiatives on economic cooperation. Among these have been a project involving Cambodia, China, Lao PDR, Myanmar, Thailand, and Vietnam, all of which border the Mekong River or contain part of it. Another is a growth triangle development project involving Indonesia, Malaysia, and Thailand. These opportunities should enable the Bank to take a leadership role and coordinate the assistance needed for regional projects.

What constitutes achievements of an institution is essentially a matter of judgment. Only those I have considered to be major have been listed, although others may assign importance to other issues. From an overall point of view, one bases a judgment on whether the Bank is contributing to the resource needs of the DMCs in the most cost-effective manner, utilizing the scarce resources available to it, particularly the concessional funds, for quality projects and programs. Development needs change over time, as do donor priorities; and the institution should have the flexibility to meet these challenges.

Some Concluding Thoughts

A debate is currently taking place in many donor capitals on the effectiveness of the multilateral channel. One issue in this debate is whether the allocations from official development assistance to multilateral institutions should not be reduced in favor of the bilateral channel in the interests of a donor's broader foreign policy objectives. (ODA is not expected to increase at the rate it did in the past; indeed, it may diminish or remain stagnant in some countries.) Questions are being asked about value for money, and whether this is being achieved by the MDBs. The decline in project quality in most of the banks in recent years has also added to the concerns. Donors review procurement statistics to determine the return to the countries of funds channelled to the relevant MDB, although this was not an objective when they first joined the bank. These are all valid concerns, and the debate will probably lead to a revision of some of the original objectives for participation in the MDBs. This is understandable, since priorities of governments change over time. The AsDB, along with the other banks in the MDB community, should respond to these demands for greater accountability and better performance and will need to compete for the available concessional assistance.

The Bank has become a major donor of ODA in many DMCs, often being among the three or four largest. The acceleration of lending over the past ten years illustrates the rapid expansion that has taken place. This has to be placed in the context of operating in the most buoyant developing region in the world where all DMCs, except for the Philippines, were able to avoid any rescheduling in the aftermath of the debt crisis that began in 1982. It is possible to rejoin the debate about the effectiveness of the multilateral channel by asking whether the bilateral donors as a group could have mobilized this volume of resources and channelled them as effectively to the DMCs without the costs being prohibitive. The answer to that question is surely a negative. Had the AsDB not existed, it is highly unlikely that, for example, Canada would have found the additional $2 billion to channel to Asian developing countries through bilateral channels; nor would it have had the administrative and technical capacity to deliver that amount. The same may be said for other donors.

However, high growth in the region had its costs. Inadequate attention was paid to infrastructure development and social concerns, making it necessary for the DMCs to give these areas high priority in the interests of maintaining political and social stability. The Bank followed the lead of DMCs and supported mainly growth-oriented projects until recently.

Recent evidence from Bank evaluations suggest a deterioration in loan performance, making it necessary to examine successes and failures closely in order to determine the corrective actions that are required, beyond slowing down the rapid expansion in lending and paying greater attention to project design and implementation. Comments made in past reviews and in the Report of the Task Force on Improving Project Quality about the volume culture of the AsDB should be addressed and efforts made to meet lending and other operational targets on a multiyear rather than an annual basis, with greater attention being paid to quality. If the recommendations of the task force are implemented, there will be implications for the project cycle, the quality of projects formulated, the levels of staff skill needed, and the budget. This will lead the Bank to correct the course in its growth path of lending and will have implications for the resource requirements of the Bank. The spring cleaning exercise recommended by the task force, to weed out problem projects in the portfolio, will also have an impact on resource requirements. In the short term, there could be a decline in the volume of lending, and the delivery of loans may well be at a higher unit cost.

The Bank has responded to donor demands to introduce strategic planning to its loan operations. The new country operational strategies are providing guidance to country programming in the choice of projects for loans and technical assistance. Agreement was reached with donors during the ADF VI negotiations to base ADF allocations on country performance. No similar agreement was reached in regard to allocations from the OCR during the GCI IV negotiations. Environmental strategies for all DMCs and assessments and initial examinations for all environmentally sensitive projects are being prepared. Action has been taken to incorporate social dimensions in Bank operations in a more effective manner than in the past. The AsDB needed to acquire new skills, particularly in the staffing of the Strategic Planning Unit, Social Dimensions Unit, and Private Sector Support Unit (to provide skill-based technical support to projects departments for the reorganization of private sector operations), and for strengthening the Office of the Environment. These developments in the preparation of country strategies, programs, and projects (and consequently on Bank operations) have made necessary a human resources development strategy. Credible staff deployment to perform these new functions is required to support the willingness of management, which agreed to the changes in successive rounds of discussions and negotiations with donors. Donors should appreciate these positive actions taken and give the AsDB time to implement the new activities before loading the institution with a new agenda. The Bank, for its part, should declare a time out to give itself breathing space to absorb the changes and to implement them effectively.

The diversification of lending modalities into program and sector lending has given the Bank greater opportunities for conducting policy dialogue with DMCs, at least on sectoral issues. The AsDB appears to have accepted this role and stayed clear of building up any capability to dialogue on or gain a full understanding of macroeconomic issues with DMCs, on the grounds that these are functionally the responsibility of the World Bank and IMF. A continuation of this role and the perception it conveys to the DMCs often leads to the

Bank not receiving adequate recognition for the substantial amount of loan funds that are provided, which in some countries are in excess of the World Bank. Bank management urgently needs to address this issue and build up the capability among staff to dialogue on macro-economic policy issues. This does not necessarily mean that it will be offering advice to DMCs that conflicts with that of the World Bank. Its own dialogue will become more effective, and the Bank will certainly improve its capacity to help DMCs with their private sector development in the manner proposed in this study. Effective coordination between the World Bank and the AsDB is also required, at an operational level in the manner proposed in the study, so that agreements reached between their managements are respected at the field level. This will lead to less confusion and enhanced effectiveness in loan operations.

The need for direct Bank intervention in support of private sector projects and programs does not exist among all DMCs. The NIEs and ASEAN-4 countries do not appear to need any general Bank support for mobilizing long-term resources for private sector investment. Accordingly, direct support should focus primarily on the countries of Indochina, the Pacific, and South Asia and China. It should concentrate on financing social and physical infrastructure projects supportive of private sector development (including BOT-type projects), DFI lines of credit, and financial sector loans instead of direct private sector operations. The primary aim of Bank operations should be to improve the existing policy framework in DMCs, remove constraints to the growth of the private sector, and harness and foster its development. Technical assistance funds could be used for carrying out sector studies for formulating and implementing policy reforms, public enterprise restructuring including privatization, institutional development, and training. In many countries, the private sector is small. It is necessary to foster the spirit of entrepreneurship and teach modern management practices to small businesses.

In carving out a role for itself for the rest of the decade, the Bank has to recognize the existence of four economic groups among the DMCs and adopt a different agenda for each of them. The NIEs should be persuaded to contribute to the development of the region by cofinancing projects and programs, providing technical expertise that they have acquired in reaching this stage of development, and undertaking foreign investments in less-developed DMCs where the policy environment for foreign capital has improved. The Bank's role in the countries of Southeast Asia should be to assist in the financing of physical and social infrastructure that have become bottlenecks to their further development and consolidate the policy improvements that have been achieved. Its financing role should be concentrated in the low-income countries where it could assist in a range of sectors. In addition, it should support World Bank and IMF efforts to improve the policy environment to enable these countries to attract foreign investment. In the microstates, the Bank should cooperate with other donors, particularly those with a special interest in the Pacific region, in order to take a holistic view of foreign assistance needs to determine the most effective means of providing financial requirements.

Such a scenario indicates the need for development banking functions to be performed by the AsDB largely for only one group of countries, namely the low-income countries, with the countries in higher-income categories seeking capital from international capital markets and through FDI. An approach of this type would be as fundamental a change of course as following through on the recommendations of the task force relating to volume culture, leading to major changes in the organization. Such changes have not been contemplated in the projections of resource requirements that have been prepared on the Bank. As it gears up to meet the challenges of the next century, an approach of this type should be worked into these projections so that its implications will be clear in the context of a reduction in ODA. To contemplate such a strategy is sensible, as it is unrealistic to assume that business can continue in the same way, even on a different scale. Not only are resources becoming scarce, but the performance of the MDBs is also coming under increasing scrutiny from donors with a view to diverting tax dollars in developed countries to alternative channels of development assistance or other purposes.

The emergence of subregional groupings, such as ASEAN, the South Asian Association for Regional Cooperation, the Economic Cooperation Organization (following the accession to membership of the six Central Asian Republics), the Pacific DMCs, and the riparian countries of the Mekong should provide opportunities for the Bank to promote regional cooperation with greater vigor than in the past. The financing of regional and subregional projects is clearly within the mandate of the Bank. It could fulfill the objective of those who set the groundwork for the establishment of the Bank better than it has done to date by pursuing initiatives with specific regional projects, such as those arising from the Mekong and growth triangle studies. One obvious caveat is that there has to be a political will among the cooperating countries to implement such projects.

While the Bank has grown to become a major financier, cast in the mold of the World Bank, it has not evolved as an intellectual center for new development thinking in the region. The concept of a Development Resource Center was promoted in the OPP Study, and the Bank has organized a number of studies and regional conferences on a variety of development issues that were funded by regional technical assistance. These appear to have fallen short of the requirements for developing a center of excellence; more effort should be made to continue the work begun in the 1980s.

The process that has just been set in motion by the recommendations of the task force on improving project quality, many of which are supported in this present study, will make the Bank a stronger institution in the most dynamic developing region in the world, which still has its fair share of intractable development problems. The Bank's strengths are widely recognized, as indeed are its weaknesses. The DMCs have a special responsibility to see that it evolves into an institution that is well prepared to assist them in the remaining years of this century. The developed members have an equally important role to create a genuine partnership to serve the interests of development in the region.

APPENDIX

STATISTICAL TABLES OF THE STRUCTURE AND OPERATIONS OF THE BANK AND DMC INDICATORS

Table A1 Bank Lending by Country and Source of Funds: 1970–1992 (amounts in millions of dollars)

Country	1970–1972		1973–1975		1976–1978		1979–1981		1982–1984		1985–1987		1988–1990		1991–1992		1970–1992	
	$m	Share %	$m	Share %	$m	Share %	$m	Share %	$m	Share %	$m	Share %	$m	Share %	$m	Share %	$m	Share %
OCR																		
China	—	—	—	—	—	—	—	—	—	—	133.3	3.3	372.6	5.5	1,399.3	18.4	1,905.2	6.6
Fiji	4.7	0.7	2.0	0.2	16.2	0.8	23.0	0.8	3.2	0.1	11.4	0.3	42.6	0.6	18.0	0.2	121.1	0.4
India	—	—	—	—	—	—	—	—	0.0	0.0	643.6	16.0	1,717.7	25.2	1,906.0	25.1	4,267.3	14.7
Indonesia	166.0	26.1	154.0	13.1	420.0	21.7	832.8	28.3	1,384.3	35.7	1,260.8	31.4	1,975.3	29.0	2,392.4	31.5	8,419.6	29.1
Korea	61.5	9.7	237.3	20.2	399.2	20.7	539.8	18.4	572.3	14.8	253.2	6.3	120.6	1.8	—	—	2,288.4	7.9
Malaysia	57.2	9.0	169.0	14.4	178.4	9.2	279.8	9.5	335.1	8.6	319.9	8.0	182.7	2.7	453.5	6.0	1,979.9	6.8
Pakistan	—	—	168.1	14.3	187.9	9.7	111.3	3.8	342.0	8.8	807.8	20.1	998.2	14.7	410.0	5.4	3,082.5	10.6
Papua New Guinea	—	—	—	—	17.7	0.9	26.3	0.9	43.3	1.1	55.0	1.4	32.4	0.5	50.3	0.7	225.0	0.8
Philippines	96.8	15.2	230.9	19.7	368.7	19.1	566.2	19.3	764.2	19.7	310.3	7.7	1,081.4	15.9	441.8	5.8	3,860.3	13.3
Thailand	60.0	9.4	158.2	13.5	262.2	13.6	507.2	17.2	433.8	11.2	219.9	5.5	288.6	4.2	484.6	6.4	2,414.5	8.3
Others	190.2	29.9	52.5	4.6	82.6	4.3	54.1	1.8	—	—	—	—	—	—	—	—	379.4	1.3
Bangladesh	—	—	14.9	1.3	—	—	—	—	—	—	—	—	—	—	—	—	-14.9	0.0
Hong Kong	21.5	3.4	20.0	1.7	40.0	2.1	20.0	0.7	—	—	—	—	—	—	—	—	101.5	0.4
Myanmar	—	—	6.6	0.6	—	—	—	—	—	—	—	—	—	—	—	—	6.6	0.0
Nepal	2.0	0.3	—	—	—	—	—	—	—	—	—	—	—	—	—	—	2.0	0.0
Singapore	81.4	12.8	10.0	0.9	42.6	2.2	34.1	1.1	—	—	—	—	—	—	—	—	168.1	0.6
Sri Lanka	10.3	1.6	1.0	0.1	—	—	—	—	—	—	—	—	—	—	—	—	11.3	0.0
Taipei,China	75.0	11.8	—	—	—	—	—	—	—	—	—	—	—	—	—	—	75.0	0.3
Vietnam	—	—	—	—	—	—	—	—	—	—	—	—	—	—	—	—	—	—
Regional	—	—	—	—	—	—	—	—	—	—	—	—	—	—	35.0	0.5	35.0	0.1
Total OCR	636.4	100	1,172.0	100	1,932.9	100	2,940.5	100	3,878.2	100	4,015.2	100	6,812.1	100	7,590.9	100	28,948.4	100

(continues)

Country	1970–1972 $m	Share %	1973–1975 $m	Share %	1976–1978 $m	Share %	1979–1981 $m	Share %	1982–1984 $m	Share %	1985–1987 $m	Share %	1988–1990 $m	Share %	1991–1992 $m	Share %	1970–1992 $m	Share %
ADF																		
Bangladesh	—	—	125.3	27.4	228.6	25.7	457.0	32.1	804.0	41.6	566.4	25.9	961.4	24.5	676.0	27.0	3,818.7	28.2
Bhutan	—	—	—	—	—	—	—	—	12.4	0.6	15.6	0.7	3.7	0.1	—	—	31.6	0.2
Myanmar	29.7	17.7	60.2	13.2	136.5	15.4	146.8	10.3	145.8	7.5	35.0	1.6	—	—	—	—	524.3	3.9
Nepal	18.2	10.8	19.9	4.4	92.8	10.4	114.6	8.0	175.4	9.1	200.5	9.2	342.4	8.7	127.4	5.1	1,102.7	8.1
Pakistan	14.7	8.8	81.8	17.9	190.3	21.4	390.6	27.4	555.2	28.7	844.3	38.6	1,080.2	27.5	781.9	31.2	3,942.5	29.1
Sri Lanka	105.3	58.7	34.3	7.5	80.4	9.1	108.5	7.6	152.0	7.9	263.0	12.0	432.0	11.0	317.6	12.7	1,402.5	10.4
Others	5.2	3.1	135.8	29.7	159.6	18.0	206.9	14.5	88.3	4.6	305.5	13.7	1,107.6	28.2	599.4	24.0	2,708.4	20.0
Afghanistan	—	—	28.9	6.3	40.9	4.6	20.1	1.4	—	—	—	—	—	—	—	—	95.1	0.7
Cambodia	—	—	—	—	—	—	—	—	—	—	—	—	—	—	67.7	2.7	67.7	0.5
Cook Islands	—	—	—	—	—	—	1.0	0.1	1.5	0.1	2.8	0.1	4.9	0.1	2.0	0.1	12.2	0.1
Indonesia	66.2	39.4	43.6	9.5	24.0	2.7	25.0	1.8	—	—	135.0	6.2	315.1	8.0	54.5	2.2	663.4	4.9
Kiribati	—	—	—	—	1.8	0.2	—	—	0.6	0.0	0.7	0.0	1.9	0.0	—	—	5.0	0.0
Lao PDR	4.4	2.6	7.4	1.6	8.0	0.9	17.2	1.2	23.3	1.2	46.5	2.1	98.0	2.5	127.9	5.1	332.7	2.5
Maldives	—	—	—	—	—	—	1.0	0.1	2.4	0.1	6.1	0.3	6.4	0.2	9.2	0.4	25.1	0.2
Marshall Islands	—	—	—	—	—	—	—	—	—	—	—	—	—	—	6.9	0.3	7.0	0.1
Mongolia	—	—	—	—	—	—	—	—	—	—	—	—	—	—	33.8	1.4	33.8	0.2
Papua New Guinea	14.3	8.5	—	—	33.6	3.8	22.0	1.5	41.0	2.1	29.4	1.3	79.9	2.0	73.0	2.9	293.2	2.2
Philippines	1.0	0.6	11.8	2.6	14.0	1.6	50.0	3.5	—	—	5.0.	0.2	550.0	14.0	200.0	8.0	876.8	6.5
Solomon Islands	—	—	—	—	9.2	1.0	5.6	0.4	9.7	0.5	13.5	0.6	4.8	0.1	—	—	42.8	0.3
Thailand	—	—	8.1	1.8	14.0	1.6	50.0	3.5	0.0	0.0	—	—	—	—	—	—	72.1	0.5
Tonga	—	—	1.3	0.3	1.9	0.2	2.9	0.2	2.2	0.1	3.0	0.1	17.7	0.5	7.3	0.3	36.3	0.3
Vanuatu	—	—	—	—	—	—	—	—	2.1	0.1	8.8	0.4	—	—	8.4	0.3	19.3	0.1
Vietnam	11.3	6.7	29.4	6.4	—	—	—	—	—	—	—	—	—	—	—	—	40.7	0.3
Western Samoa	2.9	1.7	5.3	1.2	12.2	1.4	12.1	0.8	5.6	0.3	9.8	0.4	28.9	0.7	8.6	0.3	85.4	0.6
Total ADF	167.9	100	457.3	100	888.2	100	1,424.4	100	1,993.2	100	2,185.4	100	3,927.3	100	2,502.2	100	13,530.9	100

Source: AsDB Annual Report, various issues.
Note: — = zero lending.

Table A2   Bank Lending by Sector: 1970–1992 (amounts in millions of dollars)

	1970–1972 $m	Share %	1973–1975 $m	Share %	1976–1978 $m	Share %	1979–1981 $m	Share %	1982–1984 $m	Share %	1985–1987 $m	Share %	1988–1990 $m	Share %	1991–1992 $m	Share %	1970–1992 $m	Share %
Agriculture and agro-industry	128.0	15.7	454.0	27.9	773.6	27.4	1,421.1	32.6	1,986.3	34.2	1,913.3	30.6	2,762.5	25.7	1,719.0	17.4	11,157.9	26.4
Energy	269.7	33.1	375.3	23.0	607.5	21.5	1,187.8	27.2	1,684.2	29.0	1,091.3	17.5	2,204.2	20.5	3,051.6	30.9	10,471.5	24.7
Industry and nonfuel minerals	41.2	5.0	69.2	4.2	204.5	7.2	39.4	0.9	111.2	1.9	191.3	3.1	546.4	5.1	510.8	5.2	1,714.0	4.1
DFI	114.0	14.0	272.6	16.7	405.5	14.4	468.0	10.7	407.5	7.0	702.0	11.2	1,153.5	10.7	1,046.5	10.6	4,569.6	10.8
Transportation and Communication	175.3	21.5	288.1	17.7	450.7	16.0	410.6	9.4	704.1	12.1	1,282.6	20.5	2,071.5	19.3	1,993.7	20.2	7,376.5	17.4
Social infrastructure	87.7	10.7	170.2	10.4	379.4	13.4	834.1	19.1	834.5	14.4	951.9	15.2	1,620.4	15.1	1,353.4	13.7	6,231.6	14.7
Multisector and other loans	—	—	—	—	—	—	3.9	0.1	83.4	1.4	113.2	1.8	382.6	3.6	215.1	2.2	798.2	1.9
Total	815.9	100	1,629.4	100	2,821.2	100	4,364.9	100	5,811.2	100	6,245.6	100	10,741.1	100	9,890.1	100	42,319.3	100

Source: AsDB Annual Report, various issues.
Note: — = zero lending.

Table A3 Bank Lending by Mode: 1970–1992 (amounts in millions of dollars)

Country	1970–1972 $m	Share %	1973–1975 $m	Share %	1976–1978 $m	Share %	1979–1981 $m	Share %	1982–1984 $m	Share %	1985–1987 $m	Share %	1988–1990 $m	Share %	1991–1992 $m	Share %	1970–1992 $m	Share %
Project loans	693.9	85.1	1,330.3	81.6	2,386.1	84.6	3,485.3	79.8	4,188.3	72.1	3,820.6	61.2	5,894.5	54.9	5,597.7	56.6	27,396.5	64.7
DFIs credit lines	114.0	14.0	272.6	16.7	405.5	14.4	468.0	10.7	407.5	7.0	702.0	11.2	1,048.5	9.8	1,046.5	10.6	4,464.6	10.5
Agricultural credit	5.8	0.7	15.1	0.9	6.0	0.2	54.0	1.2	167.6	2.9	144.0	2.3	238.0	2.2	240.0	2.4	870.5	2.1
Program loans	—	—	—	—	8.9	0.3	78.6	1.8	223.0	3.8	419.7	6.7	1,755.0	16.3	1,015.0	10.3	3,500.6	8.3
Sector loans	—	—	—	—	—	—	261.6	6.0	713.0	12.3	987.7	15.8	1,567.8	14.6	1,737.3	17.6	5,267.4	12.4
Technical assistance loans	2.1	0.3	11.4	0.7	14.6	0.5	17.4	0.4	51.8	0.9	14.0	0.2	5.0	0.0	6.4	0.1	122.7	0.3
Private sector loans	—	—	—	—	—	—	—	—	—	—	27.0	0.4	232.6	2.2	236.8	2.4	496.4	1.2
Multiproject and other loans	—	—	—	—	—	—	—	—	60.0	1.0	130.6	2.1	—	—	10.4	0.1	201.0	0.5
Total	815.8	100	1,629.4	100	2,821.1	100	4,364.9	100	5,811.2	100	6,245.6	100	10,741.4	100	9,890.1	100	42,319.7	100

Source: AsDB Annual Report, various issues.
Note: — = zero lending.

Table A4 Membership by Constituency Group and Date of Joining (as of December 1993)

Austria (1966); Germany (1966); Turkey (1991); United Kingdom (1966).

Canada (1966); Denmark (1966); Finland (1966); Netherlands (1966); Norway (1966); Sweden (1966).

People's Republic of China (1986).

Cook Islands (1976); Fiji (1970); Indonesia (1966); New Zealand (1966); Tonga (1972); Western Samoa (1966).

United States (1966).

Japan (1966).

Maldives (1978); Marshall Islands (1990); Mongolia (1991); Pakistan (1966); Philippines (1966).

Republic of Korea (1966); Papua New Guinea (1971); Sri Lanka (1966); Taipei,China (1966); Vanuatu (1981).

Bangladesh (1973); Bhutan (1982); India (1966); Lao People's Democratic Republic (1966); Socialist Republic of Vietnam (1966).

Australia (1966); Hong Kong (1969); Kiribati (1974); Federated States of Micronesia (1990); Nauru (1991); Solomon Islands (1973), Tuvalu (1993).

Belgium (1966); France (1970); Italy (1966); Spain (1986); Switzerland (1967).

Malaysia (1966); Myanmar (1973); Nepal (1966); Singapore (1966); Thailand (1966).

Source: AsDB Annual Report, 1993.

Note: Kazakhstan and the Kirgiz Republic completed the procedures and became members in 1994.

Table A5   Subscription to Capital Stock and Voting Power: December 31, 1992

Members	No. of Shares	% of Total	Par Value of Shares ($) Total	Callable	Paid-In	No. of Votes	% of Total
Regional							
Afghanistan	1,195	0.071	16,431	11,179	5,253	9,271	0.441
Australia	102,370	6.093	1,407,588	1,238,586	169,001	110,446	5.259
Bangladesh	18,064	1.075	248,380	218,556	29,824	26,140	1.245
Bhutan	110	0.007	1,513	1,224	289	8,186	0.390
Cambodia	875	0.052	12,031	8,181	3,850	8,951	0.426
China	114,000	6.786	1,567,500	1,379,249	188,251	122,076	5.813
Cook Islands	47	0.003	646	578	69	8,123	0.387
Fiji	1,203	0.072	16,541	14,548	1,994	9,279	0.442
Hong Kong	9,635	0.574	132,481	116,573	15,909	17,711	0.843
India	112,005	6.667	1,540,069	1,355,173	184,896	120,081	5.718
Indonesia	96,350	5.735	1,324,813	1,165,766	159,046	104,426	4.973
Japan	276,105	16.435	3,796,444	3,340,631	455,813	284,181	13.533
Kiribati	71	0.004	976	853	124	8,147	0.388
Korea	89,123	5.305	1,225,441	1,078,330	147,111	97,199	4.629
Lao PDR	246	0.015	3,383	2,723	660	8,322	0.396
Malaysia	48,175	2.868	662,406	528,876	79,530	56,251	2.679
Maldives	71	0.004	976	853	124	8,147	0.388
Marshall Islands	47	0.003	646	578	69	8,123	0.387
Micronesia	71	0.004	976	853	124	8,147	0.388
Mongolia	266	0.016	3,658	3,218	440	8,342	0.397
Myanmar	9,635	0.574	132,481	116,573	15,909	17,711	0.843
Nauru	71	0.004	976	853	124	8,147	0.388
Nepal	2,601	0.155	35,764	31,460	4,304	10,677	0.508
New Zealand	27,170	1.617	373,588	328,735	44,853	35,246	1.678
Pakistan	38,540	2.294	529,925	466,304	63,621	46,616	2.220
Papua New Guinea	1,660	0.099	22,825	20,103	2,723	9,736	0.464
Philippines	42,152	2.509	579,590	510,015	69,575	50,228	2.392
Singapore	6,020	0.358	82,775	72,834	99,412	14,096	0.671
Solomon Islands	118	0.007	1,623	1,430	193	8,194	0.390
Sri Lanka	10,260	0.611	141,075	124,135	16,940	18,336	0.873
Taipei,China	19,270	1.147	264,963	233,159	31,804	27,346	1.302
Thailand	24,087	1.434	331,196	291,431	39,765	32,163	1.532
Tonga	71	0.004	976	853	124	8,147	0.388
Vanuatu	118	0.007	1,623	1,430	193	8,194	0.390
Vietnam	6,038	0.359	83,023	65,643	17,380	14,114	0.672
Western Samoa	58	0.003	798	646	151	8,134	0.387
Total regional	1,057,898	62.971	14,546,100	12,732,132	1,849,448	1,348,634	64.220

(continues)

Table A5 continued

Members	No. of Shares	% of Total	Par Value of Shares ($)			No. of Votes	% of Total
			Total	Callable	Paid-In		
Nonregional							
Austria	6,020	0.358	82,775	72,834	9,941	14,096	0.671
Belgium	6,020	0.358	82,775	72,834	9,941	14,096	0.671
Canada	92,543	5.508	1,272,466	1,119,704	152,763	100,619	4.791
Denmark	6,020	0.358	82,775	72,834	9,941	14,096	0.671
Finland	6,020	0.358	82,775	72,834	9,941	14,096	0.671
France	41,178	2.451	566,198	498,218	67,980	49,254	2.345
Germany	76,534	4.556	1,052,343	925,994	126,349	84,610	4.029
Italy	31,975	1.903	439,656	386,870	52,786	40,051	1.907
Netherlands	18,147	1.080	249,521	219,574	29,948	26,223	1.249
Norway	6,020	0.358	82,775	72,834	9,941	14,096	0.671
Spain	6,020	0.358	82,775	72,834	9,941	14,096	0.671
Sweden	6,020	0.358	82,775	72,834	9,941	14,096	0.671
Switzerland	10,325	0.615	141,969	124,919	17,050	18,401	0.876
Turkey	6,020	0.358	82,775	72,834	9,941	14,096	0.671
United Kingdom	36,131	2.151	496,801	437,168	59,634	44,207	2.105
United States	267,113	15.900	3,672,804	3,231,841	440,963	275,189	13.105
Total nonregional	622,106	37.028	5,553,958	7,526,960	1,027,001	751,322	35.775
Totals	1,680,004	100.000	20,100,058	20,259,092	2,876,449	2,099,956	100.000

Source: AsDB Annual Report, 1992.

Table A6   Net Income of the Bank (amounts in millions of dollars)

	1975	1980	1988	1989	1990	1991	1992
Net income[a]	36.6	145.8	374.2	435.3	508.6	518.0	534.6
Assets	2,389.9	6,490.3	12,892.1	12,743.1	16,593.3	19,317.5	22,164.2
Subscribed capital	3,201.5	8,828.1	21,644.9	21,137.6	22,884.4	23,100.4	23,100.1
Net income/ assets (%)	1.53	2.25	2.90	3.42	3.07	2.68	2.41
Net income/ capital (%)	1.14	1.65	1.73	2.06	2.22	2.24	2.31

Source: AsDB Annual Report, various years.
Note: a. Net income before appropriation of commissions/guarantee fees to the special reserve fund.

Table A7   Net Transfers[a] of Resources to DMCs (OCR) (in thousands of dollars)

Country	1975	1980	1985	1990	1992
Bangladesh	532	–88	–867	–330	1,050
China	0	0	0	47,980	142,740
Fiji	2,692	7,208	–2,489	–12,280	3,990
Hong Kong	–674	8,358	–9,325	0	0
India	0	0	0	182,760	293,270
Indonesia	2,311	36,645	74,086	348,680	113,210
Korea	72,626	5,492	–19,759	–17,870	22,900
Malaysia	15,334	9,476	–18,376	–26,090	–35,180
Myanmar	42	197	–602	–790	–770
Nepal	19	–327	0	550	2,330
Pakistan	56,335	3,933	8,377	109,300	63,740
Papua New Guinea	0	5,193	1,510	14,480	–7,590
Philippines	37,750	45,696	6,568	46,170	–56,660
Singapore	13,112	1,652	–11,759	–16,760	–14,890
Sri Lanka	–470	–1,869	–1,068	0	950
Taipei,China	–4,272	–11,146	–7,006	–4,060	0
Thailand	31,885	52,244	45,459	–174,980	–89,440
Vietnam	89	561	–173	–220	0
Regional Equity Investment	0	0	0	11,730	0
Total	227,311	163,225	64,576	508,270	439,650

Source: AsDB.
Note: a. Excludes equity investment operations.

Table A8   Net Transfers of Resources to DMCs (ADF) (in thousands of dollars)

Country	1975	1980	1985	1990	1992
Afghanistan	2,466	4,140	-90	-1,320	0
Bangladesh	16,430	55,193	139,785	279,800	287,560
Bhutan	0	0	1,580	3,660	2,140
Cambodia	625	0	0	0	-1,380
Cook Islands	0	0	388	740	4,630
Indonesia	17,045	813	2,780	106,980	35,610
Kiribati	0	-5	57	670	330
Korea	655	-323	-314	-320	0
Lao PDR	2,459	209	3,613	39,320	13,430
Malaysia	757	-263	-246	-270	-270
Maldives	0	0	75	4,060	3,960
Marshall Islands	0	0	0	0	250
Mongolia	0	0	0	0	15,900
Myanmar	2,982	11,349	30,400	1,740	-5,320
Nepal	3,557	7,815	39,462	57,040	34,160
Pakistan	16,202	19,127	94,683	201,010	152,610
Papua New Guinea	487	6,904	2,593	38,200	8,330
Philippines	411	6,184	1,992	116,760	74,660
Singapore	539	-106	-249	-1,400	0
Solomon Islands	0	3,440	1,596	-1,980	680
Sri Lanka	5,923	4,145	26,849	101,820	118,350
Thailand	74	1,165	8,818	-1,280	-2,000
Tonga	33	1,279	570	800	1,220
Vanuatu	0	0	343	2,540	370
Vietnam	2,519	6,610	1,469	0	0
Western Samoa	1,433	3,093	521	9,850	2,410
Total	74,597	130,769	356,675	958,420	747,630

Source: AsDB.

Table A9   Loan Disbursements (OCR) (in thousands of dollars)

Country	1975	1980	1985	1991
Bangladesh	987	1,061	0	0
China	0	0	0	172,716
Fiji	2,893	8,486	1,419	6,884
Hong Kong	1,329	15,280	1,125	0
India	0	0	0	496,170
Indonesia	2,518	51,961	158,715	573,545
Korea	90,412	92,864	124,206	97,344
Malaysia	19,941	37,789	31,174	93,159
Myanmar	61	734	0	0
Nepal	310	0	0	5
Pakistan	60,818	35,186	62,967	291,315
Papua New Guinea	0	5,723	4,211	26,568
Philippines	42,588	83,333	109,009	182,502
Singapore	19,070	12,106	3,946	0
Sri Lanka	667	0	0	0
Taipei,China	5,963	0	0	0
Thailand	37,222	83,607	123,553	125,994
Vietnam	91	572	0	0
Total	284,870	428,702	620,325	2,066,202

Source: AsDB.

Table A10   Loan Disbursements (ADF) (in thousands of dollars)

Country	1975	1980	1985	1991
Afghanistan	2,474	4,698	0	0
Bangladesh	16,436	57,069	145,492	276,045
Bhutan	0	0	1,580	4,386
Cambodia	625	0	0	0
Cook Islands	0	0	404	1,203
Indonesia	17,698	6,119	8,786	24,017
Kiribati	0	0	60	393
Korea	657	0	0	0
Lao PDR	2,489	584	4,284	27,272
Malaysia	785	0	0	0
Maldives	0	0	83	4,240
Mongolia	0	0	0	10,000
Myanmar	2,982	12,339	33,011	8,795
Nepal	4,307	10,133	43,300	76,973
Pakistan	16,293	21,104	100,373	281,969
Papua New Guinea	691	8,084	4,044	53,838
Philippines	697	6,926	3,006	96,372
Singapore	556	0	0	0
Solomon Islands	0	3,470	1,701	644
Sri Lanka	6,172	6,394	29,861	151,065
Thailand	74	1,241	9,240	23
Tonga	33	1,310	676	864
Vanuatu	0	0	346	4,929
Vietnam	2,554	7,197	2,414	0
Western Samoa	1,471	3,621	1,176	14,437
Total	76,994	150,289	389,837	1,037,465

Source: AsDB.

Table A11   Social Indicators

	Life Expectancy			Adult Literacy			Human Development Index Value 1990	Human Development Index Rank 1990
	1975	1985	1989	1975	1985	1990		
Afghanistan	35	—	41	12	23	29	0.066	171
Bangladesh	42	51	51	22	33	35	0.189	147
Bhutan	44	44	48	—	—	38	0.150	159
Cambodia	45	—	50	—	—	35	0.186	148
China	62	69	70	—	69	74	0.566	101
Cook Islands	65	—	—	—	—	—	—	—
Fiji	66	—	71	—	86	86	0.730	71
Hong Kong	70	76	78	90	88	88	0.913	24
India	50	56	59	36	43	48	0.309	134
Indonesia	48	55	61	62	74	77	0.515	108
Kiribati	—	—	55	—	—	—	—	—
Korea	61	69	70	91	—	97	0.872	33
Lao PDR	40	45	49	—	44	44	0.246	141
Malaysia	67	70	72	60	73	79	0.790	57
Maldives	47	—	60	—	91	93	0.497	112
Marshall Islands	—	—	—	—	—	—	—	—
Micronesia	—	—	—	—	—	—	—	—
Mongolia	61	63	62	—	89	—	0.578	100
Myanmar	50	59	61	67	81	81	0.390	123
Nepal	44	47	52	19	26	26	0.170	152
Pakistan	51	51	55	21	30	35	0.311	132
Papua New Guinea	48	52	54	32	45	52	0.318	129
Philippines	58	63	65	87	86	90	0.603	92
Singapore	70	73	74	78	86	87	0.849	43
Solomon Islands	46	—	64	—	—	—	0.439	118
Sri Lanka	68	70	71	—	87	89	0.663	86
Taipei,China	71	73	74	84	90	92	—	—
Thailand	58	64	66	82	91	93	0.715	74
Tonga	58	—	67	—	—	—	—	—
Vanuatu	—	—	64	—	—	—	0.533	106
Vietnam	45	65	66	87	84	—	0.472	115
Western Samoa	—	—	66	98	—	—	0.586	98

Source: Key Indicators of Developing Asian and Pacific Countries—1992, *AsDB Human Development Report 1993,* UNDP.
    Note: — = not available.

Table A12   Populations of Developing Asian and Pacific Countries[a]

Country	1980	1985	1991
Afghanistan	13.4	14.6	—
Bangladesh	87.8	100.5	115.6
Bhutan	1.2	1.3	1.5
Cambodia	6.4	7.3	—
China	981.2	1,051.0	1,150.8
Cook Islands	17.9	17.3	18.3
Fiji	634.0	697.0	742.0
Hong Kong	5.1	5.5	5.8
India	675.2	750.9	843.6
Indonesia	148.0	164.6	—
Kiribati	56.7	63.9	73.9
Korea	38.1	40.8	43.3
Lao PRD	3.2	3.6	4.3
Malaysia	13.8	15.7	18.2
Maldives	158.0	184.0	223.0
Marshall Islands	30.9	—	—
Micronesia	73.2	—	—
Mongolia	1.7	1.9	2.2
Myanmar	33.1	37.1	41.6
Nepal	14.6	16.7	18.5
Pakistan	82.6	96.2	115.5
Papua New Guinea	3.0	3.4	3.7
Philippines	48.1	54.7	62.1
Singapore	2.3	2.5	2.8
Solomon Islands	225.0	272.0	322.1
Sri Lanka	14.8	15.8	—
Taipei,China	17.6	19.1	20.4
Thailand	46.7	51.7	56.9
Tonga	88.7	93.3	104.4
Vanuatu	115.1	129.3	150.9
Vietnam	53.7	59.9	67.6
Western Samoa	156.0	159.0	165.0
Total	2,293.2	2,516.4	2,576.2

Source: "Key Indicators of Developing Asian and Pacific Countries," 1992, AsDB.
Notes: a. In millions except Cook Islands, Fiji, Kiribati, Maldives, Marshall Islands, Micronesia, Solomon Islands, Tonga, Vanuatu, and Western Samoa where data is in thousands.
— = not available.

Table A13   GDP Growth Rate and Per Capita GNP

	Growth Rate (% per annum)				Per Capita GNP ($)
	1981	1985	1990	1992	1991
NIEs[a]	5.4	3.4	5.9	2.5	—
Hong Kong	6.9	−1.2	2.9	4.0	13,200
Korea	5.1	6.1	8.1	3.5	6,340
Singapore	8.3	−2.8	6.0	3.7	12,890
Taipei,China	4.2	3.5	3.8	—	9,070
PRC and Mongolia[a]	—	—	1.4	11.1	—
China	3.2	11.6	1.4	11.1	370
Mongolia	—	—	−4.9	−9.8	—
Southeast Asia[a]	4.3	−1.2	5.9	3.6	—
Cambodia	—	—	−1.2	2.4	200
Indonesia	5.6	0.6	5.1	3.7	610
Lao PDR	—	6.4	3.6	4.4	230
Malaysia	4.4	−3.6	7.2	5.5	2,490
Philippines	1.3	−6.6	1.7	−3.5	740
Thailand	4.1	1.6	8.5	6.0	1,580
Vietnam	—	3.5	2.7	6.4	220
South Asia[a]	4.2	4.2	3.2	3.8	—
Bangladesh	4.7	1.5	4.1	1.7	220
Bhutan	—	—	1.2	—	180
India	4.3	4.4	3.3	4.0	330
Myanmar	4.2	1.2	0.8	3.9	500
Nepal	5.5	3.3	3.9	1.0	180
Pakistan	3.7	4.4	1.4	4.5	400
Sri Lanka	2.9	3.4	5.1	3.3	500
Pacific[a]	−1.6	−0.7	−1.3	0.8	—
Fiji	2.8	−5.9	3.8	1.5	1,830
Papua New Guinea	−3.8	1.8	−3.8	0.9	820
Solomon Islands	—	—	2.9	1.2	560
Tonga	—	—	−0.9	−1.3	1,100
Vanuatu	—	—	2.4	−2.6	1,120
Western Samoa	—	—	−5.1	−5.6	930
Average for reporting DMCs	4.1	5.1	4.1	5.0	—

Source: AsDB.

Notes: a. The regional main heading figures have been estimated from the aggregates of GDPs of the countries in that region (or in the NIEs).

— = not available.

Table A14   Balance of Payments on Current Account (as percentage of GDP)

	1981	1985	1990	1992
NIEs				
Hong Kong	−3.7	6.2	—	—
Korea	−6.7	−1.0	−0.9	−1.4
Singapore	−10.6	0.0	6.2	6.5
Taipei,China	1.1	14.8	6.9	3.4
PRC and Mongolia				
China	0.8	−4.0	3.2	2.4
Mongolia	—	—	−28.3	−3.6
Southeast Asia				
Cambodia	—	—	−3.5	−1.4
Indonesia	−0.7	−2.2	−2.8	−3.3
Lao PDR	—	—	−9.2	−3.6
Malaysia	−9.9	−2.0	−3.8	−4.4
Philippines	−5.4	−0.1	−6.1	−2.1
Thailand	−7.4	−4.1	−8.9	−6.4
Vietnam	—	—	−3.6	2.3
South Asia				
Bangladesh	−7.8	−3.6	−1.9	0.9
Bhutan	—	—	−7.0	−9.7
India	−1.5	−2.0	−2.9	−2.5
Myanmar	−5.3	−3.1	−1.4	−0.5
Nepal	−0.9	−5.0	−9.3	−7.8
Pakistan	−3.3	−3.6	−4.2	−5.2
Sri Lanka	−10.1	−7.2	−3.8	−5.1
Pacific				
Fiji	−14.2	−1.1	−4.8	4.0
Papua New Guinea	−20.8	−6.4	−2.9	−4.1
Solomon Islands	—	—	−12.5	−14.4
Tonga	—	—	5.3	−4.5
Vanuatu	—	—	5.2	−10.7
Western Samoa	—	—	6.3	−22.8

Source: AsDB.
Note: — = not available.

Table A15   External Debt Outstanding (in millions of dollars)

	1981	1985	1990	1992
NIEs	42,380	58,684	34,981	45,882
Hong Kong	2,204	3,355	—	—
Korea	32,989	47,158	34,981	45,882
Singapore	2,263	3,406	—	—
Taipei,China	4,924	4,765	—	—
PRC and Mongolia	—	—	52,519	65,000
China	5,797	16,722	52,519	65,000
Mongolia	—	—	—	—
Southeast Asia	63,860	108,586	160,288	177,802
Cambodia	—	—	1,557	—
Indonesia	22,755	36,750	67,232	87,800
Lao PDR	321	476	305	402
Malaysia	9,225	20,449	18,173	1,700
Philippines	20,750	26,643	30,232	32,500
Thailand	10,809	17,528	28,207	40,000
Vietnam	—	6,740	14,582	15,400
South Asia	40,314	68,002	114,244	128,190
Bangladesh	4,462	6,535	12,222	14,800
Bhutan	—	—	83	—
India	21,106	40,886	69,138	78,961
Myanmar	1,714	3,091	4,673	—
Nepal	278	590	1,639	1,948
Pakistan	10,520	13,362	20,645	25,381
Sri Lanka	2,234	3,538	5,844	7,100
Pacific	1,548	2,712	3,305	2,896
Fiji	372	444	409	—
Papua New Guinea	1,176	2,268	2,582	2,896
Solomon Islands	—	—	121	—
Tonga	—	—	61	—
Vanuatu	—	—	40	—
Western Samoa	—	—	92	
Total for reporting DMCs	153,899	254,706	365,337	419,770

Source: AsDB.
Note: — = not available.

Table A16   Debt Service Ratio (in percentages)

	1981	1985	1990	1992
NIEs				
Hong Kong	—	—	—	—
Korea	21.7	29.3	10.7	10.9
Singapore	0.8	2.4	—	—
Taipei,China	—	—	—	—
PRC and Mongolia	—	—	—	—
China	6.9	8.3	11.6	11.0
Mongolia	—	—	—	—
Southeast Asia				
Cambodia	—	—	41.8	—
Indonesia	14.1	29.6	24.9	26.7
Lao PDR	—	12.0	10.3	6.3
Malaysia	8.2	31.2	11.2	8.0
Philippines	33.5	32.5	26.8	18.9
Thailand	20.2	35.3	17.0	10.7
Vietnam	—	53.4	5.5	7.5
South Asia				
Bangladesh	14.2	21.3	28.7	15.0
Bhutan	—	—	6.8	—
India	10.4	22.4	28.3	27.4
Myanmar	27.2	60.3	—	—
Nepal	3.7	7.5	17.7	9.3
Pakistan	14.8	23.9	22.7	20.9
Sri Lanka	13.2	16.5	13.9	14.0
Pacific				
Fiji	5.4	12.8	11.4	—
Papua New Guinea	18.2	36.8	38.4	20.1
Solomon Islands	—	—	11.6	—
Tonga	—	—	4.1	—
Vanuatu	—	—	2.1	—
Western Samoa	—	—	5.8	—

Source: AsDB.
Note: — = not available.

BIBLIOGRAPHY

Where a title is given in italics, it is a published document. Those in quotation marks are internal.

AsDB. *Agreement Establishing the Asian Development Bank and By-Laws.*
———. "Agricultural Inputs Program in Bangladesh, Program Performance Audit Report," December 1991. Mimeographed.
———. "Arrangements for Lending from ADF and TASF Operations Funded by ADF Contributions," May 1992.
———. "Asian Development Bank in the 1990s: Panel Report," January 1989.
———. *Asian Development Bank Annual Reports,* 1989, 1990, 1991, 1992.
———. *Asian Development Outlook,* 1990, 1991, 1992, 1993.
———. "Bank Operations and Country Performance," September 1992.
———. "The Bank's Human Resource Development and Management (HRDM) Operational Strategy: A Framework and Action Plan for the Medium Term (1993–1996)," May 1993.
———. *The Bank's Medium-Term Strategic Framework 1992–1995,* March 1992.
———. "The Bank's Medium Term Strategy Framework 1993–1996," January 1993.
———. "The Bank's Medium Term Strategy Framework 1994–1997," February 1994.
———. "Country Operational Program Paper 1992–1995," Indonesia, April 1992.
———. "Country Operational Program Paper 1993–1996," Indonesia, April 1993.
———. "Country Operational Program Paper 1993–1996," Pakistan.
———. "Country Operational Program Paper 1992–1995," Sri Lanka, April 1992.
———. "Country Operational Program Paper 1993–1996," Sri Lanka, May 1993.
———. "Country Operational Strategy Study for Sri Lanka," August 1993.
———. *The Eastern Islands of Indonesia: An Overview of Development Needs and Potential,* Brien K. Parkinson, AsDB Occasional Papers, no. 2, January 1993.
———. "Economic Review and Bank Operations: Indonesia," February 1993.
———. "Economic Review and Bank Operations: Pakistan," September 1992.
———. "Economic Review and Bank Operations: Sri Lanka," August 1993.
———. "Environmental Considerations in Bank Operations: Operations Manual Section 21," December 1992.
———. "Environmental Program," August 1990.

————. *A Generation of Growth,* March 1992.

————. "Graduation from Bank Assistance," October 1991.

————. *Guidelines for Incorporation of Social Dimensions in Bank Operations,* October 1993.

————. "Inter-Departmental Review Committee on Technical Assistance Operations, Progress Report," June 1991.

————. *Key Indicators of Developing Asian and Pacific Countries,* 1992.

————. *Lead Agency Role in Papua New Guinea,* May 1989.

————. *Loan, Technical Assistance, and Private Sector Operations Approvals,* December 1992.

————. "Office Report, 1992–1993, Report of the Executive Director for Canada, Denmark, Finland, The Netherlands, Norway, and Sweden," March 1993.

————. "Project Quality," November 1990.

————. "Replenishment of the ADF and Technical Assistance Special Fund," December 1991.

————. "Report and Recommendation of the President to the Board of Directors on a Proposed Loan and Technical Assistance to Pakistan for the Agricultural Program," November 1990.

————. "Report and Recommendation of the President to the Board of Directors on a Proposed Loan to India for a Financial Sector Program," November 1992.

————. "Report and Recommendation of the President to the Board of Directors on a Proposed Loan to Indonesia for the Second Financial Sector Program," February 1992.

————. "Report on Post-Evaluation Activities during 1988," March 1989.

————. "Report on Post-Evaluation Activities during 1989," February 1990.

————. "Report on Post-Evaluation Activities during 1990," April 1991.

————. "Report on Post-Evaluation Activities during 1991," April 1992.

————. "Report of the Private Sector Task Force," December 1991.

————. "Report of the Task Force on Improving Project Quality," January 1994.

————. "Review of the Bank's Environmental Policies and Procedures," November 1985.

————. "Review of the Bank's Major Financial Policies," November 1992, March 1993.

————. "Role of Women in Development," July 1985.

————. "Second Review of Private Sector Operations," October 1990.

————. "South Pacific Operational Program Paper, 1993–1996," South Pacific Regional Office, June 1993.

————. "Special Study: A Review of Post-Evaluation Findings in Indonesia," November 1988.

————. "Special Study: A Review of Post-Evaluation Findings in Pakistan," October 1991.

————. "Special Study: A Review of Post-Evaluation Findings in Sri Lanka," April 1989.

————. "A Strategy for Bank Operations in Sri Lanka," April 1989.

————. *Study of Operational Priorities and Plans of the AsDB for the AsDB for the 1980s,* January 1989.

————. "Task Force Report of the Bank's Role in Poverty Alleviation," August 1988.

Australian International Development Assistance Bureau. "Review of the

Effectiveness of Australia's Membership of the Multilateral Development Banks in Achieving Australia's Development Assistance Objectives," December 1991.

Canadian International Development Agency. "Framework for Analyzing the Financial Viability of the MDBs," April 1992.

Danish Ministry of Foreign Affairs, Department of International Economic Corporation. *Effectiveness of Multilateral Agencies at Country Level,* March 1991.

Hussain, Ishrat. *How Did Asian Countries Avoid the Debt Crisis?* World Bank, October 1991.

IMF. *World Economic Outlook,* October 1990, October 1992.

Rowher, Jim. "A Billion Consumers: A Survey of Asia," *The Economist,* October 30, 1993.

Sherk, Donald R. "The US and Japan Multilateral Development Banks," January 1993.

Standard & Poor. *Creditreview,* September 1992.

UNDP. *Human Development Report,* 1993.

U.S. Treasury. "U.S. Participation in the MDBs in the 1980s," February 1982.

"Washington on the Defensive over Loans for Vietnam," *Financial Times,* March 7, 1993.

Wihtol, Robert. *The Asian Development Bank and Rural Development,* St. Martin's Press, New York, 1988.

Wilson, Dick. *A Bank for Half the World,* AsDB, 1987.

World Bank. "Annual Review of Evaluation Results, Operations Evaluation Department," 1986, 1987, 1988, 1989, 1990, 1991, 1992.

———. *East Asian Miracle, Economic Growth and Public Policy,* 1993.

———. "Effective Implementation: Key to Development Impact," Report of the Portfolio Task Force, September 1992.

———. "Future AsDB/World Bank Relations," April 1990.

———. *Governance and Development,* April 1992.

———. "IDA 10 Discussion Paper No. 9," November 1992.

———. "Pacific Island Economies: Toward Efficient and Sustainable Growth," volume 1: Overview, March 8, 1993.

———. "Review of MDBs: Asian Development Bank," February 1991.

———. "Sri Lanka: Country Economic Update FY93, Public Sector Rationalization for Private Sector Development and Poverty Alleviation," June 1993.

———. "Sri Lanka: Strengthening for Growth and Poverty Reduction," January 1992.

———. *Sustaining Rapid Development, East Asia and the Pacific Regional Development Review,* February 1993.

———. "Toward Higher Growth in Pacific Island Economies: Lessons from the 1980s," January 1991.

———. "The World Bank and Pacific Island Countries, An OED Review," May 1992.

———. *World Debt Tables,* vol. 1, 1991–1992.

———. *World Debt Tables,* vol. 1, 1992–1993.

———. *World Debt Tables,* vol. 1, 1993–1994.

INDEX

ADF. *See* Asian Development Fund
Advisory Group for the Study of the
    Operational Priorities and Plans,
    28, 30, 41, 43, 77, 81, 102, 103, 119,
    120, 153, 164
Afghanistan, 108n5, 118; Asian
    Development Bank loans, 23*tab*,
    116, 117, 169*tab*, 176*tab*, 178*tab*;
    Asian Development Bank sub-
    scription, 173*tab*; debt servicing,
    121; income levels, 127; popula-
    tion, 180*tab*; suspension of loans,
    22, 117; war rehabilitation, 128
African Development Bank, 14, 41,
    43, 124*tab*, 125n2
Agriculture: and food self-sufficien-
    cy, 4, 28, 29, 74, 78; green revolu-
    tion in, 29, 73; loans for, 4, 28, 29,
    30, 30*tab*, 50, 54, 55, 59, 72, 73,
    170*tab*; subsistence, 72–73
AsDB. *See* Asian Development Bank
Asia: economic growth in, 1; gross
    national product, 2; population
    growth, 2, 64; subregion growth,
    64–65
Asian Agricultural Survey, 73
Asian Development Bank, 2–3;
    achievements, 157–165; allocation
    of resources, 104–106; arrears
    policies, 7; authorized capital, 17,
    113; Build, Operate, and Transfer
    Projects, 138–139, 163; capital
    stock, 16–17; country program-
    ming, 102–104, 162; development
    challenges, 127–154; develop-
    ment impact of, 64–85; develop-
    ment objectives, 6, 99–102; donor
    influence on, 37–40; evaluations,
    89–96; functions of, 14–16; gener-

al capital increases, 3, 7, 17,
    113–116; geographical lending
    distribution, 26–28; history and
    origins of, 13–44; institutional
    framework, 13–17; interest rates,
    18, 19, 45n16; Japanese role in, 14,
    33, 38–40; Japan Special Fund, 18,
    21–22; loan concentration, 124*tab*,
    124–125; loan-loss provisions,
    123–124; loan quality, 89–96; loan
    success rates, 52, 56; loan vol-
    ume, 25–26, 112*tab*; membership,
    16, 45n9, 172*tab*; nonregional
    financial support, 33–34, 34*tab*;
    operating principles, 14–16; oper-
    ations, 25–33; planning cycles,
    97–98, 98*tab*, 99, 159; policy
    changes, 121–125; political issues
    in, 34; portfolio quality, 5, 9, 89,
    90–91, 115; private sector assis-
    tance, 133–141; Private Sector
    Support Unit, 137, 162; profes-
    sional staff, 37–40; program lend-
    ing, 31–32; regional activities,
    34*tab*, 151–154; relations with
    World Bank, 5, 79–85; replenish-
    ments, 111–113, 157; resources, 3,
    17–24; sanction policies, 7, 89,
    123; sectoral development influ-
    ence, 72–79; sectoral distribution
    of lending, 28–31; Social Dimen-
    sions Unit, 160, 162; special
    funds, 17, 18, 19–21, 58, 116;
    Strategic Planning Unit, 159, 162;
    success rates, 61, 62, 90, 90*tab*,
    91–94; technical assistance, 18,
    19, 21, 25, 135–136; U.S. role in,
    14, 33, 38–40, 46n36
Asian Development Fund, 3, 19–21,

105, 111, 114, 116, 119, 125, 157, 162; Japanese domination of, 4; loan priority, 22; replenishments, 6, 17, 19, 20*tab*
Asian Finance and Investment Corporation, 43, 137
Asian Vegetable Research and Development Center, 29, 152
Association of South East Asian Nations, xi, 119, 135, 152, 153, 163, 164
Australia, 8, 16, 17, 34*tab*, 35*tab*, 132; Asian Development Bank subscription, 173*tab*; development assistance program, 43; loans to Indonesia, 30, 50
Azerbaijan, 118

Bangladesh, 46*n28*, 84, 108*n5*; Asian Development Bank loans, 4, 22, 23*tab*, 27*tab*, 28, 58, 168*tab*, 169*tab*, 175*tab*, 176*tab*, 177*tab*, 178*tab*; Asian Development Bank subscription, 173*tab*; contract procurement, 35*tab*, 36; debt service ratio, 184*tab*; economic growth, 181*tab*; external debt, 183*tab*; gross domestic product, 151*tab*; income levels, 127; investment in, 69*tab*; investment ratios, 66, 67*tab*; military expenditures, 151*tab*; population, 180*tab*
Bhutan, 31, 46*n28*, 108*n5*; Asian Development Bank loans, 23*tab*, 169*tab*, 176*tab*, 178*tab*; Asian Development Bank subscription, 173*tab*; debt service ratio, 184*tab*; economic growth, 181*tab*; external debt, 183*tab*; gross national product, 105; income levels, 127; population, 180*tab*
Brunei, 127

Cambodia, 84, 108*n5*, 127, 154; Asian Development Bank loans, 7, 22, 23*tab*, 116, 169*tab*, 176*tab*, 178*tab*; Asian Development Bank subscription, 173*tab*; debt service ratio, 184*tab*; economic growth, 181*tab*; external debt, 183*tab*; Khmer Rouge in, 1; population, 180*tab*; suspension of loans to, 7;

technical assistance to, 7; war rehabilitation, 128
Canada: Asian Development Bank subscription, 20, 34, 34*tab*, 174*tab*; commitment withholding, 53, 63; contract procurement, 35*tab*, 36; loans to Sri Lanka, 58
Capital: Asian, 14; callable, 114, 121; development, 15; domestic, 135; foreign, 127, 135, 163; impairment, 123; markets, 3, 18, 43, 52, 54, 55, 61, 76, 105, 119, 120, 134, 136, 157; physical, 2; private, 15, 65, 127, 135; public, 15; social overhead, 65–66, 67; stock, 16–17; structure, 80; subscription, 3, 4, 16, 17, 18, 113; venture, 77, 134, 135
Central Asian Republics, 46*n22*, 118, 152, 164
China, xi, 8, 46*n28*, 108*n5*, 112, 127, 153, 154; Asian Development Bank loans, 7, 22, 23*tab*, 27*tab*, 28, 78, 114, 125, 168*tab*, 175*tab*, 177*tab*; Asian Development Bank subscription, 173*tab*; debt service ratio, 184*tab*; economic growth in, 1, 65, 181*tab*; external debt, 183*tab*; gross domestic product, 151*tab*; investment in, 68, 69*tab*; investment ratios, 67*tab*; loan suspensions, 26; military expenditures, 151*tab*; population, 180*tab*; private sector in, 140; public sector in, 66; Red Guards in, 1; suspension of lending, 149
Clinton, Bill, 33
Communications, loans for, 4, 30, 30*tab*, 50, 59, 77, 170*tab*
Conflict: civil, 62; military, 1; political, 2
Cook Islands, 16, 108*n5*, 117; Asian Development Bank loans, 22, 23*tab*, 169*tab*, 176*tab*, 178*tab*; Asian Development Bank subscription, 173*tab*; population, 180*tab*
Credit: access to, 100; direct, 77; equity, 25, 58, 77, 135; guarantees, 68; lines of, 32, 75, 76, 133, 135, 159, 163, 171*tab*; long-term, 61; rural, 59, 116; small-scale, 116;

subsidized, 77; umbrella lines, 76
Currency: constraints, 60; convertible, 17, 113; dollar, 18, 20; loan repayment, 21; local, 17, 45*n12*, 49, 60

Debt: equity ratios, 80; long-term, 69*tab;* management, 121; private sector, 115; repayment capacity, 3, 19, 22; rescheduling, 115, 161; service, 57, 104, 105; stock, 57
Democracy: development of, 15, 53, 148–151; participatory, 2; suppression of, 22, 149; transitions to, 2
Deregulation, 50, 56, 57; economic, 63, 65
Developing member countries: access to Bank resources, 22–24; agricultural loans to, 74; allocation of resources to, 104–106; categories of, 3; contract procurement, 35*tab,* 36; development needs of, 9, 14, 15; economic development in, 14, 133; environmental protection in, 141–144; fear of donor domination, 6; foreign investment in, 128; infrastructure in, 138; loan commitments to, 25; loan eligibility, 23*tab;* maturation, 119; modernization in, 114; nonactive, 116–117; regional cooperation, 160; as sources of raw materials, 14
Development: assistance, 14, 127, 132, 149, 157, 160, 161; capital market, 76, 120; democratic, 15, 53, 148–151; economic, 14, 41, 70, 106, 133; goals, 13; human resource, 51, 130; industrial, 5, 70, 75; infrastructure, 53, 67, 161; institutional, 25, 46*n27,* 62, 73, 75, 76, 89, 105, 158; objectives, 6; power, 4, 63; private sector, 6, 8, 50, 68, 70, 100; programs, 15; regional, 13; resource, 144, 145, 152, 159, 160; rural, 4, 29, 73, 78; sectoral, 72–79; social, ix, 7, 106, 128–129; sustainable, 107, 119; urban, 4, 30, 50, 51, 52, 53, 54, 55,

144, 145; women in, 42, 43, 144
Development Finance Credit Corporation, 59
Development finance institutions, 4, 5, 55

Economic: adjustment, 55; competition, 130; complementarity, 15; cooperation, 13, 154; deregulation, 63, 65; development, 14, 41, 70, 106, 133; diversification, 49; growth, 1, 6, 7, 14, 15, 60, 99, 100, 107, 139, 181*tab;* infrastructure, 60; liberalization, 65; management, 106, 107, 129
Economic Cooperation Organization, 118, 119, 152, 164
Economic internal rate of return, 43, 91, 92, 93
Economies, newly industrializing, 8, 127, 163; Asian Development Bank loans, 26, 27; debt service ratio, 184*tab;* dependence on foreign capital, 127; economic growth, 64, 65*tab,* 181*tab;* external debt, 183*tab;* investment in, 69*tab,* 70; investment ratios, 67*tab;* private sector in, 135
Economy: centrally planned, xi, 66, 67, 159; deregulation in, 56, 57; export-oriented, 54, 60, 70; market, xi, 63; open, 133
Education, 42, 43, 52, 72, 78, 79; technical, 59
Embargoes, 34, 40, 116
Energy: coal-fired, 61, 74; conservation, 29, 61, 75; consumer use of, 5; crises, 74; distribution, 61; generation, 139; hydropower, 4, 57, 59, 63, 74, 75, 78, 154; indigenous sources of, 29, 74, 75; loans for, 4, 29, 30, 30*tab;* 50, 54, 55, 57, 59, 61, 72, 74, 170*tab;* planning, 74; renewable, 75; resources, 29; rural, 5, 59, 63, 75; thermal, 4, 57, 59, 63, 78; utilization, 74, 75
Environment: deterioration, 73, 74; lending for, 42; pollution, 67; protection of, 6, 7, 24, 60, 63, 68, 100, 112, 128, 141–144; sustainability of, 106

European Bank for Reconstruction and Development, 118
European Union, 58
Exchange: conservation of, 54, 75; foreign, 32, 54, 75, 127; rates, 17, 20, 32, 52, 67, 111; reserves, 2; risks, 19; shortages, 32
Export(s): growth, 1, 118; markets, 14; nonoil, 50, 51; nontraditional, 61; promotion, 68

Federated States of Micronesia, 24, 108*n*5, 112, 130; Asian Development Bank loans, 22, 23*tab*; Asian Development Bank subscription, 173*tab*; population, 180*tab*
Fiji, 46*n*28, 108*n*5, 127; Asian Development Bank loans, 23, 23*tab*, 24, 105, 168*tab*, 175*tab*, 177*tab*; Asian Development Bank subscription, 173*tab*; debt service ratio, 184*tab*; economic growth, 181*tab*; external debt, 183*tab*; investment ratios, 66; population, 180*tab*
Foreign Investment Advisory Service, 138
France: Asian Development Bank subscription, 174*tab*; contract procurement, 35*tab*; loans to Indonesia, 30, 50

GCI. *See* General capital increase
Gender issues, 6, 100, 107, 159, 160; women in development, 42, 43, 144, 145
General capital increase, 3, 7, 17, 113–116
Germany: Asian Development Bank subscription, 20, 174*tab*; contract procurement, 35*tab*, 36; loans to Indonesia, 30, 50; loans to Sri Lanka, 58
Green revolution, 29
Gross national product, 2, 3, 104, 105, 119
Growth: constraints on, 55; economic, 6, 7, 14, 15, 60, 64, 99, 100, 107, 139, 181*tab*; environmentally sustainable, 30, 50; export, 54; export-oriented, 1, 2, 56; impediments to, 2; political pressures of, 2; population, 2, 64; private sec-

tor, 159; projects, 160; promotion of, 128; social pressures of, 2; trade, 2; triangles, 153, 154, 159, 160

Health, 55, 59, 72, 145; care, 43; public, 42; rural, 78
Hong Kong, 16, 46*n*28, 108*n*5, 117, 153; Asian Development Bank loans, 23, 23*tab*, 120, 168*tab*, 175*tab*, 177*tab*; Asian Development Bank subscription, 173*tab*; debt service ratio, 184*tab*; economic growth, 181*tab*; external debt, 183*tab*; gross domestic product, 1; investment ratios, 66, 67*tab*; population, 180*tab*; private sector in, 66; technical assistance in, 121*tab*

Import(s): dependence on, 74; substitution, 60, 68
Income: disparities, 51; distribution, 51; equality, 1; generation, 145; investment, 21; per capita, 129; raising, 60; rural, 29
India, 46*n*28, 108*n*5, 112; Asian Development Bank loans, 4, 7, 22, 23*tab*, 26, 27, 27*tab*, 28, 76, 78, 114, 124, 125, 136, 168*tab*, 175*tab*, 177*tab*; Asian Development Bank subscription, 173*tab*; contract procurement, 34, 35*tab*; debt service ratio, 184*tab*; economic growth, 64, 65, 181*tab*; external debt, 183*tab*; gross domestic product, 151*tab*; income levels, 127; insurrection in, 1; investment in, 69*tab*; military conflict in, 1; military expenditures, 151*tab*; population, 180*tab*; World Bank lending in, 14
Indochina, 8, 127; private sector in, 140
Indonesia, 24, 46*n*28, 108*n*5, 112, 153; Asian Development Bank loans, 4, 23, 23*tab*, 27, 27*tab*, 28, 49–54, 78, 105, 114, 119, 124, 125, 136, 168*tab*, 169*tab*, 175*tab*, 176*tab*, 177*tab*, 178*tab*; Asian Development Bank subscription, 173*tab*; contract procurement, 34, 35*tab*,

36; debt service ratio, 184*tab;* development projects, 4; economic growth, 1, 181*tab;* external debt, 183*tab;* gross domestic product, 151*tab;* investment in, 68, 69*tab;* investment ratios, 66; military expenditures, 151*tab;* natural resources, 127; population, 180*tab;* relations with Asian Development Bank, 49–54; suspension of lending, 149; technical assistance loans, 30, 50

Infrastructure: bottlenecks, 2, 8, 30, 51, 65, 78, 128, 163; deficiencies, 67; development, 53, 67, 161; economic, 60; industrial, 75; institutional, 159; investment, 30, 119; legal, 159; lending for, 43; loans, 30*tab;* physical, 8, 30, 51, 68, 70, 72, 77, 78, 128, 138, 139, 140, 159, 163; projects, 19; regional cooperation on, 152; social, 4, 8, 29–30, 42, 50, 55, 59, 72, 77, 78, 128, 163, 170*tab;* urban, 78

Institutional Development Fund, 46*n27,* 158

Institutions: capacity of, 52, 55, 119, 129; changes in, 136–138; development of, 5, 21, 25, 30, 50, 56, 57, 62, 72, 73, 75, 76, 89, 105, 120, 135, 136, 140, 158; rural, 29

Inter-American Development Bank, 14

Interest rates, 45*n16,* 52; liberalization of, 61; OCR, 18; preferential, 68; variable, 19

International Agricultural Research Centers, 29

International Bank for Reconstruction and Development, 19, 45*n17,* 53, 71, 107, 124, 124*tab,* 126*n8,* 135

International Center for Wheat and Maize, 73

International Crop Research Institute, 29, 152

International Development Association, 71, 106, 107, 111

International Finance Corporation, 43, 120, 131, 134, 135, 138

International Fund for Agricultural Development, 43

International Institute for Irrigation Management, 29, 152

International Monetary Fund, 5, 8, 32, 45*n4,* 55, 81, 83, 84, 107, 116, 125, 128, 136, 162, 164

International Rice Research Institute, 29, 73, 152

Investment: capital, 15; direct, 61, 66; domestic, 65; efficiency of, 51, 54; equity, 18, 22, 45*n14,* 113, 133, 139, 140; flows, 2; foreign, 2, 5, 8, 14, 65, 66, 68–70, 120, 128, 154, 164; governmental, 49; and gross domestic product, 65, 66; incentives, 67, 128; income, 21; in infrastructure, 119; intraregional, 70; liberalization, 70; losses, 124; performance, 65–68; priorities, 132; private, 66, 70, 135*tab,* 136, 152, 163; public, 43, 65, 66, 67; ratios, 66; regional, 133, 152; social infrastructure, 30; underwriting, 133

Iran, 118, 119

Italy: Asian Development Bank subscription, 174*tab;* contract procurement, 36

Japan, xi, 16, 17, 153; Asian Development Bank subscription, 20, 34*tab,* 173*tab;* contract procurement, 36; domination of Asian Development Fund, 4; foreign assistance principles, 63; industrial policies, 68; loans to Indonesia, 30, 50; loans to Pakistan, 55; loans to Sri Lanka, 58, 63; per capita income, 1; role in Asian Development Bank, 14, 33, 38–40

Japan Special Fund, 18, 21–22

Kazakhstan, 118

Kimimasa Tarumizu, 38, 39

Kirgiz Republic, 118

Kiribati, 108*n5,* 117; Asian Development Bank loans, 23*tab,* 169*tab,* 176*tab,* 178*tab;* Asian Development Bank subscription, 173*tab;* population, 180*tab*

Korea Economic Development Cooperation Fund, 128

Labor: division of, ix; shortages, 65; skills, 70

Land: acquisition, 52, 53, 55; reform, 73; taxes, 56; transfers, 53

Lao Peoples' Democratic Republic, 46n28, 108n5, 127, 154; Asian Development Bank loans, 22, 23tab, 27tab, 76, 136, 169tab, 176tab, 178tab; Asian Development Bank subscription, 173tab; debt service ratio, 184tab; economic growth, 181tab; external debt, 183tab; investment ratios, 66; population, 180tab; public sector in, 66

Loans, 3, 18–19, 45n14; agricultural, 4, 28, 29, 30, 30tab, 50, 54, 55, 59, 72, 73, 170tab; Apex, 76; Asian Development Fund, 21–22; commitments, 3; communications, 4, 30, 30tab, 50, 59, 77, 170tab; concessional, 7, 18, 19, 58, 106, 113, 114, 158, 161; conditionalities of, 149; diversification of, 158, 162; energy, 4, 29, 30, 30tab, 50, 54, 55, 57, 59, 61, 72, 74, 170tab; fast-disbursing, 76; financial sector, 140; irrigation, 4, 73; multicurrency, 19, 45n16; net transfer on, 70–72; outstanding, 18; private, 5, 7, 68, 69tab, 72, 123, 157, 171tab; program, 49; project, 171tab; public sector, 7, 123; repayment periods, 19, 20; secondary, 75; sector, 50, 51, 55, 58, 158; transport, 4, 30, 30tab, 50, 52, 59, 77, 170tab; unguaranteed, 25–26, 58, 68, 69tab, 70, 71tab, 134, 135tab, 137, 139, 140, 159; water supply, 30, 50, 55, 59, 72, 77, 79

Malaysia, 46n28, 108n5, 153, 154; Asian Development Bank loans, 23, 23tab, 24, 27tab, 124, 168tab, 175tab, 176tab, 177tab, 178tab; Asian Development Bank subscription, 173tab; contract procurement, 34, 35tab; debt service ratio, 184tab; economic growth in, 1, 181tab; external debt, 183tab; gross domestic product, 151tab; insurrection in, 1; investment in, 68, 69tab; investment ratios, 66, 67tab; military expenditures, 151tab; natural resources, 127; population, 180tab

Maldive Islands, 31, 108n5; Asian Development Bank loans, 23tab, 169tab, 178tab; gross national product, 105; income levels, 127; population, 180tab

Marianas Islands, 117

Market(s): access to, 43, 79, 154; capital, 3, 18, 43, 52, 54, 55, 61, 76, 105, 119, 120, 134, 136, 157; economy, 63; export, 14; reform, 43; secondary, 61

Marshall Islands, 24, 108n5, 112, 130; Asian Development Bank loans, 22, 23tab, 169tab, 176tab; Asian Development Bank subscription, 173tab; population, 180tab

Masao Fujioka, 38, 39

Mitsuo Sato, 38

Mongolia, 8, 24, 46n28, 108n5, 112, 127, 153; Asian Development Bank loans, 22, 23tab, 169tab, 176tab, 178tab; Asian Development Bank subscription, 173tab; debt service ratio, 184tab; economic growth, 181tab; external debt, 183tab; investment ratios, 66; population, 180tab

Multilateral Investment Guarantee Agency, 134

Myanmar, 46n28, 108n5, 154; Asian Development Bank loans, 23tab, 27tab, 116, 117, 168tab, 169tab, 175tab, 176tab, 177tab, 178tab; Asian Development Bank subscription, 173tab; debt service ratio, 184tab; economic growth in, 1–2, 181tab; external debt, 183tab; gross domestic product, 151tab; income levels, 127; insurrection in, 1; investment ratios, 66; military expenditures, 151tab; population, 180tab; suspension of lending, 7, 22, 117, 149

Nauru, 45n11, 46n25; Asian Development Bank subscription, 173tab

Nepal, 46n28, 108n5; Asian Development Bank loans, 22, 23*tab*, 27*tab*, 28, 53, 168*tab*, 169*tab*, 175*tab*, 176*tab*, 177*tab*, 178*tab*; Asian Development Bank subscription, 173*tab*; debt service ratio, 184*tab*; economic growth, 64, 181*tab*; external debt, 183*tab*; gross domestic product, 151*tab*; income levels, 127; military expenditures, 151*tab*; population, 180*tab*

Netherlands: Asian Development Bank subscription, 174*tab*; commitment withholding, 53, 85*n2*; contract procurement, 35*tab*; loans to Sri Lanka, 58

New Caledonia, 118

New Zealand, 8, 16, 17, 34*tab*, 35*tab*, 118, 132; Asian Development Bank subscription, 173*tab*

Niue, 118

Nordic Investment Bank, 30, 50

North Asia: Asian Development Bank loans, 26*tab*, 27; economic growth, 64, 65*tab*

OCR. *See* Resources, ordinary capital

OPP Study. *See* Advisory Group for the Study of the Operational Priorities and Plans

Organization of Economic Cooperation and Development, 129

Organizations, nongovernmental, 63, 137, 142, 159

Pakistan, 46*n28*, 108*n5*, 118; Asian Development Bank loans, 4, 22, 23*tab*, 24, 27, 27*tab*, 28, 53, 54–57, 58, 76, 114, 119, 124, 136, 168*tab*, 169*tab*, 175*tab*, 176*tab*, 177*tab*, 178*tab*; Asian Development Bank subscription, 173*tab*; contract procurement, 35*tab*, 36; debt service ratio, 184*tab*; economic growth, 64, 181*tab*; external debt, 183*tab*; gross domestic product, 151*tab*; income levels, 127; investment in, 69*tab*; investment ratios, 67*tab*; loan projects, 4; military conflict in, 1; military expenditures, 151*tab*; population, 180*tab*;

relations with Asian Development Bank, 54–57; World Bank lending in, 14

Palau, 117

Papua New Guinea, 46*n28*, 82, 108*n5*, 112, 127, 131; Asian Development Bank loans, 23, 23*tab*, 119, 168*tab*, 169*tab*, 175*tab*, 176*tab*, 177*tab*, 178*tab*; Asian Development Bank subscription, 173*tab*; debt service ratio, 184*tab*; economic growth, 181*tab*; external debt, 183*tab*; investment in, 69*tab*; investment ratios, 66; population, 180*tab*

Philippines, 24, 46*n28*, 83, 108*n5*, 112, 139; Asian Development Bank loans, 23, 23*tab*, 27, 27*tab*, 28, 53, 114, 119, 124, 125, 168*tab*, 169*tab*, 175*tab*, 176*tab*, 177*tab*, 178*tab*; Asian Development Bank subscription, 173*tab*; contract procurement, 34, 35*tab*; debt rescheduling, 121; debt service ratio, 184*tab*; economic growth in, 1–2, 181*tab*; external debt, 183*tab*; gross domestic product, 151*tab*; insurrection in, 1; investment in, 68, 69*tab*; military expenditures, 151*tab*; natural resources, 127; population, 180*tab*

Policy: agricultural, 73; environmental, 141; exchange rate, 32; foreign, 160; formulation of, 5, 56, 130, 136; industrial, 68; macroeconomic, 5, 50; reform, 43, 50, 54, 63, 72, 76, 127, 128, 136, 140, 157; sectoral, 79

Policy and Human Resources Development Fund, 46*n27*, 158

Political: balance of power, 33–40; conditions in lending, 149; conflict, 2; macroeconomic, 79; power, 2; stability, 65, 70, 161; sustainability, 106

Population: control, 72; growth, 2; planning, 6, 100, 144, 145

Portfolio Management Task Force, 89

Poverty, ix; alleviation, 6, 24, 28, 42, 43, 51, 54, 100, 106, 112, 125, 144, 145, 159, 160; gaps, 74; rural, 43,

60, 153, 159; urban, 153, 158;
women and, 100
Power: balance of, 33–40; development, 63; economic, 2; political,
2; urban, 59
Privatization, 55, 61, 63, 136, 137,
139, 140

Reform, 56; deepening of, 114;
financial, 59; follow-through on,
62, 63; institutional, 136; land, 73;
market, 43, 54, 55; policy, 43, 50,
54, 63, 72, 76, 127, 128, 136, 140,
157; regulatory, 136; tariff, 61
Republic of Korea, 46n28, 108n5,
153; Asian Development Bank
loans, 23, 23tab, 27tab, 120,
168tab, 175tab, 176tab, 177tab,
178tab; Asian Development Bank
subscription, 173tab; cofinancing
projects, 7; contract procurement,
34, 35tab, 36; debt service ratio,
184tab; economic growth, 64,
181tab; external debt, 183tab;
gross domestic product, 1,
151tab; industrial policies, 68;
investment in, 68, 69tab; investment ratios, 66; military expenditures, 151tab; population, 180tab;
technical assistance in, 121tab
Resource(s): access to, 22–24, 106;
allocation, 3, 67; cofinancing, 5,
21, 72, 120, 126n6, 128, 129, 134,
135, 157; constraints, 129, 131;
development, 144, 145, 152, 159,
160; energy, 29; flows, 5, 65, 68;
human, 6, 51, 54, 65, 67, 68, 100,
129, 130, 131, 144, 145, 152, 159,
160; local, 75; mobilization, 6, 51,
54, 111–125, 158; natural, 6, 8, 65,
100, 127, 129, 141, 152; reduction
in, 49; transfers, 2, 57, 132; utilization, 15, 54, 99, 130
Resources, ordinary capital, 3, 4,
18–19, 58, 105, 107, 108, 113, 114,
114tab, 115, 119, 124, 125, 162
Rights, human, 15, 53, 63, 129,
148–151
Russia, 119, 153

Sector, industrial, 56
Sector, private, 6, 26, 43, 54, 58, 76,

99, 118, 123, 129, 130, 131, 138;
Asian Development Bank assistance to, 133–141; assistance to,
77; credit to, 61; debt, 115; development, 6, 8, 50, 68, 70, 100;
growth, 159; investment, 66, 163;
loans, 7, 25, 171tab; projects, 15,
22
Sector, public, 118, 123, 127, 129,
133, 138; deficit reduction, 61;
dominance, 70; investment, 43,
66, 67; loans, 7; management, 6;
performance, 65; restructuring,
63, 136
Sector, social, 30
Shiro Inoue, 38
Singapore, 46n28, 108n5, 153; Asian
Development Bank loans, 23,
23tab, 120, 168tab, 175tab, 176tab,
177tab, 178tab; Asian Development Bank subscription, 173tab;
contract procurement, 35tab, 36;
debt service ratio, 184tab; economic growth, 181tab; external
debt, 183tab; gross domestic
product, 1, 151tab; investment in,
69tab; investment ratios, 66; military expenditures, 151tab; population, 180tab; technical assistance in, 121tab
Social: development, 106; infrastructure, 4, 8, 29–30, 42, 50, 55, 59,
128, 163, 170tab; stability, 161
Solomon Islands, 46n28, 108n5;
Asian Development Bank loans,
22, 23tab, 169tab, 176tab, 178tab;
Asian Development Bank subscription, 173tab; debt service
ratio, 184tab; economic growth,
181tab; external debt, 183tab;
population, 180tab
South Asia, 8, 127; Asian Development Bank loans, 26, 26tab, 27;
debt service ratio, 184tab; economic growth, 64, 65tab, 181tab;
external debt, 183tab; income levels, 128; investment in, 69tab, 70;
investment ratios, 67tab; private
sector in, 140; resource flows,
69tab
South Asian Association for Regional Cooperation, 119, 152, 164

Southeast Asia, 8, 127, 163; Asian Development Bank loans, 26, 26*tab*, 27; debt service ratio, 184*tab*; economic growth, 65, 65*tab*, 181*tab*; external debt, 183*tab*; investment in, 69*tab*, 70; investment ratios, 67*tab*; lending in, 4

South Pacific countries, 16, 31, 127, 164; Asian Development Bank loans, 26, 26*tab*, 27, 131; Asian Development Bank role in, 129–133; debt service ratio, 184*tab*; dependence on development assistance, 127; economic growth, 65, 65*tab*, 181*tab*; external debt, 183*tab*; gross national product, 105; investment in, 69*tab*; "Pacific Paradox," 129; private sector in, 140; technical assistance to, 131

South Pacific Project Facility, 131

Sri Lanka, 46*n28*, 108*n5*; Asian Development Bank loans, 22, 23*tab*, 27*tab*, 28, 53, 57–64, 76, 108*n4*, 136, 168*tab*, 169*tab*, 175*tab*, 176*tab*, 177*tab*, 178*tab*; Asian Development Bank subscription, 173*tab*; debt service ratio, 184*tab*; economic growth, 181*tab*; external debt, 183*tab*; gross domestic product, 151*tab*; income levels, 127; insurrection in, 1; investment in, 69*tab*; investment ratios, 67*tab*; loan projects, 4; military expenditures, 151*tab*; population, 180*tab*; relations with Asian Development Bank, 57–64; suspension of lending, 149; World Bank lending in, 58

Structural adjustment, 51, 55, 107

Subsidies, 32, 56, 67, 77

Sumatra, 154

Sweden: Asian Development Bank subscription, 174*tab*; commitment withholding, 53; loans to Sri Lanka, 58

Switzerland: Asian Development Bank subscription, 174*tab*; contract procurement, 35*tab*, 36

Tahiti, 118

Taipei,China, 46*n28*, 108*n5*, 153; Asian Development Bank loans, 23, 23*tab*, 120, 168*tab*, 175*tab*, 177*tab*; Asian Development Bank subscription, 173*tab*; debt service ratio, 184*tab*; economic growth, 181*tab*; external debt, 183*tab*; gross domestic product, 1, 151*tab*; industrial policies, 68; investment ratios, 67*tab*; military expenditures, 151*tab*; population, 180*tab*; technical assistance in, 121tab

Taiwan. *See* Taipei,China

Takeshi Watanabe, 14, 38

Tariffs, 32; reform of, 61; water, 80

Taroichi Yoshida, 38

Task Force on Improving Project Quality, 6

Technical assistance, 5, 15, 57, 59, 171*tab*; availability of, 6; grants for, 43; for institutional development, 72, 105, 120, 158; loans to Indonesia, 30, 50; loans to Sri Lanka, 59; need for increase of, 95–96, 103; project preparation, 5, 25, 103, 120, 158; regional, 22

Technical Assistance Special Fund, 18, 19, 21

Technology: assimilation, 56; dissemination, 73; regional cooperation on, 152

Thailand, 46*n28*, 108*n5*, 154; Asian Development Bank loans, 23*tab*, 24, 27*tab*, 78, 168*tab*, 169*tab*, 175*tab*, 176*tab*, 177*tab*, 178*tab*; Asian Development Bank subscription, 173*tab*; contract procurement, 34, 35*tab*; debt service ratio, 184*tab*; economic growth, 1, 181*tab*; external debt, 183*tab*; gross domestic product, 151*tab*; investment in, 68, 69*tab*; investment ratios, 66, 67*tab*; military expenditures, 151*tab*; natural resources, 127; population, 180*tab*

Tiananmen Square massacre, 26, 149

Tonga: Asian Development Bank loans, 22, 23*tab*, 169*tab*, 176*tab*, 178*tab*; Asian Development Bank subscription, 173*tab*; debt service ratio, 184*tab*; economic growth,

181*tab;* external debt, 183*tab;* population, 180*tab*

Trade: foreign, 65; growth, 2; liberalization, 32, 127; promotion, 13; regional, 152

Transportation, loans for, 4, 30, 30*tab,* 50, 52, 59, 77, 170*tab*

Turkey, 16, 118; Asian Development Bank subscription, 174*tab*

Turkmenistan, 118

Tuvalu, 46*n22,* 112, 117, 125*n1;* Asian Development Bank loans, 23*tab*

Unemployment, 60; rural, 73

United Kingdom: Asian Development Bank subscription, 174*tab;* contract procurement, 35*tab,* 36; loans to Sri Lanka, 58

United Nations: cooperation with, 15; Development Programme, 43, 58, 79, 84, 116, 129, 132, 133; Economic and Social Commission for Asia and the Pacific, 13, 14, 16

United States: Asian Development Bank subscription, 20, 34*tab,* 111, 174*tab;* contract procurement, 35*tab,* 36; loans to Indonesia, 30, 50; loans to Pakistan, 55; loans to Sri Lanka, 58; role in Asian Development Bank, 14, 33, 38–40, 45*n4,* 46*n36*

U.S. Agency for International Development, 80, 142

Uzbekistan, 118

Vanuatu, 46*n28,* 108*n5,* 130; Asian Development Bank loans, 22, 23*tab,* 169*tab,* 176*tab,* 178*tab;* Asian Development Bank subscription, 173*tab;* debt service ratio, 184*tab;* economic growth, 181*tab;* external debt, 183*tab;* population, 180*tab*

Vietnam, 46*n28,* 108*n5,* 127, 154; Asian Development Bank loans, 7, 22, 23*tab,* 116, 168*tab,* 169*tab,* 175*tab,* 176*tab,* 177*tab,* 178*tab;* Asian Development Bank subscription, 173*tab;* debt service ratio, 184*tab;* economic growth, 1–2, 181*tab;* embargo on, 34, 40, 116; external debt, 183*tab;* investment ratios, 66; population, 180*tab;* public sector in, 66; suspension of lending, 149; technical assistance to, 7; U.S. involvement in, 14

Wapenhans Report, 89

Water supply loans, 30, 50, 55, 59, 72, 77, 79

Western Samoa, 46*n27,* 108*n5;* Asian Development Bank loans, 22, 23*tab,* 169*tab,* 176*tab,* 178*tab;* Asian Development Bank subscription, 173*tab;* debt service ratio, 184*tab;* economic growth, 181*tab;* external debt, 183*tab;* population, 180tab

World Bank, ix, 8, 14, 41, 43, 51–52, 58, 71, 89, 103, 107, 118, 119, 125, 128, 129, 131–132, 133, 134, 136, 138, 149, 162, 163, 164; Consultative Group for International Agricultural Research, 29; Economic Development Institute, 140; interest rates, 18; loan-loss provisions, 123; loans to Indonesia, 30, 50; loans to Pakistan, 55; loans to Sri Lanka, 58; operations and policies, ix; Pakistan Aid Consortium, 55; private sector lending, 50; relations with Asian Development Bank, 5, 79–85; sector adjustment programs, 32; success rates, 61, 62, 90, 90*tab*

ABOUT THE BOOK AND AUTHOR

The multilateral banks are powerful forces in the international community, providing loans of more than $250 billion to developing countries over the last half-century. The best-known of these, the World Bank, has been studied extensively, but the "regional development banks" are little understood, even within their own geographic regions.

This book looks specifically at the policies and projects of the Asian Development Bank, which, like the other multilateral banks, is being increasingly criticized by grassroots organizations, environmental groups, and others.

Drawing on case studies, Kappagoda responds to some basic questions: has the Asian Development Bank in fact been an effective agent of development? Has it been a mere clone of the World Bank, susceptible to that agency's weaknesses, as well as its strengths? He also assesses the bank's ability to take on the emerging challenges on the development agenda, including such issues as governance, military spending, and the need for gender-sensitive development strategies.

Nihal Kappagoda is currently an independent economic consultant. He was previously Director of External Resources in Sri Lanka. He has held senior positions in the Commonwealth Secretariat, the International Development Research Centre, and the Asian Development Bank.